Praise for *The Influential Product Manager*

"It's the instruction manual (and now my go-to desk reference) that only the most seasoned, thoughtful, honest product guru and mentor could create—guiding you through the hiccups of making truly great products and even demystifying tough topics like how to go about understanding users' needs and how to collaborate with your team while leading them too."
—Marisa Gallagher, Head of UX and Design, Amazon Music

"This book outlines stellar frameworks and, more importantly, philosophical guidance on how Product and Engineering can build relationships, collaborate effectively, and share mutual respect. While the companies I've worked for have had a variety of cultures, ultimately the core principles around effective collaboration stay the same, and this book shines a bright light on these principles for both Product and Engineering leaders to embrace."
—Eric Bogs, Engineering Leader, Facebook, and former engineering leader, Google, Spotify, Yahoo!, Etsy, and Hinge

"*The Influential Product Manager* captures the art of product development all in one place. Ken Sandy emphasizes courage, focus, commitment, respect, and openness, which strike me as values that apply to all aspects of product development, from ideation and design to implementation and delivery to the customer. I plan on recommending this book to all my product management, engineering, and design colleagues as an excellent guide to working together to delight our customers and build great products!"
—David Zabowski, Vice President of Engineering, Nerdwallet

"*The Influential Product Manager* is essential reading for both product managers looking to hone their craft and stakeholders who would like to improve their working relationship with a product organization. Ken Sandy packs his incredible talent for coaching and developing teams onto the page, providing the most comprehensive survey of the product discipline and tools for success that I've ever read."
—Matt Sanchez, Senior Vice President of Platforms, Hearst Magazines

"Ken's book is a fantastic addition to the product manager's toolbox. It's unique in that it provides a comprehensive 360-degree view into the product manager role, and it's full of practical insights that product managers can take to work right away. This is going to be an essential part of product boot camps for my team, and I recommend that all product managers in India building for the next billion users read this book to sharpen their craft."
—Rahul Ganjoo, Vice President and Head of Product, Zomato

"*The Influential Product Manager* is an in-depth playbook that's perfect for both those new to product management and those who want to have an even greater impact on product at their company. This is my new go-to resource for how to be an effective strategic partner throughout the product development life cycle."
—David Sherwin, coauthor of *Turning People into Teams* and author of *Creative Workshop* and *Success by Design*

"Ken Sandy's book does an amazing job of breaking down complex concepts, helping product managers learn the discipline it takes to wade through the sea of data to find the signal in the noise. This book gives you tried-and-true, practical frameworks for solving problems as a product manager and ultimately for your customers."
—Rachel Wolan, Vice President of Product, LiveRamp

"Early in your career, leadership comes not because you are the smartest but because you ask the right questions and have the tools to lead your team to the right answers. *The Influential Product Manager* provides a complete tool kit to help you succeed in your new role."
—**Mark Cook, Vice President of Product, Trax Retail**

"This book offers critical insight on practical product management strategies, from how to influence complex organizations and how to break down complex problems to get (the right) stuff done!"
—**Daniele Farnedi, cofounder and Chief Technology Officer, Solv; former Chief Technology Officer, Trulia; and former Director of Technology, Shopping.com**

"This valuable guide will help product managers lead their organizations and better serve their users and will help product executives uplevel their team's effectiveness and business impact."
—**Brent Tworetzky, Senior Vice President of Product, InVision, and former Executive Vice President of Product, XO Group Inc.**

"Excellent practitioner's guide for budding and experienced product managers alike. What sets this book miles apart is the way Ken draws from his experience, goes beyond theoretical advice, and provides excellent examples and pragmatic techniques to become a successful PM. This book is a must-read for every tech product manager in India."
—**Sachin Arora, cofounder of Chqbook.com and former Chief Technology Officer, Myntra.com**

"Unlike so much literature in this field, Ken has not adopted a 'one size fits all' approach but rather has drawn on deep, practical experience to craft a coherent and pragmatic guide for product managers working on any internet-based product. The net result is that by reading this book, literally all product managers will become more effective in their organization. This will be good for them, their teams, and their company. It will result in less wasted time and fewer failed projects."
—**Martin Hosking, cofounder of Redbubble**

THE INFLUENTIAL
PRODUCT MANAGER

THE
INFLUENTIAL
Product Manager

HOW TO **LEAD** AND **LAUNCH**
SUCCESSFUL TECHNOLOGY PRODUCTS

KEN SANDY

Berrett–Koehler Publishers, Inc.

Berrett-Koehler Publishers, Inc.
1333 Broadway, Suite 1000
Oakland, CA 94612-1921
Tel: (510) 817-2277
Fax: (510) 817-2278
www.bkconnection.com

ORDERING INFORMATION

Quantity sales. Special discounts are available on quantity purchases by corporations, associations, and others. For details, contact the "Special Sales Department" at the Berrett-Koehler address above.

Individual sales. Berrett-Koehler publications are available through most bookstores. They can also be ordered directly from Berrett-Koehler: Tel: (800) 929-2929; Fax: (802) 864-7626; www.bkconnection.com.

Orders for college textbook/course adoption use. Please contact Berrett-Koehler: Tel: (800) 929-2929; Fax: (802) 864-7626.

Distributed to the U.S. trade and internationally by Penguin Random House Publisher Services.

Berrett-Koehler and the BK logo are registered trademarks of Berrett-Koehler Publishers, Inc.

Printed in Canada

Berrett-Koehler books are printed on long-lasting acid-free paper. When it is available, we choose paper that has been manufactured by environmentally responsible processes. These may include using trees grown in sustainable forests, incorporating recycled paper, minimizing chlorine in bleaching, or recycling the energy produced at the paper mill.

Library of Congress Cataloging-in-Publication Data

Name: Sandy, Ken, author.
Title: The influential product manager : how to lead and launch successful technology products / Ken Sandy.
Description: First edition. | Oakland, CA : Berrett-Koehler Publishers, [2020] | Includes index.
Identifiers: LCCN 2019033798 | ISBN 9781523087464 (paperback) | ISBN 9781523087471 (pdf) | ISBN 9781523087488 (epub)
Subjects: LCSH: Product management. | New products.
Classification: LCC HF5415.15 .S26 2020 | DDC 658.5—dc23
LC record available at https://lccn.loc.gov/2019033798

First Edition
28 27 26 25 24 23 22 21 20 19   10 9 8 7 6 5 4 3 2 1

Book producer: Westchester Publishing Services
Text and Cover designer: Kim Scott, Bumpy Design
Illustrator: Michael Tanamachi

For my grandparents.

You taught me to have compassion for others and to embrace life's challenges with grace and humility.

Contents

Introduction

*What being influential means for you,
and how to use this book.*

Why "The Influential Product Manager"?

When I started working in consumer internet businesses (for a company called LookSmart), the role of product manager was largely undefined. I was labeled a "business analyst," charged with tracking and understanding product performance and gathering market insights. Over time I gradually assumed more and more of the responsibilities we would now expect of a product manager—defining and prioritizing features; designing, building, and launching the product with the user experience and development teams; and ultimately managing the full product lifecycle.

Product managers learned by doing. So in a startup environment, through trial and error, I invented new approaches and processes—creating whatever was needed to deliver a product. Leading my first product launch, I made all the rookie mistakes. I upset the engineering team by thinking I was qualified enough to design a user interface, which was roundly and justly rejected both by users and my more creative peers. I did little in the way of customer research, believing in the power of my own ideas. And I deployed a bug-filled product just days before a high-stakes PR event (to be held in full view of Australian media and government ministers), much to the anxiety of my stakeholders. Yet somehow things fell together at the last minute, and the PR event went off well.

I got lucky. And in more ways than one—because, as it turned out, I had also found my passion in product management. This was early in my career, and I never looked back. I still love working across the realms of business and technology, from high-level strategy to detailed execution. I love collaborating with a team of talented individuals who have complementary skills, coordinating and focusing our collective efforts to solve critical customer problems. There are few things more satisfying than watching an idea turn into reality through sweat (and, yes, sometimes tears), and seeing users not just use but also enjoy using your product!

Of course, the product manager's role has evolved since my early days. Techniques, processes, tools, and frameworks are now well-defined. Product management can be learned beyond trial and error, and the craft can be honed with practice.

But what makes a truly outstanding product manager? It's not just the ability to deliver a product to market. It is also the ability to empathize and determine customers' needs; to persuade, motivate, and align a cross-functional group of professionals behind a common purpose; and to navigate teams and stakeholders to achieve successful outcomes for their business and their customers.

In order to be successful, product managers must rely on the success of others. They have no direct authority—only influence. To be effective over the long-term, they must use data and facts along with conviction and vision, and they must have a deep understanding of business, technology, and user needs. Counterintuitively, they are successful because they can *only* achieve their goals by being objective and influential. They *must* optimize for the needs of the customer and business over their own goals. They *must* build trusted relationships, and they *must* collaborate and compromise to deliver outcomes—bringing their team and stakeholders with them on every step of the journey.

Who Is This Book For?

You! You may be

- an established or aspiring product manager looking to grow and advance your career;

- a career-switcher, looking to parlay your business, design, or engineering expertise to transition into product management;

- in an engineering, design, or business function working with product managers and desiring to understand more about product management best practices;

- a leader or manager of a product-management team looking for a practical self-training guide to give your team members; or

- a learning and development professional looking for a resource to help you attract, train, and retain high-impact product managers for your company.

My goal is to provide current and aspiring product managers with the tools, techniques, skills, and empathy required to be successful in navigating the critical "human" or "people" component of their role. That means building products that delight customers, avoiding common pitfalls, and establishing a strong reputation with peers, stakeholders, and customers.

The outlined practices will be useful to those managing existing products or trying to create new ones, and the products covered include those related to software, internet, mobile, web, and SaaS—whether in consumer or enterprise industries. You will likely find some sections more relevant than others. If you're working with highly technical or "platform" products, for example, you may find the sections on customer discovery and user validation less applicable. Or, if you are a product manager at a startup company, you may have little access to existing business or product data, making data-driven decisions and metrics harder (but not impossible). Conversely, if you are working in a company with well-established product management, development, and launch processes, you may find specific recommendations in some chapters less applicable but the overall concepts still relevant.

In other words, you must decide which approaches are appropriate within your organization. Far from providing a one-size-fits-all framework, this book is meant to be a "toolkit"—a series of frameworks, methodologies, best practices, processes, and ways of thinking or empathizing. Pick, apply, or adapt the right tool for you or a given situation.

How to Use This Book—and a Bonus!

This book consolidates over 20 years of hands-on experience and is your guide to learning what it takes to succeed as an influential product manager in modern technology companies.

Working as an influential product manager requires you to master effective interpersonal, collaborative, and empathetic techniques across the product lifecycle. You should be able to imagine yourself applying these techniques in your business environment:

- as you determine the mindset in which you will approach your role;

- as you build relationships within your organization;

- when you evaluate your market and validate with your customer;

- as you prioritize, define, and execute the desired product solution;

- during and after launch, in determining how you thoughtfully go to market; and

- in choosing the appropriate metrics to measure success.

The book is loosely organized around each lifecycle step—ideation, discovery, prioritization, definition, implementation, launch, and measurement. Each chapter begins with a summary of learning objectives—the three key outcomes you will take away in each. Then each concept is simply described and kept in context, telling what the concept is, why it is important, and how to apply it. You will learn about the needs and obstacles you will face and your unique role on the team—often challenging preconceived notions. I steer clear of theory, preferring simple frameworks and practical advice that you can immediately use in your work environment. I've also included examples and brief personal stories for further explanation.

This book is intended to be highly approachable and readily applicable, a complete and practical guide to becoming influential and successful as a product manager. It should be used as a reference when you need help, providing easily comprehensible solutions you can apply in likely situations and to common issues. When you need to decide how to move forward, this book is there to guide you with an easy-to-follow and likely to be successful next step.

As a bonus, you also have access to an extensive set of complementary online resources at http://www.influentialpm.com.

The resources include the following:

- Copies of introduced frameworks and templates, with completed examples.

- Additional downloadable written materials and deeper appendices expanding on what's covered in this book.

- Recommended third-party online and offline references.

- A set of exercises that will help you to put into practice the techniques outlined in a way that is immediately relevant to your current product challenges.

- Sample answers with explanations to select exercises.

Throughout this book, I refer collectively to your *team* and your *management* as your *stakeholders*. By "your team" I am referring to the cross-functional group of people assigned to work toward the product solution (engineers, designers, project managers, those in charge of quality assurance, and those who will support the product once it's in the market). "Management" refers to any (generally more senior) stakeholder; in other words, anyone who is responsible for making key decisions and has a substantial say in the direction you take (such as your direct manager, executives, and managers of other team members).

Legend

 Look for this icon for tips and tricks you can apply to implement the techniques reviewed.

 Look for this icon for a checklist of activities covered in the section.

 Look for these pointers to uncover relevant details covered elsewhere in the book.

Look for these markers for real-world examples illustrating the content covered.

First, Think Like a Product Manager

Differentiate yourself with
four powerful mindsets.

What you'll learn in this chapter

1 Four mindsets that influential product managers deliberately employ—with strategies you can use in your daily work throughout the product lifecycle.

2 How you can generate superior customer and business outcomes through a more motivated team focused on executing against the product vision.

3 Ways to detect and navigate common pitfalls and techniques and to avoid common cognitive biases you may face.

Four Mindsets Influential Product Managers Use

It's a cliché but, oh, so true—ideas *are* cheap. Few organizations are struggling for new ideas—most have too many and struggle to figure out which are most likely to be successful. And they are often challenged to execute them smoothly while maintaining highly motivated, collaborative teams.

For example, there are significant differences between the following:

- Conceptualizing a high-level business opportunity *versus* investing in understanding the customer to discover problems worth solving.

- Having product ideas of your own *versus* gathering and embracing ideas regardless of whether they come from inside or outside an organization.

- Defining a potential solution (full of assumptions) *versus* validating and prioritizing which of many options are worthwhile to pursue.

- Driving a project execution plan *versus* motivating everyone and organizing everything needed to execute well.

- Launching a product *versus* ensuring customer adoption and market success.

Influential product managers understand that success in their role lies in the latter part of each statement, not the former. They employ a set of fundamental, and sometimes contradictory, mindsets. These guide their approaches to daily work and their actions throughout the product lifecycle.

So how do you discover new possibilities and excite others with their potential? How can you prioritize and validate many potential initiatives? How do you remain balanced and objective, aware of hidden downsides and assumptions? And once you give something the green light, how do you ensure a smooth execution and keep up the momentum? Start with explicitly employing these four powerful mindsets, as highlighted by the framework in **Figure 1.1**.

Consider a simple matrix with two axes. On the horizontal axis on the far right is *imagine*. To imagine means to be open to discovering opportunities and potential solutions; to build excitement for new possibilities and to suspend long-held beliefs and ignore limitations. On the far left is *inspect*. To inspect is to gather data to build customer empathy and discover hidden insights, assess product performance, evaluate new opportunities, and uncover risks and issues.

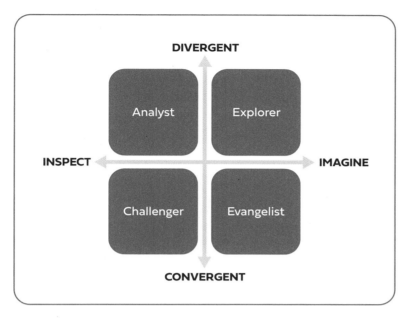

FIGURE 1.1 *Four mindsets to influential product management*

On the vertical axis (at the top), engage in *divergent* thinking to broaden your perspective. Brainstorm, discover, and share data; explore parallel paths of inquiry and make sure not to adopt any particular approach prematurely. At the lower end, engage in *convergent* thinking. Focus is essential once you have decided to pursue a path, allowing you to challenge assumptions and mitigate risks, strengthen and deepen your understanding in your plan, and to build momentum. Avoid distractions, misalignment, analysis paralysis, or constant revisiting of the options you have already dismissed.

Each of the resulting four quadrants represents a specific mindset you can employ. Each is essential to influential product management. You must be ready to imagine the possibilities and brainstorm options (the *explorer* mindset), and yet you must know when to focus and motivate a team toward a singular goal (*evangelist*). You must gather data to discover hidden gems (*analyst*) but ask the hard questions to eliminate the less-promising paths (*challenger*).

You may find yourself flipping from one mindset to the next throughout the product lifecycle; you may even appear to contradict yourself. For instance, you might be evangelizing a product opportunity but at the same time challenging assumptions and finding reasons *not* to pursue it.

Pay close attention to your natural decision-making process and biases, and make it a practice to employ other mindsets. Look, too, at the preferred mindsets of others involved in the decision-making process, as you may need to provide balance by applying a contrary point of view.

In the rest of this chapter, I will review each mindset along with actionable recommendations, pitfalls, and common biases that undermine objectivity and can lead to poor results. You can find a checklist to remind you of specific recommendations online at http://www.influentialpm.com.

Drive Innovation with an Explorer Mindset

With the *explorer* mindset, you'll understand the power of vision—and seek many, sometimes unexpected, paths to reach it. You'll use creative thinking to identify opportunities and potential approaches to address your customers' needs.

Don't adopt too specific a product implementation too early. Instead, allow yourself the flexibility to work in "problem mode"—before moving to "solution mode"—to explore and experiment.

Adopt an explorer mindset by starting with these recommendations:

1. Define your target customer, problem statement, and a product vision.

2. Canvas broadly for opportunities and ideas.

3. Validate and create prototypes of potential solutions concurrently—and continue gathering feedback throughout the lifecycle.

1. Define Your Target Customer, Problem Statement, and a Product Vision

Set a "North Star." Clearly articulate what you are trying to achieve, why, and for whom. Make sure everyone involved with your product has a shared understanding of this vision as it is the basis of everything you will do together.

Don't be surprised to discover that you have multiple customer types to serve. For example, a marketplace must attract buyers *and* sellers; the economic buyer of an enterprise solution is typically not the end user. Each customer or user type has different needs you must satisfy with your solution.

Developing empathy for your customer can only come from regularly meeting with and observing them in person to fully understanding their challenges. Use simple tools—such as personas and value propositions—to capture and communicate your findings. Focus on describing the customer, their desired outcomes, and the benefits you offer—not your business goals or the product's feature set.

A good product vision describes the underlying motivation and desired outcome for your user—not your proposed solution. Your vision must hold true regardless of which solutions you pursue. Make it exciting—a stretch, but still obtainable. You are giving your team context and permission to think big.

There are many approaches to stating your product vision. A popular one is the elevator pitch proposed by Geoffrey Moore in *Crossing the Chasm*. I recommend the following revised template, based on his:

> [Product Name] solves [meaningful problem] for [target customer] by providing [benefits or value propositions]. We're interesting because, unlike alternatives, [unique differentiator].

As an example, drawn from **Chapter 3**, I introduce a product called Babylon (more is described in that chapter). Using the revised template, the vision statement for the product might be the following:

> Babylon solves the desire of urban professionals to live a greener, healthier lifestyle by providing cost-effective and convenient access to hyper-local, fresh, organic produce. We're interesting because, unlike alternatives, our fully automated and space-efficient solution eliminates the time-intensive process to learn and maintain the otherwise manual, error-prone and complicated alternatives currently on the market.

▶ **Chapter 3** covers five key questions to answer in order to understand your customer and build a compelling vision—the "North Star" for your product.

2. Canvas Broadly for Opportunities and Ideas

Be open to finding ideas from both inside and outside your company (such as from team members, stakeholders, customers, competitors, and other products). Don't just seek solutions to known problems; also look for new problems to solve.

Schedule regular brainstorming sessions with colleagues and collect their insights. Structure your brainstorming session to be effective, constraining it around a specific, focused goal. Capture ideas in a backlog and prioritize them, bringing the most promising opportunities into your product roadmap.

Visualize Your Product (before You Build It)

Many people respond better to visuals (show) over text (talk) to communicate a vision. Here are two standard approaches to using visuals for this purpose:

1. Produce a design mock-up for a possible "end-state" for your product. For example, if your product is a website, show a mock-up of the homepage with essential functionality that would be available to users once it is entirely built—even if that is many years away.

2. Create a "customer journey," showing the before and after, helping to illustrate how the product will change the end user's life. Show each step the customer must take to solve the problem today and contrast it with how much easier this process will be once your vision is fully realized. An example customer-journey map can be found online at http://www.influentialpm.com.

Don't fall into the trap of attempting to design your product at this stage. You are *not* creating specifications to give to the user experience and engineering teams to implement: you are creating a communication tool.

And take care not to make your mock-ups too perfect looking—even a hand-drawn concept can be enough to spark rigorous conversation.

▶ **Chapter 3** outlines how to identify and evaluate your competitors—including what to look for in a teardown to learn effectively from their solutions.

▶ **Chapter 4** introduces the KJ Method: an excellent approach for brainstorming ideas and aligning stakeholders around priorities.

Use your own product frequently (surprisingly, many product managers do not). Complete product "teardowns" by identifying related products and experimenting with them, using them side by side with yours. Note how they function, how they are designed, where they are intuitive, or where they have elegantly solved a problem. In addition to looking at competitors' products, explore adjacent product categories and products with similar business models but in different industries. Take screen captures and post them on a wiki for future reference and a source for new ideas.

3. Validate and Create Prototypes of Potential Solutions Concurrently—and Continue Gathering Feedback throughout the Lifecycle

Validation with prospective customers can be challenging, particularly early in the product lifecycle when the potential solution isn't fleshed out.

▶ **Chapter 5** covers approaches to discovery, prototyping, and validation to generate optimal outcomes for your customers and business.

As a result, many product managers do it too infrequently, start too late in the process, or make it more complicated than it needs to be.

At the beginning of the product-development process, you want to improve your understanding of the problem and uncover possible solutions. Before committing to a single approach, create mock-up alternatives and test them with a group of actual or potential users (and internal stakeholders). For the best use of time and resources, keep to a couple of concurrent ideas and cull early in the process, when it's apparent something isn't working. Often, you'll find that a hybrid solution gives the best results.

By continually testing throughout discovery, design, and implementation—even if on just a few customers each time—you are always gathering new insights and refining your solution with feedback.

Using the Explorer Mindset to Find Hidden Opportunities

I was consulting for a consumer company having difficulty increasing subscriptions for their product that served college students. The number of new paid sign-ups seemed low, given the potential market and many months spent investing in optimizing the existing product.

In an all-day workshop that included business, executive, and development team stakeholders, we started by revisiting the product vision. The current product offered only incremental, occasional homework help for students—with low engagement rates. We set our sights on making it an essential, everyday study companion instead.

We reviewed research comparing what students needed versus what we were giving them. During brainstorming, we identified five high-potential opportunities including virtual study groups, test prep, access to live tutors, and personalized content collections—none had previously been considered for the roadmap.

Finally, we looked at other subscription-based products we admired (none were competitors). We identified improvements to sign-up and registration flow we could test that might encourage more trials and personalize the experience for greater conversion.

While a one-day session wasn't going to make the product instantly more successful, in exploring the possibilities, we unearthed new ideas that were deserving of testing. Together these ideas had the potential to substantially improve student outcomes and business results.

Such exploration doesn't have to take weeks or be a costly venture—you are creating lightweight deliverables, not fully working solutions. Your prototyping can be as simple as paper sketches or high-level flows (enough to communicate your overall concept), clickable mock-ups (to simulate a high-fidelity, user-facing experience) or working prototypes (where a user can interact and explore as if the product is real even though, in reality, most of the engineering is not functional).

Note that the deliverable from this process is the ability to validate a hypothesis or learn something new, not the prototype itself. Resist letting stakeholders confuse working prototypes with a finished product—you must be prepared to allow engineering to rebuild for quality.

Develop Customer Understanding with an Analyst Mindset

To understand your customer and their unmet needs, use the *analyst* mindset. Invest in direct customer relationships to build empathy and to divine insight. Dig deep into product data to understand hidden trends, new insights, or unexpected discoveries—and share your findings liberally to create a shared understanding and to set context across the team. You must be objective and intellectually curious, open to surprises that contradict your current thinking.

You'll gather and interpret quantitative and qualitative data from a broad variety of sources. Data is often not readily available, so you will have to gather it by doing your own research or running experiments.

Quantitative data are gathered by tracking user behavior or by surveying a large customer base, and they are then used to spot statistically relevant trends. Quantitative data alone might not provide clear, actionable insights that tell you exactly what is needed, however, so you must combine quantitative and qualitative data to understand the full picture.

Qualitative data help explain the underlying reasons for an issue or reveal unknowns, and while they are not statically relevant, they provide insights into underlying customer motivations. You must actually talk to users and potential customers one on one. The results of consumer or market research studies might help surface trends and observations, but real insights that catapult your product forward come from dialogue with real users.

Adopt an analyst mindset using these recommendations:

1. Set and monitor quantitative performance metrics for your product.

2. Develop a rich qualitative perspective by observing and interviewing customers.

3. Become your own analyst

1. Set and Monitor Quantitative Performance Metrics for Your Product

Select metrics that get to the heart of delivering long-term value to customers and your business. For example, simply tracking user acquisition or revenue—while giving you information you may want to know—does not necessarily tell you whether users are regularly engaging with and deriving value from your product, or whether you have a sustainable business model.

Determine and gain agreement among stakeholders for your key performance indicators (KPIs). If possible, benchmark against products with similar business models to set reasonable targets. Do this to make sure everyone has realistic expectations.

▶ In **Chapter 11**, I provide recommendations on KPIs for customer satisfaction and your product's long-term financial success, and I reveal what distinguishes good metrics from poor ones.

Recognize, especially in enterprise settings—where many different groups may have opposing goals, incentives, and metrics—that getting consensus may not be easy. For example, a sales team might emphasize goals to help them close deals, taking resources away from advancing end-user satisfaction or making it harder to find and use primary features.

Don't just monitor high-level KPIs or make do with the standard "out-of-the-box" reports delivered by many analysis tools. Explore and understand the underlying subdrivers. By breaking out your metrics into subcomponents, you will discover which levers provide you with the greatest opportunity for improvement, focusing your product development efforts where you will have the most impact to advance your KPIs.

When creating product specifications, be sure to define tracking and reporting requirements and allow time for tracking setup and testing in your project plan—a step that is often overlooked. Without it, you will not be able to measure the impact your product has had on your customers and business.

2. Develop a Rich, Qualitative Perspective by Observing and Interviewing Customers

Get out of the building regularly—several times a month at least—to build empathy and gather breakthrough insights. Join sales calls. Get involved with any user-experience or customer-research activities your company is undertaking, particularly in-person interviews. Don't just test your existing product or ideas; try to learn more about the customer, their environment, and why they use your product.

▶ **Chapter 5** includes interviewing techniques you can use to gather insights from your customers and inform your product direction regularly.

It is essential to set up your own interviews with your own objectives and not just listen in on others' sessions. Negotiate access to perform this primary data-gathering and show you can be trusted with clients (especially if you want to earn trust from sales teams in an enterprise or in B2B companies).

Read customer-service emails or reviews about your product—scan them for common themes, particularly repeating issues, concerns, or unmet needs. Find external or internal market reports to read. Write down ques-

· ·

Analyze Data to Look for Unexpected Trends

At a digital media company I worked at, we noted that our ads, when shown on mobile devices, had much lower click-through rates than when displayed on desktop computers.

It was 2011, and we were convinced that the disparity mainly came from smaller screen size and longer load times. Add to that the fact that mobile ads were simplified versions of their desktop counterparts, and were less relevant (as, at the time, mobile targeting technologies were still in their infancy). And, because mobile phones are more social, intimate devices, we suspected that mobile advertising just wasn't something people were comfortable with yet.

Interested in exploring these hypotheses, I looked at user performance for specific devices and operating systems to see if there were any patterns (such as lower engagement rates on smaller, less advanced phones or demographic differences between their user bases). With both platforms still relatively new, iPhones were performing much better than their Android counterparts overall—but that did not seem to fully explain the gap. The breakthrough came when we noticed several popular Android phones were getting a high number of ad impressions but no clicks at all.

We had mistakenly assumed demographic and form-factor differences explained the gap—but a bug in our ad-serving technology affecting some Android phones was the greatest culprit. Now we knew how we could improve our results, and it was with something well within our control.

· ·

tions as they come to you, as these can help you identify analyses you should be doing or form future hypotheses to test. Do not take results at face value—get to the "why."

3. Become Your Own Analyst

While some organizations have a team to provide analyses and reports, you should not rely entirely on others for your needs. Why? Consider the following:

- Unless you cut and slice the underlying data yourself, you can miss anomalies or surprise realizations, or fail to see data that has been misinterpreted. You're unlikely to get the full story from canned reports and secondhand information.

- Your ability to learn and iterate quickly may be slowed if you need others to provide you with all your analysis. Whether you're relying on your marketing, sales, or business-analytics team, all of them typically have many other internal customers they also need to service.

- If you can self-service your reporting needs, you can reframe and tweak your questions without delays. Asking the right question up front is hard; more than likely you'll have to go back to re-analyze or augment your data, requiring additional requests.

Practice the skills that allow you to gather raw data from trusted sources. As needed, in addition to partnering with your data analytics team, perform your own quick-and-dirty analyses, so you can learn and iterate quickly. Do not be afraid to learn new tools and techniques—especially SQL and advanced Excel functions. Answering a question that's been on your mind can be a fun downtime or late-week activity.

> ▶ **Chapter 11** details five categories of metrics that product managers analyse to uncover insights—surfacing the areas of greatest opportunity within their products.

Segment and cohort data to find insights otherwise hidden in the "averages." Averages are a trap. Insights come from understanding unusual distributions or trends over time, or observing unexpected behavior within a particular user segment.

Conversely, many products are data-poor or badly instrumented. Misinterpretations can quickly arise if you're not careful. Your entire week can quickly become occupied with wrangling a difficult data set. Push for

Techniques to Equip Yourself for Self-Service Analytics

Depending on your organization's policies and level of maturity in data analytics, consider the following options:

- Become an expert in using your company's reporting tools.

- Learn advanced Excel—especially pivot tables, charts, look-up functions, filtering/sorting, and VBA.

- Learn SQL so you can manipulate data yourself. Product managers often have to fight for attention from data teams, so empower yourself to DIY.

- Negotiate read-only access to non-production databases or ask for a daily (or weekly) data dump for select data.

- Subscribe to one or two key market-research companies serving your industry.

- Negotiate direct access to customers and users for interviews to gather supporting qualitative insights.

- Petition for dedicated analysts to be assigned to support the product team.

- Make a close friend in data analytics.

clarity and understanding of data definitions, escalate to your manager any need to support the purchase of better tools or training, and understand that even with data in hand, not all decisions are easy—especially as people interpret data with different lenses.

Identify and Mitigate Risks with a Challenger Mindset

The *challenger* mindset shines a light on contrary data, flaws, and hidden assumptions, helping you to preempt potentially serious issues. Your goal is to seek out what can go wrong, even when everything looks overwhelmingly positive.

Look for gaps in your understanding and guard against cognitive biases. Approach each step as simply a hypothesis that requires validation or disproving. Remain objective by critically validating your assumptions. You'll poke holes in some bad assumptions, but you'll also strengthen good ideas. You may identify risks that can be easily mitigated or raise the alarm when the risks require more thoughtful decision-making.

Maintain healthy skepticism. Be open to the possibility of being wrong and accept criticism without becoming defensive; instead, be unafraid to embrace constructive conflict as it battle-hardens your product. And, when warranted, recommend a change in course.

Finally, be ruthless in prioritization decisions, so that you and your teams can focus on the highest-value activities.

Adopt a challenger mindset using these recommendations:

1. Approach all opportunities as hypotheses requiring validation.

2. Embrace dissenting voices and constructive conflict.

3. Focus, prioritize, cut.

1. Approach All Opportunities as Hypotheses Requiring Validation

Do not assume your product plans, no matter how compelling, are sure to be worthwhile. This holds true whether you are prioritizing small feature enhancements or embarking on entirely new product initiatives. And it's true even, and perhaps especially, when the idea comes from someone highly respected and more senior than you.

Start with a hypothesis. A simple framework for creating one is as follows:

> We know that [data or observation] and believe that [need or issue]. Through delivering/testing [concept] for [target user], we expect [measurable outcome].

The framework forces you to articulate what facts you know, what you suspect is the underlying cause, what your product idea or concept is, and what metric you expect to move. It is a powerful context-setting device for your team that also leaves you space to collaborate on and craft the solution. It drives focus and accountability, and it establishes a platform in which you will likely learn something new (even if the idea fails).

It is even more powerful to propose a null hypothesis. For example, when testing whether something lifts sales for retailers, the null is that the action does *not* make a difference. Your new feature drives no new sales. By trying to prove the null hypothesis true, you can be at your most objective.

The Psychology behind a Hypothesis-Driven Approach

Switch to hypothesis and test mode, and you can help offset any personal attachment you have to an initiative. Rather than staking your reputation on being right or feeling it's not in your best interests to dissent with the consensus direction, your approach should be seen as that of making judicious use of scarce resources to guide the business to success.

Oh, and being "wrong" is okay—if you learn something new. It is powerful when a product manager says that they are wrong in front of a team. It demonstrates that you are unconcerned by ego and are objective in your search for the right answers.

▶ **Chapter 6** covers how to start with a hypothesis and define your product specification to build the minimum product scope necessary, speeding your time-to-market and your learning as quickly as possible.

▶ In **Chapter 4**, I introduce how to approach split-testing and incremental product optimization.

For incremental optimizations requiring little effort, you can build and deploy a split test—an experiment that definitely determines whether the idea causes better outcomes. For larger product efforts, continuously gather qualitative and quantitative data during definition and implementation to increase confidence and adjust direction in response. Post-launch, be sure to measure outcomes and seek optimizations if you have not hit your goals.

2. Embrace Dissenting Voices and Constructive Conflict

New opportunities can seem exciting, and their potential promising. When they're enthusiastically endorsed by a majority ("*groupthink*"), those who disagree or are less convinced will often stay silent (or be silenced). Pretty soon, all the data presented seem to support pursuing the current path ("*confirmation bias*").

Seek out and embrace dissenters—peers, stakeholders, or customers that appear unsupportive or even negative. Do so one on one, rather than in large groups, so that later you can help frame and present concerns to a broader set of stakeholders without discrediting the dissenter.

Avoid defensiveness or dismissing concerns out of hand. Respect the value of diverse personalities, skills, and experience. Try to understand their objections and integrate these into your evaluation. Seek to prove them right, not wrong. And don't take to heart everything they say—they usually aren't attacking you personally.

▶ **Chapter 2** covers powerful techniques for engaging stakeholders, including surfacing potential areas of misalignment.

▶ In **Chapter 3** you will find advice on identifying risks and assumptions— before you start building solutions.

Don't be afraid to challenge others diplomatically or to communicate bad news thoughtfully. If you don't confront issues that may undermine the success of the product and, at large, the business, you're not doing your job. But remember to critique content, not people—constructive conflict comes from a position of trust and assumes all parties are approaching the issue with good intent.

Share all data and insights you have, so that others can confirm or challenge your conclusions. During product updates and in decision-making forums, don't just present your initiative in

Challenging Assumptions and Communicating Bad News

One of our company goals was to ready our platform to support the globalization of the business with all that entailed—multiple languages, currencies, marketing platforms, pricing, and packages. I was among a team of product managers and engineers asked to assess all the activities and time required to complete this mammoth task— nothing short of the rewrite of a platform that had been built to serve only a single (U.S.) market. To their credit, the team did not shy away from presenting the bad news: it would take three years.

Not surprisingly, this didn't fly. We set about challenging our assumptions, in the hope we could reduce the scope or find creative approaches. We asked questions such as these:

- Is there a smaller set of customers (still accounting for a sizable portion of the opportunity) we can build for first?
- Do we need to offer a full-featured solution, or will local markets be okay with a simplified offering?
- Can we partner with third parties in some markets, until we're ready to launch our own solution?

We realized that 80 percent of the market opportunity came from serving a subsegment of enterprises that required a much smaller core offering. This would reduce the work by half (such as local marketing, pricing, or currency support). By partnering (licensing a partner platform but with our brand and content), we could support consumers in three other markets.

The original plan assumed everything was required out of the gate, without considering whether this was necessary. While the new plan was ultimately agreed upon, we would have saved time had we asked all the pertinent questions earlier.

a positive light so that it will be approved. True, your role is to garner support, but include assumptions, scenarios, and risks that might paint a less rosy picture so that sound decisions can be made.

And if you happen to win them over in making the idea a success, then all the better!

3. Focus, Prioritize, Cut

There's no shortage of problems to solve and ideas to pursue. So as much as you decide what to do, also determine what *not* to do. Prioritize the ideas with the most potential and explicitly deprioritize the rest.

You will add more value by avoiding distractions and ensuring a thorough evaluation of each initiative in the development pipeline. Get this right, and you will avoid not only significant direct costs but also *opportunity costs* (which are often hidden and more insidious). Imagine, for example, that you have one high-potential idea and another that's not; both require the same investment, such as development resources ("direct costs"). Pursuing the wrong idea sets you back not only the direct cost but also the opportunity cost of delayed revenues or forgone growth in *not* pursuing the high-potential idea earlier.

Your process to decide which ideas to prioritize should be well defined and robust, but it need not be time-consuming or involve too detailed a cost-benefit analysis or business case. Many initiatives have too many unknowns to quantify the outcomes accurately at the outset.

Instead, it is equally valid to use methods that endeavor to establish shared outcome-oriented goals and then (using the best data you have) collaboratively score or rank initiatives to fulfill the goals. Such methods inherently drive stakeholder alignment—permitting focus on the items likely to have the highest impact, empowering product managers to drive toward outcomes rather than specific projects, and reducing context-switching between many competing alternatives.

▶ In **Chapter 4**, I present techniques for collaborative prioritization among a stakeholder group—focusing first on aligning objectives and then on determining the initiatives likely to advance these goals.

▶ In **Chapter 9**, I outline one of the trickiest challenges facing product managers—navigating and communicating scope-time-quality trade-offs.

Take care not to waste time revisiting and discussing the same ideas repeatedly or exploring left-field ideas that have little to do with your business priorities or customer needs. You can add them to an ideas backlog for possible consideration in the future.

Challenging Others: How to Say "No" Nicely

Particularly with senior colleagues, but also with peers, you want them to see you as supportive, aligned, and undemanding. Try not to challenge others too directly unless you have built a healthy relationship where this is appropriate, but neither shy away from confrontation when you believe an alternative path is the right thing for the customer and business. Importantly, do not fall into the trap where you are merely responding to stakeholder demands (also called an order-taker, where the product organization is simply a service organization doing the bidding of other departments).

When you must challenge others, start by reiterating the useful insights they bring. Then try using the following questions and approaches:

- "Given that our objective for this quarter is X, how does your idea help us with X?"
- "What data might we gather to confirm which path to take?"
- "Who else would need to be involved in deciding a trade-off?"
- "Thanks for the idea—compared to existing priorities A and B, help me with why we should prioritize this higher?"
- "Walk me through your thinking about…."
- "Have you considered Y alternative?"
- "Here's the data I see. What am I missing?"
- "I'll put the idea in the idea backlog." This shows that you won't forget about it—but avoids setting expectations as to when you will address it.
- Rather than debate, recruit them to help you address current priorities. Ask them to own an important task.

Even agreeing to evaluate an idea is still committing resources away from core priorities. Be aware of pursuing too many parallel lines of inquiry with limited resources. Sometimes you just have to be firm and say no.

As a project gets underway, be prepared to make tradeoffs early and quickly—starting at the scoping and specification stage. Nobody likes to compromise, especially once you have put work into defining an elegant product solution you think is sure to solve all your customers' needs. Unfortunately, sticking with your best intentions can slow your time-to-market (and postpone your learning from real customers). Or you may unintentionally make engineering take shortcuts so they can meet a deadline, which, over time, accumulate to undermine the quality of your product (known as "technical debt").

Scrutinize every feature during the definition stage and manage scope creep aggressively. You need to ensure that everything is essential to delivering customer value and that no features are incrementally so demanding that they mean you can no longer ship quickly. The sooner you ship, the sooner you can start learning from customer feedback and know what's required in the next iteration of your product.

Likewise, be very cautious about making timeline commitments before you and your engineering team have time to discover and assess the work ahead of you. Nothing diminishes respect for a product manager faster than committing an engineering team to an unreasonable deadline with a scant, unvalidated product scope.

Build Momentum with an Evangelist Mindset

With the *evangelist* mindset, you can motivate your team and build company-wide support. Your goal is to get them to focus with enthusiasm on the initiative's potential. You want to turn stakeholders into believers. You want the team to unleash its creativity on the problem at hand—so that the solution generated is even better than you thought possible.

Develop trusted internal relationships early, then leverage these to excite and align stakeholders behind your plans—while enabling their teams to take ownership and guide the solution's direction. Understand there is greater power in articulating the "why" over the "what" or "how."

Adopt an evangelist mindset by starting with these recommendations:

1. Communicate plans to your stakeholders proactively and keep them updated regularly.

2. Set context rather than prescribing solutions—and lose ownership to your team.

3. Carefully manage planning, collaboration, and communication before, throughout, and immediately after product launch.

1. Communicate Plans to Your Stakeholders Proactively and Keep Them Updated Regularly

Identify internal stakeholders and share with them your plans and data; then gather their input and incorporate it. You want to build goodwill toward you

▶ In **Chapter 2**, I discuss how to identify and maintain strong relationships with stakeholders effectively—setting context and keeping them up to date and supportive.

and your product, reminding everyone of the beneficial impact for customers and the business. Share your assumptions and your understanding of the risks, possible trade-offs against other initiatives, and investment needs. Share how your current product, if in the market, is performing, while stressing that continued investment is beneficial to the company.

Even after you receive approval or support from decision-makers, don't stop the roadshow. Find opportunities to reinforce why your plan is a priority, especially to those who will be implementing a product initiative, selling it, or otherwise supporting it.

2. Set Context Rather Than Prescribing Solutions—and Lose Ownership to Your Team

Team members are usually most motivated by their impact on customers and the business (the "*why*"). They are much less enthusiastic about being prescribed a specific solution (the "*what*") and are especially sensitive to being told "*how*" to go about building the solution or "*when*" it has to be completed. So get them excited about potential customer and business outcomes. Provide them with support and air cover from distractions. Show

Finding Evangelism Opportunities

- Develop your 30-second elevator pitch and a ready-to-go set of slides outlining the customer problem, the business opportunity, and your vision and solution. Walk through the information with stakeholders.

- You may be asked to provide product updates at important meetings or the company all-hands gathering. No matter how nerve-racking, embrace these opportunities—or even volunteer.

- Hold a "brown-bag meeting" at lunchtime for interested parties to attend. Topics can include your product roadmap, things you've learned about the customer, interesting trends, or outcomes of new feature launches. Keep it to about 30 to 45 minutes and include time for Q&A.

- Send a weekly email to team members that includes notable achievements, learnings, customer quotes, and callouts. Keep your emails lively and not just full of status updates. A template is available online at http://www.influentialpm.com.

respect for the problem-solving abilities of your team and emphasize the goal over your own solution.

Allow others to take control and make the product theirs. This can be hard if it has become your "baby." But you need a cross-functional team with diverse skills to make it a reality. Let them set the approach and break down the plan. Articulate a need from the customer's perspective and leave plenty of room for others to influence the target solution. Whatever they come up with will usually be better than, or at least as good as, what you imagined.

▶ **Chapter 7** outlines how to take a user-centric, goal-driven approach to requirements. User stories leave extensive opportunity for your team to shape the product solution.

▶ **Chapter 8** details how to effectively engage engineering and guide your product through the development process—keeping your team focused and energized, and continually delivering value.

You've probably had much more time to understand your customer's problems, evaluate options, and develop potential solutions than others around you have. It is natural for you to be further out in front— and frustrated when your team don't seem to "get it" quite like you do.

Recognize this and patiently take them through your thought process and data, and then let them arrive at similar outcomes or possibly a different interpretation of the same data. Having conducted a thorough analysis, you'll be ready to preempt and answer many questions—building their

Losing Ownership

The idea was to revamp and thoroughly redesign the website. As the site had evolved, many features had been tacked on over time without much thought about the user interface—reducing discoverability and overall usability. The problem was just going to get worse as more interactive features were added.

As the product manager, I led the redesign, outlining the vision and roadmap, and partnering with the user experience team to explore different approaches. This was a major refresh, and there were many concerned stakeholders. I conducted a roadshow to excite colleagues and address as many concerns as I could.

Simultaneously evangelizing and executing the project soon became an overwhelming task. As I was spending so much of my time addressing stakeholder needs, my development team was spinning wheels, uncertain what to prioritize next.

I realized I would be of most benefit discussing the best ideas and stakeholder feedback with the team and then letting the team independently define and own the new design and functionality.

Empowered to enact the best decisions they could, they developed a better product than they would have had they relied on me to lead everything.

confidence in your product plan and in you. You'll often find this is enough to get their buy-in.

3. Carefully Manage Planning, Collaboration, and Communication before, throughout, and Immediately after Product Launch

As your product initiative takes shape, it is essential that you prepare your organization for its eventual launch. As the product takes shape and its launch date draws near, your product's stakeholder visibility increases.

Invariably, people beyond your immediate team—those across many functions—need to be involved, consulted, or informed.

> ▶ In **Chapter 10**, I discuss "deploying gently" to guide your organization through the process of bringing your product successfully to market.

Start early, so you don't take other departments by surprise or surface new needs late in the game. Instead, build excitement and anticipation. Ask for their contribution to the go-to-market plan. You will likely find many internal needs, such as documentation, process-setting, and approach for roll-out, need to be discussed, agreed upon, and put into place.

Finally, take responsibility for your product's market success—not just its technical delivery. Launch is the start, not the end. Once your product is out in the world—as it is used at scale—you will see bugs surface, receive a high volume of customer feedback, and gather your first performance data against your KPIs. Stay on top of all this, communicate proactively, and seek to optimize the product to ensure long-term success.

Top Five Pitfalls to Avoid

Deploy the four mindsets explicitly and in a disciplined way, and you will avoid the most common pitfalls product managers run into when identifying, exploring, validating, and executing product opportunities. Look out for the following pitfalls and learn how to recognize and address them.

Pitfall 1—Playing Only to Your Strengths

You are likely stronger at one mindset (or a few of them) than others. Perhaps you are deeply analytical—a wizard at working with data and spreadsheets, and deriving insights—but weaker creatively. Or maybe you're one of those people who can easily find and tackle problems, but getting on stage to evangelize your ideas terrifies you. This is normal—product managers are human, after all. Don't think that to be successful you need to be good at everything. Be conscious of what you naturally do well and deliberately move out of your comfort zone to practice other skills. Consider asking a friendly colleague who is strong in a skill you want to gain to coach you or give you pointers.

You also need to compensate for the natural "go-to" strengths of others. Look at your team and stakeholders: What are their strengths and what are yours? Here are three examples of what that might look like:

- **A visionary and thrilling founder or leader**—It might be easy for you to get swept up in their vision and skip detailed critique or customer validation; however, they may be overly optimistic and scarce on details. You may need to use the analyst and challenger mindsets more often as a counterbalance, to ground their enthusiasm and help the visionary add rigor by providing data that may support or refute a path.

- **A strong, decisive, and respected peer or stakeholder**—Rarely wrong and demanding of action, they may be prescriptive on solution and light on rationale. Nonetheless, be aware that overconfidence or a lack of context might be taking them down the wrong path. You may need to use the explorer and challenger mindsets more often as a counterbalance, to determine alternative solutions and to ensure the problem is of high priority. Be disciplined in gathering data and developing your own point of view. Likewise, be aware they might have context or insights you don't that you should seek from them.

- **A profoundly technical or data-driven manager**—While they have a good handle on the problem and solution, they tend to be highly detail-oriented and analytic. Perhaps the excitement and big-picture view are lacking. You may need to use the explorer and evangelist mindsets to help them set a vision, generate momentum, and motivate the team.

Pitfall 2—Applying the Mindsets, but Not Objectively

Your role is to guide the organization to a logical outcome, though there may still be risk and unknowns. So try to avoid the many cognitive biases that flaw much of human decision-making.

There are many cognitive, beliefs-based, behavioral, and social effects that undermine objective decision-making. Just by being aware of the most common that undermine product management decision making, you will be more likely to detect them (whether in yourself or others) and counteract them.

CONFIRMATION BIAS

The tendency to look for data that confirm a held belief, preferred outcome, or expectation. This bias is manifest through

- locking onto data that support what you want to hear;

- dismissing data that seem to disagree with your hypothesis (calling such data "outliers," for example); or

- interpreting data in a way that generates optimistic insights to confirm your preconceptions

Counter-strategy Actively seek to *disprove* your hypothesis (such as by testing the null hypothesis). Embrace data that contradict your assumptions or seem misaligned with your beliefs.

AUTHORITY BIAS

A manager, key customer, or other person—in a position of power or expertise (perceived or real)—may assert information to be true or a course of action to be the preferred or correct path. The tendency is to skip a critical assessment of their directive, perhaps out of deference to their authority, fear, over-eagerness to please them, or an assumption that they must "have all the facts."

Counter-strategy Diplomatically negotiate for time to complete discovery: through analysis, testing, talking to customers, and exploring solutions. Explain the need for you and the team to have firsthand experience of the customer problem you are solving to develop a solution that makes the best use of scarce resources.

SURVIVOR BIAS

A common flaw bedeviling customer research, user behavioral analytics, and user testing is to concentrate your efforts on those most active with your product. These users are generally more positive about your product. Active users are more visible, more easily reached, and typically more responsive, and therefore are overrepresented in collected data.

Counter-strategy Balance your research efforts by explicitly seeking out users who have stopped using your product or customers who purchased a competitive product instead of yours.

REPUTATION RISK

Once you propose and communicate support for an approach, you become personally invested. It is very easy to fall in love with your own ideas (this is called the "halo effect"). Or you may see the failure of something you have supported as a reflection of your personal failings. You become defensive and inflexible, and you reject data that contradict your belief.

Counter-strategy Be mature enough to divorce your personal feelings and professional reputation when deciding whether an approach is working or not. Embrace potential failure as a *learning experience*. Communicate what you learned and the benefits of figuring this out to others earlier rather than later. Usually, your colleagues and stakeholders will see such maturity as a strong character trait.

GROUPTHINK

Also called "herd mentality," groupthink is the tendency to believe in something because many other people do. Perhaps these beliefs are long-held or are organizational norms. Perhaps they are ways of doing things that have "always been done that way," so ingrained that no one has thought to challenge them. In such situations, the easy path is to conform and go with the status quo.

Counter-strategy Consider the possibility that entire groups can convince themselves of the infallibility of their path. They create an echo chamber, building false confidence by agreeing with one another. In such circumstances, you mustn't skip the critical step of gathering independent, external data, which may potentially invalidate these.

SUNK-COST FALLACY

Sometimes an investment is made in pursuing a path that turns out to be less promising than initially thought. With time, resources, or reputation already invested, it's common to justify further investment based on the cumulative prior investment, despite evidence to suggest the original decision was probably wrong. Of course, this is throwing good money after bad.

Counter-strategy Declare milestones you must meet along the way to justify continued investment. Separate and report on future investment versus past investment. And be prepared to "cut bait" (after two or three tries to make something work).

More Techniques for Guarding against Biases

- Rather than just testing your product, also test using your competitors' products. You have so much less personal attachment and may well learn that users are quite happy with the existing solutions. Or perhaps you'll find clues to differentiate your product and make it stand out.

- Ask the opposite question to your hypothesis—can you disprove it?

- Divide customers into five groups—"friendly current customers," "dissatisfied current customers," "elapsed customers," "competitors' customers," and "potential customers." Then try to interview a sample from each group.

- As a rule, during early discovery, and as resources allow, explore two potential solutions simultaneously. One-horse races are easily won.

- When prescribed a feature request or particular solution as priority, ask why. Keep pushing (commonly called "five-whys") until you feel you have enough context to identify the root problem they are trying to address. Then work backward from there, to decide priorities and devise solutions.

- When interviewing customers, ask open-ended questions first, so that respondents can tell you what's on their minds before you suggest your own options or solutions.

Pitfall 3—Ambiguity vs. Certainty and Analysis Paralysis

To delay or not to make a decision is a decision in its own right. Time marches on, resources are deployed on projects that were understood to be the next priority, and eventually the decision is made for you.

It is entirely valid, however, to kick the can down the road, delaying a decision that does not need to be made immediately in order to get more information first. Data can be inconclusive. Sometimes the data are lacking or not good enough for you to be sure of the outcome. But to keep moving forward, you must be ready, when needed, to make choices with partial, incomplete, or contradictory information. Otherwise, you will fall victim to analysis paralysis, where you (or stakeholders) seek more information, and then even more, hoping to increase your confidence in making a long-overdue decision. Perfect, as they say, is the enemy of good!

Collecting, synthesizing, and generating insights is a significant investment in time and resources. But information-gathering can be endless if you are not careful. Therefore, collect only those data that will usefully affect the actions you can take—those that will inform with *reasonable probability* the best option to pursue. You can always revisit your choices once you learn more. It's rare that you can't reverse a decision should you learn something material later.

Pitfall 4—Conflict Avoidance

Few people enjoy confrontation; however, it's essential you embrace healthy conflict as you develop and execute your product plans.

Constructive conflict occurs when trusted professionals, who mutually respect each other, come together to share diverse points of view, challenge one another's assumptions, debate alternatives, and develop a more thorough outcome. It is then that the best decisions are made—either by creating a hybrid decision, through compromise, or by one side convincing the other of the validity of their arguments. Embracing and pursuing new directions is hard work; criticizing or just keeping the status quo is easy.

Individual personalities and cultural backgrounds affect how comfortable someone is with conflict. Many individuals are profoundly uncomfort-

· ·

Embracing Conflict

A product manager on my team was struggling. He wouldn't listen to his stakeholders, was suspicious of communicating openly, and was extremely overprotective of plans or initiatives he was working on.

Over time, I became more and more frustrated. "What was going on?", I wondered.

At some point, one of his peers (another product manager) was discussing what they liked and didn't like about the company environment. Later the conversation was shared with me by the product manager who was struggling.

> "I don't feel trusted. I am asked too many questions by our manager and other product managers. I feel like I'm being tested all the time."

The other product manager expressed surprise.

> "But that's what I like about our culture. Our team is only challenging you to make sure your ideas and plan are as good as they can be. They do that to me too—it helps me find the flaws and improve my thinking. Far from feeling tested, I feel like they are pushing me to be successful—so when I go back to the engineering team or speak with a senior executive, our ideas are bulletproof."

The conversation had a profound effect on him. Years later, though we no longer worked on the same team, he frequently contacted me to help him challenge his plans and seek alternative points of view.

· ·

able with conflict and may think challenging others is rude or inappropriate (especially those in more senior positions). And social norms might prevent someone from saying what they genuinely believe, to avoid offense or to "fit in."

In other cases, you may face a particularly challenging team member who seems to enjoy arguing—frequently disagreeing, finding new options, challenging the rationale and data. So long as this remains a constructive process, try to be patient and embrace their dissent.

When you find yourself disagreeing with your peers or manager, speak up and avoid sugarcoating your message. Think about appropriate forums to do so (not, for example, in front of the entire company at an all-hands meeting). It's also your responsibility to invite and encourage others to speak up—especially to balance louder, more frequent contributors.

Pitfall 5—Not Trusting Your Instincts and Dismissing a New Opportunity Too Easily

At the start of their lives, ideas are very fragile. They are easily dismissed or ignored. Upon first glance, they might not seem to be very good at all. Lacking data or validation, it may be hard to imagine their application; challenging the status quo, they may look too audacious to be obtainable.

Don't let new ideas be easily overridden. When assessing their validity, try to separate opinion from sound reason. When a new idea comes up, positively acknowledge the parties that contributed and look for its merits.

Resist immediately pointing out all the problems and reasons the idea might not be workable. In holding back from immediate judgment, you send a signal that you welcome creativity, and you will be, in turn, rewarded with more ideas.

Even in the face of contradictory data or doubt, don't entirely dismiss your intuition (your gut feel) and that of others. Data, or rather our interpretation of data, can mislead. Stakeholders and customers may be slow to warm to a particularly bold or innovative idea but, afterward, they may wonder how they ever lived without it. Look for the balance, knowing when you have enough data to walk away from an idea and when to keep believing in your intuition and vision.

Delivering on your product vision requires you to be persistent, try new things, and take risks. Listen to your heart as much as you rationalize with your head.

Lead through Influence

Establish context across your organization and communicate effectively with stakeholders.

1 What's meant by the (often misunderstood) term "leading (or managing) through influence" and how you can apply it.

2 Powerful but simple techniques to help you develop strong relationships with stakeholders across your organization.

3 How to avoid common communication pitfalls that can undermine your effectiveness when working with senior management.

What Is Leading through Influence?

Product managers are in a catch-22 situation. They are expected to be strong leaders, respected across an organization. They must deliver outstanding products that drive business results. They do so by leveraging the talents of a cross-functional group of people—individuals with their own personal, professional, and business objectives to consider. Product managers take responsibility should something not work out, yet they are liberal in praise for the efforts of others when they do.

As a product manager, however, you have no direct *authority* over those you depend on—a team that will include engineers, designers, marketers, product support personnel, executives, and more. None of them report to you, and they may be more experienced or senior, or of longer tenure.

To achieve your goals, you will need to rely on *persuasive power*, not *positional power*. (See **Figure 2.1**.) Your role is independent of and central to the organization's goals, yet it is dependent on the success of others. Far from being a handicap, this can make you more effective. You are more likely to be seen as impartial. Rather than instruct and direct your team, you will rely on

- objectivity and data to drive decision-making,

- cross-team collaboration and compromise to deliver outcomes, *and*

- the needs of the customer and business to guide your priorities.

Influence	Aligning beliefs, behaviors, actions, and outcomes behind a common, shared purpose
Authority	Directly controlling actions through organizational seniority, power of relationships, apparent or real expertise, or threat of consequences
Manipulation	Convincing someone to do something that is primarily in your interest

FIGURE 2.1 *The difference is clear*

Leading through influence is a subtle but essential skill to master if you are to be successful. For others to willingly follow your lead, they must trust you, fully believing in the purpose behind your actions.

> Product managers are careful to ensure their motivations are best for the **customer first, company second, team third,** and **themselves last.**

That's not to say that leading through influence works every time—far from it. Product managers can still be hamstrung by politics, dependencies on resources they have no control over, and others' irrational behavior.

Stay clear of office politics and you'll preserve your relationships and reputation. Resist resorting to *manipulation*: it's a quick way to kill your career. That doesn't mean you should let someone walk all over you. If you're having trouble with someone, provide them honest, open, constructive feedback (if they are open to it), and do your best to work through or around the issues.

Using Positional Power Rather Than Influence

In one of my first product management roles, I was tasked by a C-level executive to lead an important and urgent initiative. He asked me to get a team assembled to work on it right away. Ambitious and hungry for leadership opportunities, I readily agreed.

I called a meeting together, including people from the marketing, engineering, and design teams. I gave a rousing speech, asking that they drop what they were doing and commit themselves to this new goal—as it was of great importance to the C-suite.

Distressed by the urgency of this new priority, the team reluctantly agreed to switch gears and focus on what had been asked of them.

A few days later, the C-level executive approached me and asked to speak in private—he was visibly angry. He proceeded to explain that several team members had come to him to complain that I had steamrollered them into working on this new initiative.

I protested. "But you asked me to. This is something you want, isn't it?"

"Yes, I want this, but no, I didn't ask you to operate that way," he replied. "Instead of pushing them into doing something, I wanted you to motivate them. You should have explained *why* it was important—provide business context and discuss the customer need. Just because I want it and asked you to lead it, doesn't mean you can suddenly direct others. You used my position and my seniority to transfer authority to yourself. That weakens me. I want to inspire my team, not simply order them to work on something."

I was shocked and will never forget that lesson.

Sometimes leading through influence is called "managing by influence." While they mean the same thing, I prefer "leading" since, strictly speaking, you aren't managing others.

You may well think the advice and techniques outlined in this chapter are just common sense—and you would be right. However, you'd be surprised how little product managers and other professionals remind themselves every day to make use of these influencing techniques—to their own detriment. Instead, they focus on only those techniques that are expedient in achieving short-term goals. However, with deliberate action, you can put them into everyday practice, helping you build strong, lasting professional relationships, become more effective in your career, and have greater impact on your organization.

How to Lead through Influence

Essentially, influence is at its most effective when you see it primarily as creating the context in which everyone understands and shares an appreciation of the same goals, data, approach, and constraints—and their unique contribution but interdependent roles—in pursuing the vision.

> Context describes the underlying reasons that guide a specific course of action or direction. It is "why" you are doing something, not "what" or "how."

Inexperienced product managers can be prescriptive on the "what" and "how" but not provide enough of the "why." That's a problem: teams that don't understand or don't believe in the "why" tend to be unmotivated, even rebellious. They don't feel connected to or valued by the business. They aren't convinced that they are working on something useful to the business or to customers.

By setting context, others will more often than not reach similar insights as you. Be patient and share, in detail, the bigger picture and all of your supporting data. Ask them open-ended questions, without directing them to your conclusions. Ask them to voice their thoughts and reach their own conclusions about what needs doing—perhaps they will surprise you with new perspectives or something you missed. And you'll get a more motivated team.

Here are actionable techniques you can employ to set context in your daily work environment. Use them repeatedly, and over time you'll increase your ability to persuade others, and persuade them with conviction.

1. Constantly Reinforce Product Vision, Strategy, and Business Goals

Don't assume that everyone understands and appreciates the desired outcomes. For any initiative, this can be true at any time, but especially when

- you're introducing a new, possibly daunting and vague concept;

- everyone is heads-down, hard at work in the trenches executing against the plan; or

- the first data, bugs, and change-requests start coming in after launch.

Losing sight of the underlying purpose is easy. Despite your best efforts, the objectives might not be well understood by all. Likewise, business goals frequently change, typically quarterly, but sometimes suddenly. Your team might feel disconnected, unsure of how what they are doing fits in.

As opportunities arise, remind your team of the "why" behind what they are doing. Link every product initiative to a central goal of the business, ideally with a measurable target. Periodically revisit your progress toward the goal and share the results.

2. Introduce Change and Constraints Clearly—and Appeal to the Team to Creatively Work through Challenges

Change is inevitable. It may be that business performance is off-track or you've discovered something during product testing that requires a reset. Or decision-makers set a new priority or reallocate resources away from your product. You may or may not understand and support these changes. And even when you do, the rationale may not be evident to others. Seek clarity as to why the changes are needed, consider what adjustments you'll need to make, and share the underlying causes with your team.

Give control back to your team to whatever extent possible. Work with your team to develop a new path forward—don't prescribe an answer. Allowing them to solve the problem and take ownership means they're less likely to feel powerless or like victims of change.

Regardless of your true feelings, never complain about management in an attempt to sympathize with the team. This creates a "them" and "us" mentality and is terribly unproductive and unhealthy.

Similarly, every team believes they could achieve so much more if only they had more time and resources. They believe they'd be more productive if they didn't have to contend with attending meetings, addressing emails, training new team members, fixing bugs, writing documentation, creating work estimates, or communicating updates to others outside the team. You may even be tempted to join in with your team in complaining about all these limitations. But every business has constraints, especially with allocating scarce resources across competing priorities. Help your team understand constraints, appreciate the value of the perceived overhead activities, and find constructive ways to work within the limits.

3. Liberally Gather and Share Quantitative and Qualitative Data—Demonstrate You Are Objective and Impartial

It might surprise you to know how many strategic discussions are based on opinion alone. But even the most experienced expert isn't going to be right all the time. And as product managers lack direct authority, it's rare they win a debate solely on opinion. Just because you're charged with making prioritization decisions for your product doesn't mean you can make decisions based on your own "expertise."

Rather than simply present and argue for your opinion, arm yourself with persuasive, supporting data—quantitative and qualitative. Likewise, when stakeholders present choices that seem based on opinion alone, listen to different points of view, and ask yourself what data you need to validate or invalidate them. Remain objective and open to being challenged. Do not react emotionally. Keep your ego and personal goals in check. By introducing the relevant data into the conversation and presenting a compelling case, you can effectively align others behind a course of action.

But you'll need to be prepared with more than just the top-line data points. You will also need to prepare the following:

- **Different levels of detail**—Don't overwhelm your audience with complex reports and tables with too many data. Conversely, don't show data at such a high level that it limits discussion and understanding of the details when needed. The trick is having multiple levels of data ready—summaries, with more detail on hand to support your position if questions come up.

- **Methodology**—Understand how the data has been collected, have confidence in its accuracy, and be able to explain where the flaws might be. Your data will only be persuasive if you can defend its validity and eliminate your own biases. Common issues include the following:

  - Overuse of averages or canned reports from analytics tools (hiding trends within segments and distributional patterns).

- Selecting data trends that are unduly influenced by external factors or edge cases (not under a product manager's control).

- Difficult-to-reproduce data or results extrapolated on too few data points (such as relying on input from only one or two customers).

- Confusing correlation with causation (therefore jumping to conclusions about what product improvements will bring).

- Lack of a common definition among stakeholders (leading to different interpretations of the same data).

- **Insights and recommendations**—Don't present a raft of remarkable data but leave your audience not knowing the implications. Be prepared with a "so-what": a set of actionable insights that draw conclusions from the data and a set of recommendations for proceeding. Stakeholders will want to discuss the implications and next steps. Come ready with your plan.

The most potent source of data you can gather and present is the *voice of the customer*. You must be the customer's advocate—validate that the decision is in their best interests. Speak up, if not. With many different roles and departmental goals, it can be easy to lose focus on the customer and get caught up in internal challenges or over-optimize for short-term business outcomes.

> ▶ In **Chapter 11**, I share best practices for developing useful metrics, and in **Chapter 5**, I discuss techniques for gathering customer data to inform product decisions.

Gather and share customer testimonials and unfettered feedback. Few things are more powerful at motivating a team than hearing the customer speak to them in their own words. Don't seek only positive feedback, but don't overwhelm them with too much negative feedback either. Find a balance to generate motivation and optimism while identifying constructive improvements.

4. Create Opportunities for Stakeholder Involvement and Open Discussion

Senior stakeholders love to feel useful. Figure out ways to recruit them in your efforts. You might use them as sounding boards or involve them in problem-solving sessions. You might want their help in getting the support of their teams or have them boost morale by reaching out and thanking

Effective Leading through Influence Tactics

REINFORCING GOALS

- Put your product vision, Objectives and Key Results (OKRs), and roadmap up on the wall where they are highly visible. Be sure to avoid ambiguous, wordy vision statements, however well-intended—otherwise you'll invite cynical eye-rolls.

- Ask your team to describe where they think their work fits into company priorities. Discuss and clarify their responses to help them see their work's relevance and impact.

- Hold occasional offsite sessions to discuss team progress toward the product vision. Invite them to participate in brainstorms and provide feedback on ideas, priorities, and process improvement. Allow the conversation to become critical, so long as it remains constructive.

- To the extent you can share results publicly, regularly update your team on key business metrics and product KPIs. Display them on a TV screen, clip them from reports, and send in emails—or set aside time every other week for team review.

SHARING THE VOICE OF THE CUSTOMER

- Ask the customer service team to send you a selection of incoming emails or call records about your product. Share these with your team, providing your own editorial overview. Ask customer service to select specific, actionable messages, both positive and negative. "Good job" isn't as effective as "Thank you for launching the updated dashboard—now I can find everything in one place."

- In each customer interview or user survey, ask users for a personal story of how the product has impacted them. You may get some deeply moving, highly compelling stories to share.

- Take a team member with you on customer interviews so they can hear first-hand accounts of both enjoyment in and struggles with your product. These experiences are more likely to generate empathy and drive home critical insights than your secondhand messages. Rotate your team through multiple interview sessions so you don't have too many people attending each session, which can overwhelm the interviewee.

INTRODUCING CHANGE AND CONSTRAINTS

- When introducing any change, always start by giving the rationale that drove the outcome. Here are some examples:

  "Last month we set a goal to increase user engagement by 10 percent, but we fell behind; therefore,..."

"After testing the product with customers, we received feedback that the current feature is confusing; therefore, …"

"At last week's product-review meeting, we reprioritized X higher than Y because …; therefore, …"

- When something changes, don't immediately prescribe the new path you want to take. Instead, communicate the context and rationale to your team and ask them to share their observations and identify possible solutions. Often, they will arrive at the same conclusions as you will, but they will be far more committed to the new approach.

- Understand what other people in your company are working on. Share the value of the contribution of all competing priorities (the overall portfolio) with your team.

- Discuss the value of, and opportunities to improve, "overhead" activities. For instance, regular email communication and update meetings drive support and minimize disruptions, training others spreads the workload, setting milestones provides clear goals and alignment, and bug fixes reduce tech debt.

ENGAGING STAKEHOLDERS

- Ask a senior executive to swing by to chat with the team about the importance of the project the team is working on, focusing on the business results the executive hopes to deliver.

- Ask your team to suggest any questions they have for management regarding quarterly business goals and where your project fits in. Find an appropriate forum to ask these in—such as in emails or in all-hands or weekly meetings.

- Ask whether your team feels comfortable with your sharing their concerns over business goals, process, or culture (anonymously) with management, and promise to come back to the team to discuss management's perspectives.

- Never propose taking team members from another project to increase those working on yours, without understanding the relative impact on other priorities. Instead, discuss the idea with stakeholders and project leaders who will be affected before you make any formal proposal.

hardworking team members. The more they feel involved, the more they'll provide support.

A little secret: stakeholders, even executives, are often misaligned with each other. They are too busy, too focused on achieving their specific goals, and too harried by their responsibilities. They haven't had the time to identify all the cross-department issues and hash them out. These issues, if left unresolved, can impact product quality, timelines, and customer value.

Sometimes influencing merely requires you to get a group to meet to tackle a tough blocking issue. Get key stakeholders into a room and set a clear agenda for discussion. First, you structure the discussion, explaining the problem and sharing all the data you have. Then you can sit back and let them talk. About halfway through, ask a couple of probing questions and suggest possible courses of action. Often, everyone in the room has already reached the same conclusions, but now they feel involved and committed to solving the problem.

Stakeholder Discussion and Finding Compromise

Our company was attempting an international launch. We had tried twice before but had been delayed due to resource issues and last-minute priority changes. While we had agreed on the need to grow internationally, the strategy wasn't clear, and the execution plan was cumbersome. The project would have taken three years to deliver.

The key stakeholders—the head of international, the CTO, the CEO, and the CFO—were all highly frustrated. It felt like we were trying to do too much at once. I wondered if there might be a compromise.

I first worked with the head of international to understand his business goals, explore different business models, and prioritize high-value clients. I discovered that 80 percent of the revenue opportunity would come from one industry segment, but he was being held to a higher target requiring much more complex product solutions to serve many segments.

I then worked with development leadership to explore reducing the scope and determine resource requirements. The aim was to dramatically speed the time-to-market (from 3 years to 12 months). Finally, I worked with the CFO's team to put together a revised budget (much lower than before), which implied setting new revenue goals in keeping with the reduced scope.

After understanding each stakeholder's goals and needs, I called a discussion, putting on the table all the options, points of view, and recommendations for focus and reduced resourcing levels. After much debate on the pros and cons, everyone agreed the new option was the right balance between reducing scope and achieving revenue targets. The plan was adopted, and the stakeholders committed to and owned the new approach.

While scheduling stakeholders to meet might be a challenge, attempting to resolve a complex issue over email is ineffective and can quickly spiral out of control as misinterpretations start to stack up. Likewise, trying to fix a problem in a series of one-on-one meetings usually leaves you playing the role of go-between. All that back and forth is very inefficient, and confusion is likely.

Managing Up: Working with Senior Stakeholders

Contrary to what it sounds like, *managing up* does not mean you manage your manager. Managing up means understanding and preempting your manager's needs (and the needs of other key decision-makers), providing information proactively, and seeking guidance from others when needed (while also respecting their time). Influential product managers—like all good employees—look to make their manager, other stakeholders, and the overall business successful. When you do so, you build trust and confidence in yourself and your direction.

By regularly practicing the following six principles, as illustrated in **Figure 2.2,** you can master managing up.

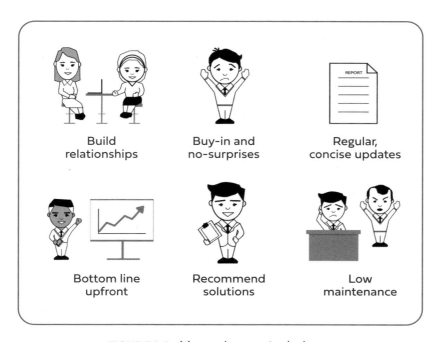

FIGURE 2.2 *Managing-up techniques*

1. Build Relationships before You Need Them

Build strong rapport with your direct manager, other senior stakeholders, and team members long before you need their assistance. If you leave it until you need their help, they may be less inclined to expend their own time and political capital in assisting you.

Start with identifying your stakeholders. Think broadly—don't limit your thinking to those with whom you work directly or those who are more senior to you. Consider peers and trusted independent contributors too. Anyone who is a decision-maker or influencer providing support or input on your product should be on your list. If you can, get a copy of your organizational chart. Traverse through each function to ensure your list is complete.

Here are some questions that will help you identify stakeholders:

- **Who guides my work and career?** Your manager (obviously), but also your manager's manager. A word of caution: be open with your manager about any "skip-level" conversations you plan to have before you have them and always demonstrate commitment and support for your manager during those discussions.

- **Who else guides or decides priorities that affect my product?** This may include business leads, colleagues charged with strategic planning, and anyone who approves investments.

- **Who guides or decides resourcing for my projects?** The leaders to whom your engineering, QA, and design team members report. Be liberal with positive praise for your team's work ethic, capabilities, and results, while being honest and sincere about challenges you collectively face.

- **Who keeps the trains running on time?** Members of project management, release engineering, and technical operations teams who manage the development process, handle timelines and dependencies, and support in-production software. When something unexpected happens, you want them on your side.

- **Who has access to data I might need?** Analytics, consumer insights groups, or market research groups can provide reports, dig up data, validate your assumptions, or conduct quick-and-dirty analyses to help you make decisions. Usually, they are in high demand and are overworked.

- **Who sells to potential customers?** Sales and marketing. When you wish to speak to customers, it's essential you have a supporter who will connect you and trust you to handle those conversations diplomatically.

- **Who else talks to users regularly?** Don't overlook your customer success teams (such as account management or customer service). They often know more about customer issues than anyone. They're usually delighted to be asked to contribute to share insights on what they hear every day from the field.

- **Who are the most trusted and respected independent contributors?** Look for long-term employees and individual contributors who are frequently invited to participate in strategic discussions—or for seasoned engineering leads who can come up with creative solutions to otherwise technically challenging problems. Seek their input and appreciate their access to strong, informal internal networks.

- **Who might be a good role model or mentor?** Consider senior product managers or experienced people managers outside of those you report to. They are often open to coaching you or acting as a sounding board. Most are flattered to be asked and, as they aren't part of your chain of command, are an excellent "low-risk" source for constructive feedback.

- **Who addresses everyday challenges?** Support staff such as executive assistants, front-desk people, human resources employees and recruiters, and the IT help desk. Share your project goals with them, and engage with them where possible. If they understand your goals, they can expedite the little things, whether that's scheduling last-minute meetings, quickly resolving IT issues, or ordering lunch as a reward for your hardworking team.

Before your first meeting with a stakeholder, put yourself in their shoes. Although there are company goals, each stakeholder has their own goals to meet, and those other goals may well conflict with your desired course of action. Ask yourself the following:

- What goals and incentives do they have and how might my goals be aligned or in conflict with theirs?

- Do they know what I'm working on for the business? What concerns or questions might they raise?

- What needs do they have that I haven't considered yet? What product feedback can I gather from them?

- How will they and their team benefit (or not) from my plan of action?

- What commitment and support can I ask them to provide?

As you meet with each stakeholder for the first time, here are some fundamental questions to ask them:

- What are your key goals (and how are these measured)?

- What does your team do to achieve these priorities?

- How can I help you achieve your goals?

- What data, resources, or relationships do you have access to that will give me the information I need to promote, prioritize, and address your needs?

- How best can I work with you and your team? What has worked well or not so well in the past?

- What do you like or dislike about my product?

- What more do you wish it could do? (When you respond to their wish list, make promises only if you can keep them.)

- How, and how frequently, would you like me to keep you updated on my initiatives?

- Who else on your team should I meet with?

Finally, consider their preferred communication styles and determine how to keep in regular contact with them:

- Do they prefer email updates or in-person dialog?

- Do they want regular, scheduled one-on-one meetings, or catch-up only as needed?

- Do they want time to process new information before responding, or do they prefer to jump into problem-solving mode—such as whiteboarding—immediately?

- Are they "water-cooler" types, preferring informal discussions where you bat around ideas? Or do they prefer short, formal meetings with clear agendas, where you quickly get down to business and make clear-cut decisions?

Don't expect all stakeholders to be able to dedicate much time to you. However, most should be willing to at least grab a coffee and chat with you for 20 minutes or so. Come ready with questions and let them do the talking.

Always discuss these meetings with your direct manager, ask for their permission, and invite them (at their option) to meetings with anyone more senior than they are—especially their direct manager. It's both courteous and a sound practice to keep them in the loop.

Also consider the importance of informal relationships. While personal commitments outside of work, or culture and beliefs may limit your involvement in some activities, go out to lunch, hang out after work, participate in the happy hours or office parties, join the sports team, or volunteer for the social committee. Express authentic interest in others in conversations. The more you know everyone at deeper levels, the more trust builds and the easier it gets.

Don't think that building relationships is "sucking up" or means you have to sugarcoat your communications. Superficial relationships quickly crumble when under stress. Building a relationship is about finding common ground—a mutual passion for the company's mission or shared personal values—and developing a deep respect for each other's contributions and complementary talents. You don't need to be the best of friends, but you do need to move beyond simple professional courtesy.

2. Seek Buy-In and Practice a No-Surprises Policy

Influential product managers master the techniques for getting buy-in across a large group of stakeholders. Buy-in is a process through which you "prewire" group consensus by previewing key points individually with stakeholders, ahead of a group discussion. It gives them a chance to digest the information and to respond and get onside with your recommendations. It reduces the likelihood of negative reactions and forewarns you of issues that might derail you when meeting in a larger group.

If you learn something that may be important for stakeholders to know, proactively share it with them, even when doing so is uncomfortable for you. Don't let them be surprised to hear about an issue for the first time in a meeting or from someone else in the organization. Likewise, never present controversial data or recommendations in a group setting where they are seeing it for the first time. Not only do you risk causing a commotion, but you miss a golden opportunity of giving them time to come around to your thinking and speak in support of your challenging new insights.

The perfect meeting is one where you know you have consensus on your desired outcomes with stakeholders and you receive unanimous public support. Buy-in increases the chance of that happening. A group meeting still enables everyone to share perspectives and debate, and you may yet have unexpected outcomes should the group uncover additional implications. But it's less likely a single stakeholder will express surprise or strongly disagree with you.

When seeking buy-in, consider stakeholder "hot buttons," and adapt your message and delivery to their preferred style. Consider the following, for example:

- Are they highly analytical, detailed-oriented, or data-driven (finance people, business leads, data scientists)?

- Are they visionary, brand-sensitive, and long-term thinkers (founders, CEOs, CMOs)?

- Are they determined to ensure time for thoughtful planning, execution, and quality (project managers, engineers, technical operations people)?

The Value of Buy-In

My meeting with the VP of operations was going to be tough.

There had been no progress on some of his workflow automation goals for over a year. His team's processes remained very manual and time–intensive. But other initiatives were always justifiably higher in priority. We would save a few hundred thousand dollars per year in costs, sure, but other projects with similar engineering effort could generate ten times that amount in revenue.

The latest roadmap did not address many of his needs. Knowing he would object, I asked to meet before its presentation. I planned to share what I was going to recommend and get his input. Over lunch, I told him I couldn't see a way to prioritize his initiatives. I reiterated his pain points (showing empathy) and acknowledged that he'd been promised commitments (by others) at previous planning sessions that still would not be delivered.

He was disappointed and argued for some time—even getting emotional at times (he was obviously frustrated). I presented data to show the value of other priorities while reiterating my appreciation for his position.

By the end of our meeting, he'd accepted the outcome and agreed these were the right decisions. He also made it clear that he'd still bring up his objections in the group meeting so everyone understood the issue—but signaled he would support the roadmap. Which he did.

He also thanked me…expressing gratitude for hearing him out. We met regularly after that, treating each other with renewed trust and respect.

- Are they concerned with how customers will respond and how the company will hit revenue targets (sales reps, marketing people, customer success/support employees)?

When you know what's important to each stakeholder, you can customize your message accordingly.

3. Proactively Deliver Regular, Concise Updates

To a stakeholder, no news *might* be bad news. Don't wait for stakeholders to follow up with you to get the latest update—give them one less thing to worry about by updating them proactively. An email, sent mid-Friday afternoon, is both a suitable medium and time—in just a few minutes at the end of the week, recipients can read it and respond (or peruse it on Sunday evening before the week starts).

Make updates concise—no more than a couple of paragraphs (or, better yet, outlined using brief bullet points) and well under one page. Only you care how you and your team spent every hour this week. And while there are always hundreds of small wins and completed tasks, they aren't all weighty enough that stakeholders need to know about them.

Long emails will not be read. Recipients should be able to glean key points at a glance. (Confirm with recipients that they are indeed finding them useful.)

Stick to a couple of key points such as these:

- What were your notable achievements this week? (And how are they aligned with progress towards your goals)?

- What are your priorities next week?

- What are the significant upcoming milestones and dates in the next month and beyond?

- What are the challenges, issues, obstacles, concerns, and outstanding action items inhibiting your progress?

- What specific action items do you want your managers or other leaders to take?

- What interesting data can you share (customer testimonials, charts, research, relevant articles)?

- Who on your team should you call out (for going above and beyond), and precisely what did they do?

As with the buy-in process, don't surprise anyone with an unexpected, bad-news update late in the week, just when everyone is ramping down.

Done well, product updates by email are excellent for keeping stakeholders feeling confident and in the loop, while allowing you to promote the value of your product initiatives.

In addition to a regular email, schedule a one-on-one meeting with your direct manager for about 30 minutes each week (or longer, or more or less often if they desire). Instead of expecting them to run the meeting, send an agenda ahead of time and come prepared with talking points.

Your purpose is to build confidence by

- providing a status update,

- asking questions and seeking feedback,

- clarifying and aligning business priorities,

- engaging your manager in your problem-solving, and

- asking for specific support where they can give it.

How to Write an Effective Email Update

- Use an email distribution list so you can control who you add or remove. If they have follow-up questions or reactions, you want recipients to be inclined to reply just to you rather than reply to all. An email list provides an extra barrier to unnecessary or disruptive group-wide communication, since the replier may not know who is on the list.

- Ask people if they want to be put on the list and provide an easy option for people to unsubscribe.

- When new stakeholders start at your company, don't forget to offer to add them, and forward helpful recent updates.

- Consider a more detailed email update for your manager and a briefer one for general distribution. Send the latter to everyone you identified in your stakeholder group.

- Save your manager some time by making it easy for them to copy and paste an exec summary from the top of your email update into their own weekly update email to forward onto their own stakeholder group.

- Don't use the "bcc" (blind carbon copy) function. When a recipient later discovers you have also been sending to hidden recipients, the unfortunate assumption is that you have not been transparent with them.

Always start your one-on-one with "How are you?" One-on-ones are perfect for building a personal, trusting relationship.

Also, a regularly scheduled one-on-one helps you and your manager resist the temptation to send too many emails or hold meetings to resolve every single issue that arises. You only need to meet when there are urgent issues; others can wait until your next one-on-one. Often, an answer to a problem will come up in the meantime.

Occasionally, utilize your one-on-one for a career development and personal growth discussion—seek feedback and identify areas of skills development. Create and share a simple individual development plan (IDP). Review roughly once per month to understand how your manager perceives your progress—making adjustments as necessary and asking your manager for support.

An email template, IDP template, and further advice for running your one-on-ones is available online at http://www.influentialpm.com.

4. Communicate the Bottom Line Up Front—Don't Keep Them Guessing

Whether in emails, one-on-one meetings, group discussions, or informal chats, nothing is more frustrating for a stakeholder than waiting for you to get to the point. While you ramble on, they are asking themselves questions such as the following:

- Why am I reading or listening to this? Don't make me guess.

- What are the implications? Don't make me worry or think for you.

- Where is this conversation going? Can you stay on point?

- What do you want from me? Action? Is this just an FYI? Am I about to be asked to make a decision?

Instead, *bottom line up front*: deliver the "so what?" points first, then fill in the details. Be clear about implications and any actions you want your listener to take. Not sure where to start? Imagine you've been asked a question about each of your priorities, decisions, or issues. Start with the conclusion first and finish your answer within 30 seconds.

In emails, start with the outcome first—so your communications stand a higher chance of being read. If you want to go into more detail, write an executive summary (you can start the summary with the acronym TL;DR which stands for "too long; didn't read") and include details "below the line" or add links to documentation the recipient can choose to read should they want further information.

Don't pad bad news between good news or roll it in with small talk to soften the blow. It isn't rude to skip the small talk if there's something that needs immediate attention. Managers get hundreds of demands on their time each day—you stand a better chance of getting their attention if you quickly get to the point.

5. Always Provide a Recommendation and Options When Communicating a Problem

When you approach a manager with a problem, know that just passing it on to them doesn't mean the problem has gone away. You may feel better after describing in detail your struggles, frustrations, barriers, constraints, and complaints, getting it all out of your system. You might think that you have done your bit by escalating the issue and that it is now someone else's problem to resolve. But don't be surprised if your manager replies, "Well, what are you going to do to solve that?"

Usually managers want you to feel confident in addressing issues without involving them every time. They may be happy to guide you, contribute to the team effort in resolving the problem, or intervene in high-impact urgent problems, but they won't want to do all the thinking for you.

So be ready to own the problem by doing the following:

- Before escalating the issue, think about two or three possible solutions. Some might be within your power to solve; others may require your manager's help.

- Don't include options that are unfeasible or unpalatable, just to get your manager to support your desired solution. That is manipulation.

- In your communication, describe the problem, followed immediately by your solution options.

- Recommend your preferred solution. Let your manager either agree with you or suggest an alternative approach.

6. Be a Low-Maintenance Employee—You'll Earn Trust and Become Part of the Inner Circle

You have probably heard the saying "the squeaky wheel gets the oil." While that might be true for some, it isn't a particularly attractive trait in a product manager. Accept the challenges that come with your role. New

Come with Recommendations

With hundreds of people reporting to him and constant requests from the president and other executives of the company, demands on this Fortune 500 COO were intense. He was trying to make an engineering organization work more effectively, while managing a tight budget and addressing slower-than-expected customer growth.

I was called to a meeting with the COO by one of his peers—a general manager for a business unit. The agenda wasn't clear, but I soon learned that the general manager was pushing the COO to make decisions on several of our product priorities. He was unprepared for the meeting and didn't have any suggested solutions or recommendations for all the problems he wanted the COO to fix. I could sense the COO getting frustrated and alarmed—here he was being pressured to make critical decisions without having either the time or data to process them.

I turned to the general manager and suggested, "How about we take this discussion offline, you and I, and then come back to the COO with a recommendation? We'll try to come up with something we think we can all support."

The relief in the COO's face was apparent. I had just lifted a load from his shoulders. He readily agreed to a follow-up meeting once we were ready with our recommendations. A few days later, he came by to thank me for being prepared to step in. I told him it was nothing and joked that "one of my jobs is to try to make us all more successful—that way I can be successful too."

Years later, when he moved to a different company, that same manager reached out to recruit me for his team.

business priorities, changes in direction, conflicting needs, resource constraints, unexpected disruptions, aggressive deadlines, and conflicts with other departments are all to be expected. How you handle them is what matters.

Managers have only so much time to make their teams productive. While they may have more sway in an organization, they, too, are often highly constrained. They certainly don't want to spend much of their time on a single employee. You don't want a reputation for being difficult to work with when something doesn't go your way. Instead, you want your manager to see you as their go-to person, especially when it comes to addressing complex issues or changes.

As a rule, then, build the following practices and attitudes into your work life:

- **Be judicious as to what issues you escalate**—Try to be self-sufficient but communicative. Escalate only what truly needs their attention (even if it means a little more pain for you).

- **Monitor your emotional response**—Be wary of complaining (about your workload, about other team members, etc.) or getting emotional with your manager. Save such expressions for times (hopefully infrequent) when you have a serious issue and need to jolt your manager into action.

- **Focus on making the company and your manager as successful as possible**—Understand your manager's goals and support them. Your efforts will be all the more appreciated.

- **Develop empathy for the rest of the organization**—Understand how each team does its job, along with its needs and challenges. By doing so, you'll be more likely to assume good intent and appreciate where others are coming from when conflict arises.

- **Accept what you cannot change**—Understand, for reasons that may not be entirely clear to you, that your manager may occasionally overrule you or task you with an essential (but less fun) initiative.

As a low-maintenance employee, you often become a trusted insider, sending your manager the message that they can delegate tough jobs to you, value your involvement in key meetings, and think of you as someone who will get the job done with a minimum of fuss.

Product Governance

You might already benefit from a regularly designated check-in with senior decision-makers that allows you to communicate and receive guidance on overall product priorities and progress. However, if not, perhaps you are experiencing misunderstandings or having trouble gaining agreement on your product priorities or desired outcomes. There may be a lack of clarity in regard to roles and responsibilities, or resourcing may be misaligned with delivery expectations. Maybe you lack sufficient input on business objectives to inform your decision-making. At a regular meeting—say monthly—your key stakeholders can collectively review, discuss, and align behind your recommended product direction.

If you don't currently have such a forum and feel one might be helpful, suggest it to a senior product leader as a means to improve collaboration and visibility. You need to be empowered and confident that you are focused on delivering what the organization believes to be the highest-value initiatives. For the most efficient use of your time, you and other product managers can team up to run a single session.

The benefits of such regular check-ins include the following:

- **An opportunity for stakeholders to influence and align**—Product managers present roadmaps and recommendations, gather input on decisions, and identify tradeoffs between competing objectives. Stakeholders voice concerns and ideas and provide perspectives. Importantly, other stakeholders hear them and join the debate. It helps to have opposing views surface at the same time to accelerate alignment. You can identify hidden issues and flag these for later follow-up, to get resolution.

- **A review of the allocation of resources**—It's common to have more priorities than can be adequately resourced. And what can get done with the available resources within the time available is often overestimated. A product forum provides an opportunity for a reality check, reviewing how resources are deployed and what reasonably can (and cannot) be worked on. It can help inform which priorities should progress in the near future and which should not. To ensure they set realistic expectations, make sure that your product forum participants discuss both roadmaps and resource allocation together (not separately).

- **Goals, commitments, and risks**—A forum provides a stage for product managers to remind the organization of why specific initiatives are being worked on and to ensure business goals haven't shifted in the meantime. Project KPIs are shared, so stakeholders understand what success looks like. (Don't just recite a laundry list of initiatives; emphasize the business reasons behind them.) Risks and mitigation plans can be agreed upon. If for any reason, a commitment looks to be in jeopardy, the product manager can request help, whether to remove obstacles or enlist assistance from other teams.

- **A green light**—A product forum can serve as a place in which to review substantive (potentially high-investment, high-risk, or both) ideas and initiatives. You can discuss their business benefits and formally approve their implementation. Alternatively, if a project looks less promising than initially hoped, the forum is a place for product managers to recommend whether to halt it.

Guard against the tendency of the product forum to become primarily a place for tactical discussion, which is ineffective and disempowering.

Product forums must be kept high-level. Product managers must take care to make sure they do not become occasions for simply providing status updates, gathering requirements, or enabling stakeholder to constantly overrule or second-guess the product manager's decisions. If you observe any of the following issues, you may be slipping into dangerous territory:

- Someone other than a senior product leader runs the meeting. A product forum is meant to be a place for the product team to lead the discussion and build confidence.

- Individual or team performance, date slippage, or delivery pace is a regular topic of conversation. This can lead to finger-pointing between the product team and engineering.

- Past decisions are consistently revisited. Pet ideas resurface again and again for re-evaluation.

- Meetings include detailed feature reviews or demos. There's discussion about scope, design, or functionality instead of goals, metrics, and roadmaps.

- Project timelines are presented and specific delivery dates mandated.

- Product managers abdicate their responsibility to make prioritization decisions and leave such decisions to the forum instead. While they should welcome the opportunity a product forum provides for everyone's point of view to be heard, product managers should own a clear data-driven case for what initiatives matter most.

Designed well, a product forum can serve to align stakeholders behind product roadmaps, keeping everyone focused on the business priorities that matter. Product managers should take input from forum meetings but remain responsible for deciding product priorities (and accountable for those decisions).

CHAPTER 3

Understand Your Customer

Answer five key questions to define the customer you serve and why.

1 The five questions you need to ask (and answer) about customers and their needs—before you endeavor to create a solution.

2 How to use powerful but simple frameworks to define your target customers, including the ways in which they address their own needs today and your risks and assumptions about them.

3 How to devise compelling value propositions and differentiation statements that communicate the benefits of your solution to your prospective customers.

First, Understand Your Customers and Their Needs

Stop. Before you define requirements for (or further implement) your product solution or feature set, ask yourself these questions:

- Does your team have a clear perspective and shared understanding of precisely who the solution is intended for?

- Are you solving a significant problem, and is it important that the problem is solved? Are you clear about why this is a priority for your customer? Will they pay you for a solution to their problem?

- Can you articulate exactly how customers will benefit? Is this a message that can be compellingly communicated to them?

- Have you understood how to position your product as a unique improvement over the way customers solve the same problem today?

- Do you have more than one type of end user or customer? If yes, do you know for which one you should optimize your solution?

- Do you know what risks might derail your initiative? Do you know how to deal with them should they eventuate?

- Do you have the agreement of all internal stakeholders on why, and for whom, the company is tackling this initiative?

- Have you established useful constraints and context that will serve to focus your team, making sure to limit the project's scope?

If you answered no to any of the questions above, then take a step back before proceeding.

In this chapter, I will discuss the importance of answering five questions (as outlined in **Figure 3.1**) about your customer and the problem you intend to solve for them—before you start defining and implementing a solution. Doing so for any major initiative is immensely beneficial and does not require an intensive, costly effort. And it need not delay your project. Rather, by using lightweight, informative, and focusing frameworks, you can save time and cost, and align everyone behind a common goal.

To illustrate, I will include excerpts for a hypothetical product called "Babylon," a home-hydroponics system for growing herbs and seasonal vegetables in a convenient, space-efficient system. Target customers include urban professionals who rent apartments and developers who build units that they want to make more attractive to rent out. For brevity, the examples

1. Who is your target customer?

2. What problem are you solving for your customer?

3. How is your customer solving the problem today?

4. What is unique in your approach to solving your customer's problem?

5. What don't you know yet about addressing your customer's problem?

FIGURE 3.1 *The five key questions*

contain much less information than you will need to provide when you complete your analysis, but they show how to make the frameworks actionable. More details and examples for Babylon are available online at http://www.influentialpm.com.

Don't Jump into Solutions: Part I

A few years back, I was meeting with a product manager in my team. He was updating me on his project, one that I had initially supported, and progress looked good. He described details about the features he'd defined, the results of discussions with engineers, and the designs for the technology platform.

At one point, I realized the initiative didn't seem to make as much business sense as it had a few weeks before.

"Wait," I asked, "why are we doing this again?"

"We prioritized it."

"Yes, and the product plan is excellent," I replied. "But given the changes happening in our business, I'm not sure it makes as much sense to do it anymore."

Taken aback, he asked, "Didn't you like this project?"

Now it was my turn to be alarmed. "Just because I think something is a good idea doesn't mean it is."

We were lacking a clear understanding of the scope of the problem we were addressing, had not questioned our assumptions enough, and had not ensured alignment across stakeholders (myself included).

We'd jumped into solving a problem without clearly defining *why* working on it was a priority.

Why You Should Ask (and Answer) the Five Questions

As covered in **Chapter 1,** ideas need to be rigorously explored and evaluated. Once a promising idea becomes a potential candidate for implementation, it can sometimes have so much momentum that less-experienced product managers, feeling a sense of urgency, jump straight into execution (*solution mode*). Instead, stay longer in *problem mode*, so you can:

- **Avoid opportunity costs**—Uncover hidden assumptions that challenge your suppositions. Validate that you are working on a meaningful customer problem, and if you are not, work on something of more value instead.

- **Reduce later confusion and lack of clarity**—You and your stakeholders may have different ideas of what the problem is, why it is important to solve, and what success will look like. Without establishing common understanding early on, your product initiatives may be disrupted as goals or plans are revisited. Provide context and a focused statement of intent to inform and align stakeholders and motivate your team toward a common purpose.

- **Establish principles for communicating to customers**—Confirm a clear picture of who you are solving the problem for and why it is important to solve. This will help you to determine testing and validation strategies, build empathy toward your customer, and inform your marketing message.

- **Set a baseline for defining success**—Draw a clear picture of why solving the problem is interesting for your business, along with the market environment and risks you face. As you learn new information, you'll want to check periodically that your answers are still valid. Establish post-launch success criteria to determine whether you

Problem vs. Solution Mode

Make "problem mode" and "solution mode" part of the language of your team and explicitly guard against jumping into execution too early. As in, "Wait! We are still in problem mode; we don't understand it well enough yet to define the answers."

met your goals and to hold yourself accountable if the results are not to expectations. If you didn't achieve your goals, what did you underestimate? What needs addressing to get your product on track?

However, answering the five key questions is not useful unless you follow these guidelines:

- **Do it before you start defining solutions**—Don't jump into solution mode without knowing the scope of the challenge. Ignore the product or features you already have in mind. Take a moment to fully comprehend why and for whom you are solving the problem before you commit to building a particular solution.

- **Do it for any and all initiatives**—Conduct analyses when developing new products, making major product enhancements, taking existing products to new markets, undertaking anything of significance. Even if the issues seem to be well understood, if you are about to commit resources to a project, you owe it to yourself and your organization to define precisely why you should pursue the opportunity.

- **Remember it's not a pitch**—While your analysis can be used to explain an idea in a succinct and compelling way, it should not be viewed as an attempt to sell an idea to decision-makers. The intent is to gather data, organize your thinking, and communicate how best to proceed. Be objective and avoid emotional attachment. Embrace

Don't Jump into Solutions: Part II

At one enterprise SaaS company, a product manager asked the sales team to provide feedback when they lost deals due to missing product functionality. Once sales provided the product manager with a list, she immediately set about adding the missing features.

After a few releases, many of the gaps had been closed—but customers were not using many of the new features, and there were few additional sales.

Many requested features were specific to one particular customer and not reusable across a wider market (or set of customers). Some of the features automated business processes that were needed relatively infrequently—such as pulling reports required only once a year—and, as such, were of limited value. Others solved only a component of a much larger customer need. The remainder had been requested merely because competitor products had these features and clients wanted "feature parity."

Had the product manager taken time to assess and confirm the market opportunity, the team may have avoided wasteful investment.

challenging questions with balanced, in-depth answers. Be willing to state assumptions and articulate risks, weaknesses, and unknowns.

Why only five questions? They're probably not the only questions you should answer about your customer, but they will give you a useful starting point for establishing a baseline. You are creating a *living* document. As you proceed, update it with new information and answer other questions that come up along the way.

Keep Documentation Lightweight

As a rule—as with any documentation outlined in this book—try to keep your analysis to a few pages that are easy to comprehend and summarize.

Analysis needs to be informed by actual customer and market research. And you should make extensive use of expertise available to you— collaborate with teams involved in understanding the customer such as user experience, consumer insights, data analytics, product marketing, and sales. But don't think you have to put everything on hold until you have completed lengthy, up-front research. Your goal is to state and support a direction and hypothesis—which might change, as you learn more as you go.

Use simple language, along with data, diagrams, and bullet points, and link to more extensive data if required. Producing a short, visual summary presentation for stakeholders is an effective way to communicate why your solution is necessary.

Some organizations favor *Market Requirement Documents* (MRDs). These are lengthy documents that include extensive market data (often with a list of customer and sales requests) and a business case to justify the investment. MRDs, as a rule, have become increasingly discredited as a useful means for evaluating and communicating opportunities for four primary reasons:

1. Rather than offering a critical assessment of the opportunity, they are often written to impress and win over stakeholders. Rarely does an MRD recommend *not* pursuing an idea.

2. MRDs take time to write—and they are usually too long to read. As a result, they are often ignored and go quickly out of date when business and market realities change.

3. They are uninspiring and prescriptive. Lacking vision, they often preempt specific solutions and don't leave room for learning and adapting. At worst, they define a wish list of customer "must-haves."

4. MRDs generally precede actual customer validation. A document is created based on scant research or third-party opinions, and then it moves quickly through approval, team formation, and kick-off. It is soon too late to seek out and substantially adapt the idea in response to new market insights.

Similarly, *business plans* outline the project-launch timeline, expected user growth, revenues, engineering and support resourcing levels, and profitability. They can be useful when analyzing future investment for existing, well established products—but not for new-product development. Full of "scientific wild-ass guesses" (SWAGs), they set unreasonable expectations around a mostly unscoped, untested, risky initiative. An attractive business case might mislead you into a false sense of security and into skipping validation. Business plans are rarely revisited after launch to ensure you delivered all you promised. So instead, use simple tools such as the *Lean Business Model Canvas*.

You can find an example stakeholder presentation and business model canvas—along with a basic overview on Profit and Loss (P&L) statements—online at http://www.influentialpm.com.

Who Is Your Target Customer?

Your *target customers* are those for whom you are solving a problem. Even though you may believe your product to be mass-market (and therefore everybody is your target customer), or your product is in its early days and its appeal within customer segments is unclear, you should not define your customer too broadly. Do so and your target customer becomes too abstract to inform your product-development decisions. Define your customer too narrowly, however, and you may fail to recognize that your product can appeal to prospects you hadn't initially intended to serve resulting in an overly specialized solution with limited market potential.

Not everyone who is a customer of your product or service must *pay* you—although, obviously, some must. Your *buyers* are those who pay you—they may or may not be users of your product. *Users* utilize your product to achieve their goals—they may or may not pay you directly for this. For example, if you have a media or content website, advertisers are the buyers who pay you for access to your readers' attention. Your readers are your users and are possibly receiving content for free. Similarly, in a business-to-business (B2B) example, the EVP of branch banking and CTO choose a bank's branch software and teller automation solutions. They are the buyers. The branch employees and tellers are the users.

Your product must solve the needs of both buyers and users. When I discuss "target customers" throughout this book, I'm including both buyers and users (unless specified).

There are three main advantages in defining your target customer:

1. **Focus on exactly who you do (and do not) serve**—As you evolve your product, you will prioritize many competing ideas and feature requests. Knowing precisely who you are doing what for, and why, is essential in providing clarity for you, your stakeholders, and your development team. If you don't know who your target customer is, you risk one or more of five poor outcomes:

   ■ Producing a one-size-fits-all product that isn't sensitive to your specific customer's preferences.

   ■ Creating a product with too many features, but one that does nothing particularly well.

   ■ Making product decisions that favor short-term business needs (often at the expense of your customer's long-term needs).

   ■ Over-optimizing for one customer type over the needs of others. This is particularly destructive in marketplaces (where you must balance the needs of buyers and sellers), in media products (where it might be easy to give way to advertisers' needs over those of readers), and in enterprise services (where buyers may provide a long list of needs that are of little value to end-users).

   ■ Creating the product *you* want (because you mistake yourself as a proxy for the customer).

2. **Draw attention to hidden customers and users**—You may have an "obvious" target customer. But in conducting more thorough analyses, you may discover other types of users unexpectedly using your product. They need not be large in number but may indicate a new opportunity that you can explicitly address.

   Second, beyond your primary target customer, you may also have other decision-makers and influencers, all with a say over where and how a product is used. This is particularly common in enterprise services, but it can also occur in consumer services.

   For instance, consider a hypothetical product targeted to high-school students. In addition to this target user, you might consider the needs of (and the need to deliver value to) other influencers or decision-makers: parents, teachers, principals, and school districts. For a medical product, in addition to the patient, you might consider how nurses, doctors, hospital administrators, and insurance companies are also served by, or (if it is disruptive) perhaps are resistant to, the product.

3. **Build empathy with customers**—By usefully describing your customers, their lives, and their environment, you can create a picture that will allow you to "walk in their shoes." When making product and design decisions, you are then more readily able to reflect on the impact these decisions will have on your target customer. Furthermore, when conducting user testing, these attributes become useful for qualifying users or discovering additional unmet needs you might address.

▶ In **Chapter 5**, I cover customer discovery in more detail.

It is critical at this juncture to emphasize that you cannot accurately define your target customer in a vacuum. It is essential that you seek to personally interview existing and prospective customers and study any customer-insights research your company has already undertaken, to validate your assumptions and iterate on your understanding. Interviews can be done informally (such as in a coffee talk with friendly customers) and formally (such as in structured consumer research).

Do so early and often—and start well before you invest in solutions. User-testing your product implementation is not the same as understanding your customer!

How to Define Your Target Customers

Defining your target customers is not a one-off exercise. As your product grows, you may acquire entirely new customer segments you hadn't initially intended to attract. Or you may learn more information, identifying flaws in your original assumptions about who your customers are and what they need.

1. You Likely Have Multiple, Complementary Target Customers

Your product may simultaneously serve several target-customer types, with different but complementary needs. Each type will need to understand how your product addresses their needs, and you will need to design different parts of your product solution to meet these. Their interests may even compete with one another, demanding that you discuss trade-offs and perhaps rank one customer type as more important than another.

Customer combinations are often two sides of the same coin:

- **Enterprise services**—The *economic buyer* makes the purchase decision. This person usually requires your product to serve a business need in both a secure and cost-effective way. The *end user* is the person operating or using the purchased system—perhaps employees of the company. End users need functionality to achieve their work goals efficiently and easily (much like consumers). End users may have little say, however, about which solution the company purchases. Poor enterprise services pay little attention to the end-user experience, optimizing primarily on delivering sales. Unfortunately, these products build a negative reputation, might go unused (shelf-ware), and struggle to retain customers when the product is up for renewal.

- **Media sites**—Consumers of content from media, social media, gaming, and other ad-supported products make up your *audience* (otherwise known as readers, traffic, or visitors). They want to be kept interested, informed, and entertained. *Advertisers* pay to gain access to and get the attention of your audience, usually to promote their brand or to illicit a direct response (generally encouraging your readers to click on an ad and go somewhere of the advertiser's choosing).

- **Marketplaces**—*Buyers* want to find, purchase, and secure reliable delivery of quality merchandise or services at a reasonable cost. *Sellers* want trouble-free transactions, reasonable prices for their merchandise, minimal returns, and quick receipt of payment. Marketplaces are common and may not result in a direct financial transaction between the buyer and seller. Think, for example, of a job-search website: it provides candidates with the ability to search and apply for jobs, while businesses use tools to manage applicants and the recruiting process.

- **Nonprofits and social enterprises**—The *end user* receives some service at a discount or for free. But to make these types of offerings sustainable, they require funding from *agencies* or *donors*. Agencies and donors are customers too—they are expecting value from their generosity (such as recognition or the achievement of a policy goal).

2. Sub-Segment Target Customers, Even If You Will Deliver the Same Product Solution to All of Them

For consumer products, the same product may serve different end-user segments, and each segment may use it to achieve different goals. GoPro, a light, water-proof camera, for example, serves sports enthusiasts, divers, hikers, and travelers. LinkedIn Learning, an online education subscription service, is used by hobbyists (such as amateur photographers), small-business owners, self-employed consultants, and creative professionals. While there may be much in common with these segments, their goals for using the product are different.

> ▶ You can learn more about customer lifecycles and funnels in **Chapter 11**.

Another way to "slice" consumer product users into segments is to map them into their *lifecycle stage*. It may be useful to think about them in this way if you are undertaking specific enhancements to a product designed, say, for a highly loyal expert user versus a first-time novice.

Lifecycle segments might include the following:

- A *first-time visitor* is someone considering your product, learning more about what you offer.

- A *trial user* has completed some task that might later lead to purchase of your product, perhaps signing up for a free trial or setting up an account.

- A *paid customer* is someone who values your service enough to pay you at least once.

- A *loyal* or *repeat customer* is an ongoing payee for your service. They're happy with the value you deliver and are adept at using your product and its advanced features.

- A *lapsed* or *former user* is a user who has stopped using your product for any number of reasons. They can be a wealth of sobering insights and a target for re-acquisition.

Enterprise services can also be segmented (often by *size*). There is no definitive classification system for size: some define categories by employee headcount, others by revenue. Definitions vary by country and industry. Combining common definitions used in the United States and European Union, one might propose the following segments as shown in **Table 3.1**.[1]

TABLE 3.1 Enterprise classifications by size

SEGMENT	SUB-SEGMENT	EMPLOYEES
Small-medium businesses or enterprises (SME or SME)	Sole proprietors	Self-employed professionals (who may contract or outsource occasional help)
	Micro businesses or small-office-home-office (SOHO)	1-10 employees (in addition to owner)
	Small businesses	<50 in EU <100 in USA*
	Medium-sized businesses	<250 in EU <500 in USA*
Large enterprises		<10,000
Very large enterprises		10,000+ (includes most Fortune 500 companies)

* varies by industry

Sole proprietors, micro businesses, and small businesses make up 98 percent of all businesses in the United States. They often act more like consumers in their behavior and product-purchasing habits. The larger the enterprise, the more attractive it may appear to you as a lucrative, prospective customer. However, they can also be more demanding, take longer to progress from a lead to a paying client, and require you build a specialized sales and support organization.

A second method for enterprise segmentation is by *Industry Classification*. The North American Industry Classification System (NAICS), as of 2017, maps industries into 17 top-level and 99 second-level categories.[2]

For enterprise products, your target customer (or market segment) should have the following in common:

1. They buy/need similar products that solve similar problems requiring the same benefits and features. Can you productize a single solution for them?

2. They have similar sales cycles and decision-makers. Can you create a sales process that is largely standardized?

3. When you gain key customers in a particular segment, others in the same segment view it as a validation of your product. Are prospective customers likely to respond well to your reference customers? Will they talk with each other (creating word of mouth)?

Keep segmenting until your target customer largely shares these three things in common. For example, "Fortune 500" is not as useful a segment as "financial institutions in the Fortune 500." Fortune 500 financial institutions tend to have the same needs and similar processes for decision-making, and they will want to see that you've completed successful implementations for other companies like them.

3. Constrain Your Target Customer by Their Attributes

Broad and all-encompassing target-customer definitions, such as "students" or "parents with small children" are usually not useful. To focus on a more specific target, add qualifiers to your customer segmentation, as relevant. Here are some examples of such qualifiers:

- *Demographics* such as age range, gender, and socioeconomic factors (education, social status, occupation, income, industry).

- *Geography* if you are focusing on a location-specific market (country, state, city) or environment (urban, suburban, rural).

- *Goals and values* such as aspirations and interests (relative to the problem you are addressing).

- *Motivators and inhibitors* such as intrinsic factors such as personality, frustrations, incentives, or work culture.

- *Technology comfort and preferences*, which may inform the kinds of solutions you should pursue.

When defining attributes, resist the temptation to do so in terms of your proposed solution—you're not exploring your product at this point but rather the market opportunity. For example, "Babylon is for people seeking a home hydroponics solution to grow greens" is stated as a solution. Better—although still not perfect—is "Babylon is for affluent urbanites who want to eat better as part of a healthier, more sustainable lifestyle."

4. Create a Persona to Bring Them to Life

Personas are intended to describe your target customer as a stereotype or archetypal user. They help you empathize with your intended target audience by describing their busy lives, their competing priorities, and their needs, wants, and desires. Personas help you look at the world—and your product's role in it—through the customer's eyes.

They also provide a reference for effective communication within your team. When designing and implementing your product, personas are a convenient shortcut to discuss trade-offs. Ask, for example, "What would Debbie think about that?" Immediately everyone can reference your persona, Debbie, and imagine her using your product.

Personas are closely related, but not identical, to your target market. Generally, the target market is much more diverse than the average or typical user. Personas capture many of the common attributes within that target, but not all target customers will have all attributes. For example, your target market might be in the 24- to 39-year-old range and be 70 percent women. Your principal persona should be 29 (assuming that is the median age) and be a woman.

Build secondary personas for one or two others—but only if they represent a large segment of your user base. (If they make up a small percentage of your revenue or usage, then you should not make explicit product trade-offs in favor of them.) In this example, the 24- to 39-year-old male may not be representative of the average user but might warrant a persona if they exhibit materially different behaviors or needs.

Personas aren't just for consumer products. You can also use them when selling in enterprise environments (as you sell to people, not companies), to describe the economic buyer of your product (the person deciding to

Using Personas

My e-commerce client had developed a powerful set of personas. One was a detailed definition of the life of a *busy mom*—dropping her kids off at school, working full time, and making major purchasing decisions for the family. Convenience and simplicity were of utmost importance to her.

Another persona described the motivations and values of a *comparison shopper*—wanting to review options side-by-side, making trade-offs, and shopping across a variety of online and offline stores (with little loyalty to any of them). Choices and low prices were of the utmost importance to this persona.

Although both personas used the same e-commerce site, their needs (and the product features required to support them) were different.

Impressively, these personas were ingrained into the client's culture. Large posters summarizing each persona, including a first name and a photo, were displayed throughout the offices. Rarely did a meeting go by when one or the other persona was not invoked to determine which decisions stayed true to the needs of the customer. Most employees did not resemble either persona, but they had developed true empathy and sensitivity for their target customers.

acquire your service, often a senior manager) or other influencers in the decision-making unit (DMU), including technology executives who support your product and your end users (employees who will use your product day to day). Each can be represented by their own persona.

End-user personas are particularly helpful in sales-driven enterprise companies where the client relationship centers on the economic buyer. When end users have little choice over whether they use your product, product priorities tend to favor the economic buyer's needs. Create an explicit end-user persona, and you can raise awareness of their needs, making sure their experience and satisfaction is considered by your team too.

Internal users can also have personas. Think, for instance, of the people in your organization who are responsible for product support, marketing, business operations, and development and then create personas for them where warranted.

Base your personas on real research and be cautious of your own biases—made-up personas likely do not represent your actual user base. It is fine to propose personas as a hypothesis, so long as your customer research aims to validate and adapt them. Include only those attributes that are relevant to the decision to use your product and those that help your team empathize with your users.

Finally, when creating personas, don't focus on how they will use your product. Keep specifics of the solution out of it—especially features. Concentrate on the overall context in which your target audience lives and works.

You can build personas using the framework and examples in the supporting online materials at http://www.influentialpm.com. In the framework, I have included descriptions of 27 attributes to spark your thought process and help you generate rich personas to bring your customers to life for both you and your team.

What Problem Are You Solving for Your Customer (Value Propositions)?

Value propositions articulate the benefits you promise to deliver to a specific target customer for the problem you aim to solve—in their terms.

They are a powerful way to turn "it" statements that focus on the product into "them" statements that are all about the customer. They change your perspective from the internal-facing "what" into the external-facing "why." Using the customer's point of view, they aim to confirm why your new product or product enhancement should exist.

Here are three advantages in using value propositions. They:

1. **Help limit scope**—Prioritize only the features and functionality that will be core customer benefits. Anything that isn't necessary to delivering on a value proposition is either superfluous or addressing a different need.

2. **Align stakeholders**—Good value-proposition statements are compelling and exciting. Even before your product is defined, they can be used internally to provide context for the problem you will solve and the impact on your customers.

3. **Set the stage for talking to your customers**—They describe why customers should buy or use your product. Whether getting validation from users that you are solving a meaningful problem or marketing your newly released product, you must be able to explain succinctly the benefits to potential customers at any time during the product development process.

How to Create Value Propositions

A simple approach for developing a value proposition is to start by summarizing the problem you will solve and then identify about three compelling statements that, together, deliver the benefits your customers seek. Frame your statements from the target customer's perspective and avoid mentioning features.

1. Start with a Problem Statement

A problem statement explains precisely the *pain point* or *unrealized opportunity* the target customer experiences today. It should be supported by evidence. It sets the context for the problem you aim to solve and tells us why your solution matters. Writing out the problem statement clarifies your thinking and, with practice, can become part of a spoken pitch to stakeholders.

Here is a brief example for Babylon (though yours should be more thorough):

Finding and buying fresh, organic, GMO-free produce is often quite inconvenient and costly. While users desire a healthier lifestyle, supporting a healthy diet comes at a premium that many families cannot afford. Furthermore, when purchasing produce, shoppers can be challenged to know exactly what is in the food they buy. Urban apartment dwellers are particularly disadvantaged since they rarely have room for or access to a garden. There is a need for more afford-able, more readily accessible, guaranteed organic produce.

In some cities, housing developers are hard-pressed to increase the value of their properties while differentiating themselves in the rental market—leading to downward pressure on rents. Renters expect amenities, yet it is difficult to find low-cost solutions that are also attractive, useful, and unique. New policies (some subsidized with tax incentives) aim to promote healthy and sustainable living.

An opportunity exists for a cost-effective solution to support a greener lifestyle, one that intercepts the needs of housing develop-ers and urban dwellers.

For supporting evidence, include *both* quantified and qualified data. Data are essential to understanding the extent of the need or pain point; illustrating the problem has high impact and is common to your target audi-ence. Qualified data might include imagery, quotes, or a walk-through of the daily struggles of your customer (in a world without your product).

In our Babylon example, we may include the following supporting evidence:

- A chart showing the growth in awareness and consumption of healthier foods.

- A summary of the costs of funding a healthier lifestyle.

- Examination of the relative difficulty for urban dwellers to get home-grown food, compared to those who live in rural environments.

- Examples of cities under rental-market pressure and data showing declines in rental charges.

- Examples illustrating renters' increased expectations for amenities.

- Breakdowns of tax-incentive programs.

- Quotes from renters frustrated with the choices available at grocery stores.

2. Don't Assume You're Addressing a Meaningful Need

Many well-designed, highly functional products fail simply because the problem they address isn't actually that important to customers. While potential customers may *say* the problem is important, in practice, it may not be—not when compared to all the other demands on their time and money. Perhaps the problem doesn't happen very often, and the difficulty is quickly forgotten. Or the value of resolving it just isn't worth paying for.

Unless you already have a product in the market, it is difficult to be certain that solving a problem will impact your customers and business. And even if you do have a product in the market, evaluating which of the many potential enhancements would be of most benefit is equally challenging. Treat your problem statement as a hypothesis that requires constant data-gathering, validation, and challenging. Use the iterative methods outlined throughout this book to test them continually on potential customers—then practice, and present or pitch them just as you would with internal stakeholders to observe their reactions and gather feedback.

Potential problems belong to one of three categories, and knowing which category your proposed problem statement addresses can help you gauge how critical the problem is that you are solving:

- **An unmet need without a current solution**—Have you spotted an opportunity that doesn't have a solution? You may require intimate knowledge, firsthand experience, and unique new technology to address the opportunity. Tackling unmet needs comes with greater risk; solutions are harder to explore, evaluate, and market because customers are often unaware of the problem (and have learned to live with it or find manual workarounds). However, developing a solution to an unmet need can be very lucrative if you succeed.

- **A significant pain point with current solutions**—Pain points can be rational or emotional. Many useful products have addressed deficiencies in current solutions—they solve the same problem in a better way.

  Consider these common pain "motivators":

  - Too costly

  - Inefficient/laborious/slow

  - Unreliable/low-quality

  - Inconvenient

  - Inconsistent

  - Unusable

  - Uncertain/risky

  - Lacks control

- Lacks transparency

- Discriminatory/unfair

- Designed for a different user/situation

The worse the existing alternatives are, the greater the opportunity. If the existing solution is "good enough," you will run into significant barriers (switching costs) in your attempt to dislodge an incumbent or change customer behavior. To succeed, you must do an extraordinarily better job—not just a marginally better job.

- **A desire or want**—These opportunities tend to be less compelling and may appeal only to a niche audience. Customers embrace your product for its technology or for its ability to act as a fashion statement, enhance their reputation, provide emotional satisfaction, or make a personal statement. If you are to be successful, brand, design, marketing, and uniqueness are of paramount importance. Early adopters may love your product, but this may not translate into success with a mainstream audience.

3. Define about Three Statements Per Target Customer

While not a hard and fast rule, a potential customer can easily comprehend a few value-proposition statements. Three is a good target—less, and you're unconvincing or too vague; more, and you risk appearing unfocused and confusing.

Value proposition statements should do the following:

- Start with "*You*" (or "I" or "We," if written from the customer's first-person view).

- Be mutually exclusive—each one describing a compelling benefit, different from the other benefits.

- Collectively deliver on the overall goal of the user.

- Be relevant and important (not trivial) to the target customer.

- Be singular (be careful not to link benefits together with "*and*").

- Do not confuse your own business goals with those of the target customer.

For example, say you have a subscription product and your business goal is to convert visitors into paid users. You should define a set of value-proposition statements in terms of the underlying benefits you deliver to customers, so that, in turn, they value the paid product enough to upgrade.

Each separate target-customer segment has its own set of value propositions—even if you are addressing both with what is more or less an identical product solution. They likely value different benefits or see similar benefits as deserving different priority. Our example, Babylon, has two customer segments, and what appeals to urban dwellers will not appeal to housing developers, even though the one product is offered to both.

For the urban professional, these value propositions are appealing:

- You can save money compared to buying from grocery stores, by removing the middleman and harvesting only what you need.

- You will save time with convenient access to a local source of greens and vegetables right in your apartment complex.

- You control what goes into your food to deliver a healthy, sustainable lifestyle for your family.

For the urban developer, these value propositions are appealing:

- You can increase the value and appeal of your housing developments with unique and differentiated amenities.

- You will make the best use of limited, common apartment spaces and budgets.

- You may qualify for tax incentives that are available for healthy urban-living policies.

A company's value propositions are often evident in the messaging used in customer acquisition and channels, such as a website's homepage, an email, a mobile-application download screen, marketing or advertising materials, white papers, or sales pitches. When communicating directly to users, the company may not use "you" statements, but the benefit to individual customers is implied in the visuals and language.

4. Value Propositions Are the Reasons People Buy— Your Features and Functions Make It Possible

Do not include specific features or details of the solution in your value propositions. Stick to "why" your target customers will benefit—not "what" or "how."

If you already have specific features or a solution in mind, use a *feature-benefit-value* map (**Figure 3.2**). It will help you to group and link features to

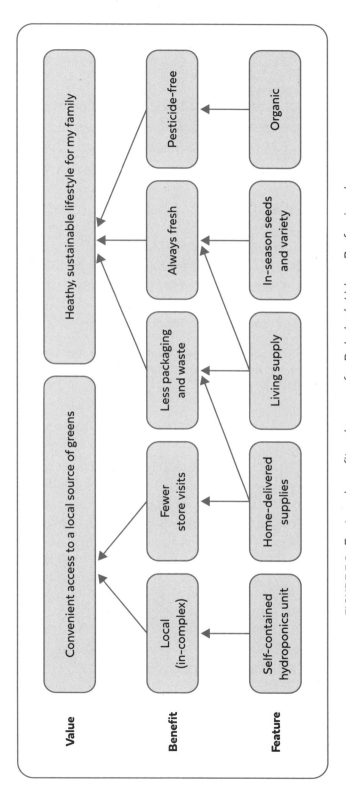

FIGURE 3.2 *Feature–benefit–value map for Babylon's Urban Professional*

common benefits and, ultimately, to a high-level value proposition. You may find some features deliver against more than one benefit or value proposition.

How Are Your Customers Solving the Problem Today (Competitors and Alternatives)?

The purpose of understanding the existing market is to extend your understanding of your target customer, their needs, and how well they are being served.

If your company is an incumbent in a market, competitive intelligence serves to defend against threats, keeping you focused on maintaining and increasing your unique advantages over other solutions. If yours is a smaller company that's new or yet to establish itself in the market, it helps you identify where incumbents fail to serve and satisfy customers—that could be your opportunity to be disruptive.

There are three key advantages in conducting competitor analysis. You can:

1. **Identify and benchmark your customers' choices**—Monitor customer satisfaction levels. Test competitor products with your users and your competitors' users to learn what they like and don't like about each one and to uncover hidden usability issues or functionality gaps in your solution.

   When competitors invest in new functionality or technologies, or in entering new markets, it indicates potential growth opportunities or better ideas to solve customer problems. If you can get competitor business and product-performance data, you will have excellent benchmarks for your metrics and targets. You will also be able to focus on the areas of weakest product performance, and the data will help in prioritizing new features.

2. **Position yourself in the market**—Your differentiators are crucial to establishing your market position relative to your competitors'. But you should also be aware of any differences in how you and your competitors view your target market and its needs. By reading, interviewing, and doing other research, you can discover how competitors talk to their customers and how they position themselves relative to other options, including yours. Where your solution is stronger or weaker, clarify your positioning.

Having Competitors Is a Good Thing

Here are some reasons why:

- *Market validation*: Having competitors validates that the problem is worth solving. If you don't have any competitors, you need to ask yourself a tough question: Am I working on a meaningful problem?

- *Customer interest*: Competitors provide you with clues. They can help you find attractive markets or customers and develop successful marketing strategies.

- *Benchmark KPIs*: You might be able to benchmark performance and compare estimated business metrics. If a competitor has better customer retention than you, for example, then find out why.

- *Efficient operations*: Competitors can provide insight into more effective or cheaper marketing, operational, or distribution models.

- *Investment and unit economics*: Competitors might be spending a lot more or a lot less than you on, for instance, engineering, sales, marketing, customer service, and support. If so, why? And what are the implications for you?

- *User testing*: You can test competitor products with your customers to learn where your product's usability is better or worse. You can interview the competitor's customers about their likes, dislikes, and unmet needs.

- *Execution insights*: Competitors might have advantages or challenges internally with their culture, decision-making, or speed of delivery. How do you replicate the advantages and avoid the disadvantages?

- *Sense of urgency*: Psychologically, competitors provide a rival, motivating a team to band together and focus on winning—creating a sense of purpose and urgency.

3. **Prepare your marketing and sales teams**—Your positioning and a summary of competitor strengths and weaknesses will help your product marketing team develop persuasive messaging. At the same time, avoid drawing attention to any problems with your solution.

   In enterprise organizations, you may be expected to provide sales materials for training and objection handling. This is essential because customers often directly compare several similar offerings in their evaluation process.

How to Analyze Competitors and Alternatives

Define a broad competitive set. New entrants, players in adjacent geographic or industrial markets, solutions on different technology platforms, and even non-technology-based solutions—they are not always obvious, yet can be potential threats.

Maintain a healthy respect for competitors, but keep your primary interest in serving your customers. Competitive analysis is useful only if actionable, so focus only on information that can influence your product direction.

Your organization may have a competitive intelligence-gathering function, often conducted by a business strategy team or corporate development group. But don't rely solely on them. You are likely, as a product manager, to be more focused on understanding your competitors' products and comparing them with your own. You will have a unique customer-centric view of competitors.

A set of competitor-analysis frameworks for product managers is available online at http://www.influentialpm.com.

1. Define Your Competitive Set Broadly—Look for Alternatives Too

Uber and Lyft are direct competitors with similar technology platforms and end-user services. They both enable easy access to transport through a mobile application. However, that's not the problem they are solving; that's their solution.

The problem they are solving is getting people from A to B affordably, safely, and conveniently. That means they are also in competition with taxis, private cars, public transportation, bikes, carpools, and even people walking. Both have also realized that the emerging technology of self-driving cars is a huge threat, and they have taken steps to incorporate it into their strategy. In general, the same cannot be said of the taxi industry.

Alternatives can be created from dramatically different technology or without technology at all. Customers don't care how you solve their problem so long as you solve it and do so efficiently.

In Babylon's case, it might be tempting to limit their competitive set to grocery stores, especially up-market organic suppliers. However, a short brainstorm and a couple of user interviews later, this would likely be broadened to include

- home, window, and community gardens;

- restaurants and chains emphasizing organic, fresh produce;

- healthful direct-to-home delivery services (premade food or recipes with ingredients); or simply,

- higher-quality, pre-packaged food.

As a team thinks further about the landscape, the challenge ahead of them becomes clearer—but so do the ways in which they can position their product, preemptively address weaknesses where alternatives are stronger, refine their target audience, and conduct effective customer research.

2. Don't Take Competitors Too Seriously—But Learn from Them

Strike a balance. You neither want to be ignorant of nor arrogant toward competitors. You also shouldn't react with concern every time they make an unexpected turn. Some industry leaders claim to ignore competitors entirely, focusing only on their own innovations and customer needs.

But even if you have a superior solution or are the market leader, it is better to be modest. Keep tabs on how your competitor landscape is evolving. You might find that a competitor is nibbling away at a lucrative niche market, attracting loyal customers they can leverage to move aggressively into your market. Or perhaps new entrants are developing innovations that could be disruptive. While this may or may not be a problem, it's always best to reduce the likelihood that you will be surprised.

At the other extreme, do not get caught up in time-consuming, exhaustive analysis. Do not allow competitor activities to distract you from your core purpose—to keep existing customers happy and attract new customers.

If a competitor does something innovative, learn from them and observe how they address customer needs. Don't react with panic or denial if an existing competitor announces an unexpected initiative or appears to threaten your direction. Observe trends, but engage stakeholders and customers before taking considered action. Competitive analysis informs your understanding of the customer and provides team motivation, but it should not dictate your vision or roadmap.

Chase *your* vision—not that of your competitors.

3. Make Analysis Actionable

A competitor analysis is not a feature-parity matrix, showing a side-by-side comparison of who has what features. All this does is promote the idea that having more features equates to a stronger service (and all you have to do is "keep up" or "catch up"). Such thinking can distract you from working on the key initiatives that *your* customers need.

Use hypotheses-driven approaches and be clear on what you will do based on the outcomes. I recommend the following process:

1. **Research the competitor's product**—In addition to online research, product teardowns (where you use and detail every observation of their products) are particularly powerful. Capture details such as

   - messaging and positioning;

   - pricing, tiers, and trial offerings;

   - first-time experience;

   - discovery and navigation;

   - learnability;

   - steps to achieve goals;

   - delighters;

   - what use-cases they don't support (perhaps deliberately);

   - how they engage you outside of the product (such as through email and notifications); and

   - overall, how well the product meets customer needs.

2. **Produce a "value summary"**—Highlight high-level similarities and differences between your solution and theirs. Rather than focus on features, describe elements such as

   - value proposition and pricing,

   - target market/segments and key customers,

   - differentiation and delighters,

   - a summary pitch, and

   - marketing and selling activities.

3. **Complete a SWOT analysis**—Using a variety of lenses, evaluate your

- strengths (internal factors that give you an advantage over others),

- weaknesses (internal factors that put you at a disadvantage),

- opportunities (external factors you could take advantage of), and

- threats (external factors that could disadvantage you).

4. **Develop an action plan**—Stick to a couple of recommendations at a time.

At http://www.influentialpm.com, you will find a thorough walk-through, with examples of a process that is ideal for evaluating competitors. Included is a rich SWOT template with 21 attributes to consider.

Serve your customers well. If they are happy, they have little reason to leave you, and they won't over just a few features. Instead, understand your competitor's strategy, target market, value proposition, and differentiators—and use that to inform, but not dictate, your decisions.

Remember, imitation is the highest form of flattery. Don't flatter your competitors.

. . . .

Feature Parity Is Not a Goal

A mobile social-networking client was in discussions with a new investor over competitor disparities. The investor worried that the client was behind in one of its key markets (China) and asked for a side-by-side feature comparison between their product and those of competitors.

The most useful outcome of the exercise was my getting to know the competitors' products much more intimately. However, the result—a three-page spreadsheet that included mind-numbing detail—was of little use.

Instead, I asked myself what the strengths and weaknesses of our product were in comparison to theirs, and where their opportunities were. Instead of the spreadsheet, I used a SWOT process to ask myself a variety of questions about the attributes that made our product stronger or weaker relative to our competitors'.

We knew we had fewer features—that had been deliberate, to keep the product to a single purpose and elegantly simple. Too many features lead to clutter. Counterintuitively, far from being "behind," the analysis highlighted that a lack of secondary features had made our product both easier to use and more useful.

However, one insight did stand out: a smaller competitor had introduced an innovative live "TV-style" broadcast-video function. Further research indicated this might be an opportunity for us in the Chinese market—one that could create higher engagement and revenue potential.

What Is Unique in Your Approach to Solving Your Customer's Problem (Differentiators)?

Your *differentiators* outline how you uniquely address your target-customer problem. They are the one or two key advantages you will offer customers that competitors do not, and they define your position in the market. Differentiators are sometimes called *unique selling propositions* (USPs).

Apart from customer communication, the major reason for defining a differentiator is to articulate your *core competency*. This is one of the most critical product decisions you will make. Much of your product development will focus on improving differentiation, putting as much distance between you and your competitors as possible. Knowing your differentiator will help you prioritize the features and functionality to deliver to customers—other features (which are similar to competitors') can just be just "good enough," or you may not even invest in them at all. A differentiator helps prevent your roadmap from becoming a race to feature parity with competitors.

That said, while differentiators capture a potential customer's attention, delivery of your entire value proposition is why they stay. You will have to build a range of requisite features to ensure your product does not lag too far behind alternatives and that it keeps your customers happy.

Focusing on Your Core Competency

I was working for an online photo-sharing and printing business that had two strong competitors. We all offered the ability to upload photos, share albums with friends and family, print photos, and order photo merchandise such as custom-made books.

Every quarter we'd run a customer survey, gauging satisfaction in using each key feature of our service compared with the use of the same features offered by competitors. For many features, such as upload speed, sharing capabilities, shipping costs, shipping speed, photo editing, and album management, we wanted to do only *as well as or slightly better than* competitors. While each feature was a vital component of the service, none was reason enough to choose our service over competitors'.

Instead, we differentiated our service on the highest-possible image quality and beautiful merchandise. Ours was the quality brand, and we invested heavily in making sure we retained that position. This included creating superior prints with our proprietary image-correction software, using professional advanced-printing labs, and investing in the most beautiful photo-book design templates possible.

How to Define Your Differentiators

Customers should see your differentiator as unique and substantive. A good differentiator is sustainable and provides you an "unfair" advantage over competitors. You want to make it hard for customers to stop using your solution and make it difficult and costly for competitors to replicate what you have.

1. Unique: Not Otherwise Available to Customers

Search for exclusive assets or approaches that you have or can develop. These may include

- access to proprietary technology or infrastructure;

- content that only you have or can produce;

- exclusive access to partners, suppliers, vendors, or channels;

- a large community of users (creating a *network effect*, where a product or service gains additional value as more people use it—meaning even if a competitor has all the same features, users will not switch);

- data about your customers that allow you to deliver an exceptional, personalized experience;

- a superior brand associated with quality, reliability, and trust;

- organizational expertise, functions, processes, or relationships;

- a platform with seamless product integrations across many tools or services (providing customers with a convenient one-stop shop for their various needs); and

- a unique cost structure or scale (so you can be cheaper *and* more profitable than your competitors).

Protecting Differentiation through Patent Protections

As a defensive strategy, companies should seek patents for the important technologies they have developed. However, in mainstream, fast-paced internet and software industries, you can't rely on patents alone as a defense against competitors. Many companies are simultaneously tackling the same customer problems and are bound to come up with very similar ideas and solutions. What's more, patents are frequently subject to costly legal challenges and can be overturned. And by the time the legal process reaches its conclusion, the opportunity for commercial success may have come and gone.

Don't forget to state why these are of value to your end customers. Unique technology, for example, is not in itself a differentiator unless it allows you to do a better or cheaper job in solving your customers' needs.

2. Sustainable Advantage: An Advantage Competitors Cannot Easily Replicate

If it's easily copied, you won't have a differentiator for long. Being "easier to use" (offering a better user experience) or less expensive (unless you have superior cost structure) aren't sustainable differentiators. User experience can be readily copied, and undercutting on price alone will simply lead to commoditization. Cost and convenience offer temporary advantages, but do you have something that will maintain your edge?

If you are working on a new product, your differentiation might be more an aspiration than a reality. That's fine—it just means you need to focus on execution, building your core competency quickly to capture a market position.

3. Substantive: Not Trivial, Too Broad, or Too Narrow

Your differentiation should neither be too broad nor too trivial. Don't make the mistake of attempting to appeal to as many people as possible or being so specific that you will only attract a niche audience.

- -

Intellectual Property in Technology Companies Is Hard to Defend

I was called on as an expert witness in a case, in which an Australian company challenged the rights of other companies to make use of their patent.

The company bringing the legal action claimed it had been awarded an Australian patent for the technology behind its targeted advertising. It used sophisticated analysis of search phrases and user behavior to serve more effective and relevant adverting, while also making the experience more palatable for targeted users. But despite the patent, various technologies for something similar had been in use for several years.

The expensive court case ran for a few months, eventually concluding that multiple companies had concurrently worked on and launched highly similar technologies—there was "prior art" that invalidated the patent.

In modern-day technology companies, it is very hard to prove an invention is truly unique and patentable, and defending such patents is costly and time-consuming. The fast pace of technology companies means that even if you have a rare legal success, by the time you do, the invention could be obsolete.

- -

Ask yourself what the appeal is to potential customers and then directly test your assumptions with potential customers. Force-rank or place on a 1-to-10 scale some possible statements to get a relative sense of what matters most to them. If your differentiator is of interest to only a small segment of your target customers (and, in particular, if it is of interest to just early adopters), then it won't be compelling enough to build a sustainable product.

Be careful not to define your differentiation factor purely around an advanced or rarely used set of functions. (There may be exceptions: for instance, when you have a "freemium" product that offers a basic service for free but aims to capture a small segment of power users ready to upgrade for premium features.)

Babylon's differentiation statement highlights unique technology and customer experience. It describes a fully automated, end-to-end solution that, if executed well, will give the company an enormous lead over competitors in both convenience and quality control:

> Babylon's differentiation is its intelligent harvesting process, which is entirely automated, meaning that the only labor required by the user is to plant the seeds, track their growth progress, and collect the produce when it is ready. Automation decreases the risk of human error; guarantees fresh, organic produce; and eradicates the distrust often experienced with third-party produce exporters who can't guarantee the absence of GMOs or the degree of cleanliness that affects the quality of the produce.

What Don't You Know Yet about Addressing Your Customer's Problem (Risks and Assumptions)?

The purpose of *risk analysis* is to identify the critical potential *external* disruptions that, if not monitored or mitigated, are the most likely causes for your product to fail.

There are three major advantages in completing risk analysis:

1. **You can prioritize early product-discovery activities**—By surfacing risks in advance, you can identify development or research activities that should be addressed early in the project. You increase your knowledge of customer needs and are more confident in your decision as to how or whether to proceed with a project. You can save time or resources.

2. **You clarify your assumptions about the future**—You have probably made a couple of assumptions that can only be proven once development of your product is more advanced. By calling out your assumptions, you can set boundary conditions. These effectively act as "trip wires"—if an assumption you made later turns out to be wrong, you can revisit your plans and make accommodations.

3. **You communicate to decision-makers**—Most stakeholders are very comfortable with taking calculated risks. Explain the dangers and articulate your plan for addressing them. Include conditions, such as if a test fails, for reviewing further investment (to build their confidence in you and your product plans).

How to Assess Risks and Assumptions

Every product initiative has risks. New products tend to have significant risks since you must establish a new market and create a profitable, scalable business. But existing products also have risks—keeping customers satisfied, sustaining growth, and protecting an existing market from competitors and new entrants.

· ·

Setting Trip Wires

Our business goal was to increase engagement and content consumption by subscribers (which would improve retention rates). We determined that the ability to create a personalized list of content (which we called "playlists") could achieve the goal.

After the feature launched, we indeed saw increased content consumption by those who used it, meeting our main goal. Customer feedback was all very positive, and we had almost declared success...until we revisited our assumptions.

We had assumed that 25 percent of subscribers would adopt the feature—but the actual adoption rate was only about 5 percent. Despite our launching a highly successful feature, 95 percent of users weren't even using it.

After further research, we determined that we had a discoverability issue. Without realizing it, we'd made the feature hard to find. We also had not done a good job in letting people know what to expect from the new feature—many trying it for the first time abandoned it before giving it a chance.

These barriers needed addressing. We moved the new feature to the homepage and created a series of preconfigured playlists so that users could experiment more easily.

Neither issue would have been found as quickly if we hadn't been clear on our incoming assumptions and vowed to revisit them.

· ·

Risk assessment does not need to be complicated. You and your team's knowledge and consensus opinion is often enough to surface your most significant concerns. So identify a few key risks, their implications, and how you will manage them. Then revisit as you learn more. The key is not to be "right" the first time but to keep validating your assumptions and surfacing new concerns as you progress.

A fun way to approach risk assessment is to hold a "pre-mortem" before kicking off a product initiative. Assume your product initiative failed. Then brainstorm why.

You'll find a useful risk-assessment framework in the online materials at http://www.influentialpm.com.

1. Focus on Risks Not Readily in Your Control

A proper risk assessment does not focus on obvious or internal risks that are theoretically in the company's control. Securing adequate resourcing, obtaining executive approvals, validating the product with customers, or testing secure and robust technology—none of these factors should be overlooked, but they are all within your control.

External risks may not be readily apparent, and if they are, you have probably figured out how to address them. Likely product risks include the following:

- Customer comfort level or willingness to change behavior.

- Customer interest and desire to pay.

- Ability to market to or reach target customers.

- Discoverability and adoption of product/features.

- Invention of new technologies.

- Systems, data, or technical complexity or stability.

- Competitor reaction.

- Partner or supplier cost or dependency.

- Regulatory/legal guidelines.

2. Your Assumptions Are Also Risks

Don't overlook assumptions you've made along the way, such as those in your target-customer and competitor analyses. Are you assuming how much your users will pay for your product? How many users you'll convert into paying customers? How aggressively you can grow? Where the sensitivities are in your model? What, if wrong, could be problematic? Those are risks too!

As introduced in Chapter 1, it is natural to have cognitive biases (such as seeking data to support existing views or to be overly optimistic). This is particularly true when you are publicly advocating that your company is pursuing an idea—it's natural to choose assumptions that put the product initiative in a good light. So balance those biases by objectively challenging your assumptions.

3. Prioritize Critical Risks and Have a Mitigation or Response Plan

Surface the risks that matter most—identifying and addressing a few (three to four at most) key risks. These tend to be risks that are both high in *probability* and *impact*.

A risk assessment is not valuable unless you make it actionable. Increase your chance of success by communicating the risks you are taking and how you plan to address them. Mitigating risks means acknowledging them beforehand—in your product discovery and development plan (for example, through testing early with users). Responding to risks means having a plan to address them if and when they occur (but not before).

4. Revisit to See Whether Things Have Changed

As you learn more, some risks will be replaced by new ones. Don't become too focused on assessing risks, but occasionally revisit them. Look to see if anything has changed and whether further actions are needed. Critically, review your risks when you launch your product and monitor them closely.

Be proactive in communicating and responding to issues as they arise. Especially for new innovations, the risks might be high enough that stakeholders are concerned about dedicating resources towards the initiative. To address, start with a smaller scoped initial product, and ask decision-makers to commit enough to allow you to demonstrate whether the risks are material or not and then later to decide to invest in a complete product, should the initial step be a success.

If your risks are substantial, promise to do sufficient work to reduce or mitigate them, then go back for additional support. Don't expect the full backing of decision-makers for a risky project without providing plans to mitigate or nullify the risks you've identified.

For example, in addition to gathering a small, but invaluable, amount of consumer insights from customer interviews and using the collective wisdom of the team and some trusted advisors, the Babylon team brainstormed potential risks and scored them as shown in **Figure 3.3**. They identified issues with user confidence, local regulatory challenges, competitor moves, product predictability and stability, and supplier risk. They were then able to pursue customer discovery with more focus.

RISK	DESCRIPTION	PROBABILITY
Lack of consumer knowledge and comfort-level with hydroponics	• Users do not trust automated farming • Users think they need technical knowledge	High
Laws, community guidelines, and developer restrictions	• Local government regulations restrict installation • Developers can't or won't dedicate space for units	High
Hydroponic farming system failures [internal risk]	• Fully automated farming system at scale not yet proven • Yields may be substantially lower than expected	Medium
External technology or services threats	• Users prefer just going to stores that provide cheap, local, organic produce • More convenient solutions for healthy eating (online delivery services)	Medium
Farming supplies increase in price beyond that which can be supported by unit costs	• Supplies needed to run the system (seeds, nutrients, tools, delivery) become too expensive for a large portion of users	Medium

FIGURE 3.3 *Example risk action plan for Babylon*

IMPACT	PLAN
High	1. Stress the fully automated nature of the product 2. Push for media coverage of hydroponic farming 3. Create user friendly guides
High	1. Dedicate a legal team to research legislative barriers 2. Lobby with local communities and policy decision-makers to advocate for acceptance 3. Proactively talk with developers, boards, and committees as product is evolved
High	1. Dedicate more resources during discovery and testing to ensure technology is stable 2. Invest in a customer success team 3. Include a food guarantee in GTM and business model
Medium	1. Market the personal and customizable features (grow what and when you like) 2. Stress the hyperlocal aspect of the product, highlighting small carbon footprint 3. Assess strengths of new competitive technology applications and alternative business models
Medium	1. Partner with seed companies to ensure sustainable prices and supply for the future 2. Order supplies in bulk to lower the price per unit 3. Create financing plans and alternative pricing strategies (such as subscriptions)

CHAPTER 4

Collaborate to Set Priorities

Focus on the highest-impact opportunities and align stakeholders behind your product's goals.

What you'll learn in this chapter

1 Your role as a product manager in evaluating and driving alignment of product priorities and the frequent challenges you will face.

2 Techniques you can use for collaboratively prioritizing product initiatives, whatever your company culture, while balancing the need for speed and precision.

3 How to approach the incremental optimization of existing features using user-behavior feedback loops through split-testing.

Why Product Prioritization Is Hard

If there is one responsibility that keeps product managers on their toes more than any other, it is deciding what to prioritize. Deciding what to build—and, critically, what not to build—is arguably the most important role you, as a product manager, will play in driving value for your company. Building the wrong thing can be incredibly costly, not just in time and resources but in opportunity cost. Your credibility, as well as team morale, will be negatively affected if you work on initiatives (regardless of origin) that have marginal value to the business and your customers, fail to challenge rationale and assumptions, or gather insufficient data to inform prioritization decisions.

Yet failure, at some level, is inevitable.

Prioritization is about striking a balance between two competing needs. Yes, you want *always to be building, always to be shipping, and always to be learning.* But you also need to gather and use the best information you can get ahold of to make sure your team focuses on what is most important.

Failure is okay if you could not have anticipated it. It is not okay if you did not do the hard work up front to evaluate a proposed project or feature carefully.

Here are the most common challenges you might face as you navigate prioritization, with tips for making the journey smoother.

1. Process Is the Easy Bit; People Are the Hard Bit

Throughout your organization, you will have many stakeholders who have an opinion on what you should build next. They all consider themselves experts—and they all are, within their respective domains. Your user experience team might see ways to enhance the product flow to improve customer satisfaction; a business lead might see opportunities to increase customer acquisition and revenue; a founder might imagine dozens of potential new features that, if implemented, take the product closer to realizing his or her vision; the sales team might request short-term features as demanded by a big prospective customer they want to land; and an engineering lead might see ways to rework some core technology, so it scales and performs better.

They all feel emotionally attached to their ideas—and have a sense of urgency about them. And all think that the company does not appreciate and act on their ideas fast enough.

The answer is to see prioritization as a *collaboration*, not simply a process. Give your team, stakeholders, and even your customers the opportunity to provide input and influence decisions in two discrete ways:

1. **Discuss user, business, and product goals (not features) and their relative importance**—Stakeholders will need to agree on the vision and objectives of the product before they ever agree on projects and features. Get senior stakeholders in alignment and be explicit on low-priority (or no-priority) goals.

2. **Gather features and enhancement ideas**—View ideas as mere candidates and never evaluate an idea in isolation from others. Document the idea, why it is being proposed, and any supporting evidence.

Do each step separately. By first aligning on goals, you can set the context in which to make feature level decisions. Prioritize ideas relative to one another to determine which are more likely than others to advance your goals. If you receive further stakeholder pushback, then the question becomes "Have the goals changed?" rather than "Which is the more important feature?"

Later in this chapter, I will introduce frameworks you can use to manage your prioritization process, but don't use them in a silo. Instead, collaborate and be transparent. Don't sacrifice progress trying to get unilateral buy-in, however; you will rarely—perhaps *never*—reach a unanimous consensus. Stakeholder groups have far too distinct and conflicting goals.

2. Saying No Is Unpleasant

Product managers want to please both stakeholders and customers, and each group can sometimes be convincing, or even forceful, in their demands. Perhaps they've put a lot into thinking about and communicating their ideas. The absence of a solution might cause them more pain; for instance, a lack of tools or features makes their job a lot more difficult. Saying no to their request might feel, to them, like a personal rejection, because emotions invariably get involved.

By definition, however, prioritizing an item of work over other work is a zero-sum game due to limited resources. Saying "yes" to more than the team can do sets you up to miss expectations—either something you promised to someone else earlier will get bumped, or the new request won't be worked on anytime soon. Whatever you do, you're going to upset somebody.

▶ See **Chapter 1** for more ways to handle stakeholder ideas, including nice ways to say no.

Recognizing what not to prioritize is as important as knowing what to prioritize. If the work you've planned doesn't make sense in the broader context of your strategy and goals, then don't work on it. Furthermore, don't let inertia allow you to continue to work on something that no longer makes sense. When necessary, it's better to bravely cancel a project.

3. There Is Never Enough Data

You can't always be entirely confident that you are setting the right priorities. Even if you do have lots of data, you may have conflicting input from customers, stakeholders, your team, and your research.

If you're endlessly collecting more data to inform choices or win over stakeholder objections, you're experiencing analysis paralysis. Recognize that the mere act of analyzing a potential project is to prioritize working on it. Approach prioritization as an ongoing task. Set the expectation with your team and stakeholders up front that you will frequently revisit priorities as you continually gather new data. Blend techniques that you can implement quickly and collaboratively, with more detailed analyses of customer needs and business opportunities as needed.

Your objective should be to seek proof points so you can confirm priorities with supporting data, research, and tests. Focus on learning and tweak priorities as you discover new information. But never prioritize a project without some convincing evidence that it may be valuable to customers and your business.

Second, break larger projects into smaller ones. Because prioritization is about making progress toward goals, focus on the critical part of each initiative first. The Pareto Principle[3] suggests that 20 percent of the effort is likely to generate 80 percent of the benefit toward your goal. It is better to stop working on a priority once you've done enough to deliver on the highest-impact components and then move onto what's next on the list. You can always return to it later if you think there are additional business opportunities to capture.

▶ You can read more about validation and prototyping in **Chapter 5**.

Finally, do not forget your project list is just a list of candidates—a set of hypotheses about what might advance your product goals. It should not be interpreted as a list of commitments. Conduct validation, including prototyping and launching a small increment of the broader feature set first. Be prepared to eliminate a priority that has turned out to be less promising.

4. Dealing with the Loudest Voices in the Room

Perhaps a senior leader is asserting their opinions as truth, prescribing priorities without providing context and data, and not understanding the consequences for other potential projects. Or maybe a strong type A personality has debated others into a corner, presenting the illusion of having achieved consensus. While you must win over stakeholders, their opinion is still just one among many; and though they're experts, gut feelings are not a good way to prioritize work.

Sometimes it is okay to give in if, in the long run, it will build trust and the idea seems solid enough. But if it is a recurring issue, giving in can undermine the quality of the product and set the precedent that this is how the company sets priorities.

There is no simple approach to this issue. Each situation is different given individual personalities and leadership styles (for example, you may feel overwhelmed if the challenging individual is senior to you); however, here are a few methods you can try:

- **Bring data**—Negotiate more time to complete and share some analysis before declaring the project a priority. The act of presenting objective, challenging insights might be enough for the stakeholder to change their mind; but even if they do not, the decision can be taken with a greater understanding of the risks.

- **Include resourcing, dependencies, and consequences in the conversation**—They may change their mind once they learn that the cost is too high or that another critical project will be delayed to pursue theirs instead.

- **Return the conversation to goals and objectives**—If goals have changed, that needs to be reflected in the overall priorities, not just in the priorities for this project; in other words, such change would likely impact projects. Reinforcing the currently agreed overall goals might be enough to convince them to deprioritize the request.

- **Reiterate what is in the plan**—Busy stakeholders often forget what is already being worked on. Issues that arose earlier and are now being addressed by the development team are considered resolved in the mind of the stakeholder, so they move onto new issues. Remind them that you're working on what were previously agreed to be the topmost priorities. Be specific (list the specific initiatives you're working on, for example) and tell them that there is no excess capacity—if necessary, show them how each person on the team is currently allocated—and, to switch priorities, a tradeoff would have to be made.

The longer-term solution is to structure a methodical and transparent prioritization process. Doing so puts you in the driver's seat—you provide data, prepare recommendations, and invite input. You will build trust through transparency and, perhaps, see most of your recommendations adopted. At the same time, stakeholders feel they can strongly influence outcomes and that you are open to their input. Use one of the techniques discussed later in this chapter to formalize how goal-driven prioritization occurs.

▶ See the section on product governance in **Chapter 2**.

5. Disruptions out of Nowhere Always Jump to Priority Number One

Perhaps a product outage requires all hands on deck to address. Maybe a key customer is insisting on specific features. Or sales may ask for something that's likely to help them land a big client.

For the unavoidable disruptions, plan to make slower progress against priorities. Surface the issue and show the impact. If it happens consistently, then you may have a dire quality issue. Or it may simply be that urgent issues keep jumping the queue whether or not they are actually important.

For example, in sales-led organizations, especially those selling to large enterprise companies, stakeholders may escalate urgent requests to land a large client, effectively sidestepping the prioritization process. Try not to react to incoming requests from sales or customers; instead, escalate the issue to your product leadership. This may be challenging. If so, remind them that you're developing a solution to be used by many customers, not just one. If you hear the same request frequently, however, that is indeed cause to consider the item for prioritization.

What matters in determining priorities is understanding the core of what customers need (value), how they want to use your product (usability), and what you can reasonably build (deliverability).

Techniques to Make Product Prioritization Easier

No prioritization approach works consistently across all organizations, given their different sizes, product lifecycle stages, decision-making structures, and cultures. Even within one company, a single methodology may not be suitable for the full range of initiatives under consideration.

How, for instance, can you prioritize an initiative that is innovative and strategic but has a high risk of failure, an unknown scope, and a payback period well into the future against others that are well defined and of easily quantified business value?

The best techniques work top-down: they provide context and assessment criteria by prioritizing high-level customer and business goals first. You then map feature level details to these goals and evaluate their importance based on where the most value will be created. This approach is also highly adaptable. Top-level goals should change infrequently and be clearly visible to product managers and their teams. That way, product managers are empowered to move to the next priority should one that appeared promising turn out not to be so.

If your organization does not already have a standard prioritization approach, then select from the many techniques available and adapt them to suit your situation. Use them consistently so you can make relative assessments among options and refresh (rather than reinvent) your priorities regularly. I recommend you use several complementary methods concurrently—looking at your priorities from different angles will give you a better perspective.

Ultimately, regardless of which methodology you use, what matters is that you collaborate and discuss the priorities. You and stakeholders must agree on

1. the process for making prioritization decisions,

2. the overall goals and criteria to make evaluations, *and*

3. your rationale for and assessment of the initiatives that you believe will have most impact on those goals.

Your objective is to develop a plan that will allow your team to focus on the essential work and to leave other initiatives out of scope (for now). Your plan will be one your stakeholders can buy into even if they don't necessarily agree with everything.

Referring to **Figure 4.1**, you can categorize prioritization techniques into four groups:

Quantitative methods attempt to convert goals, project impact, and effort into numbers and calculate a set of ranked priorities. They can also be used to determine whether a project is financially viable or not.

Qualitative methods try to frame business goals and customer needs, using the collective wisdom of your team, stakeholders, and customers to identify priorities most likely to achieve those goals. The accuracy of

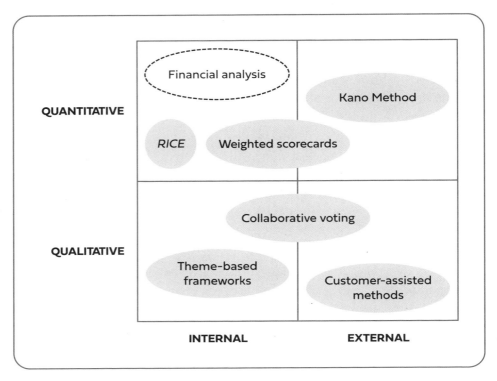

FIGURE 4.1 *Example collaborative prioritization techniques*

qualitative methods is not necessarily lower than that of quantitative methods; a set of assumptions converted into numbers are still assumptions and can give a false sense of precision.

You can further categorize these methods into the dominant set of inputs that go into the prioritization process. *Internal* approaches rely more on the data and perspectives already found within a company. They might include business goals, product performance data, stakeholder opinions, and existing-customer insights. Internal approaches are best when you already have a lot of knowledge to digest and to use to drive decisions. However, internal approaches might miss crucial new market information and are subject to groupthink bias.

External approaches leverage input from customers directly—helping determine needs, as well as areas of satisfaction and dissatisfaction, and getting buy-in and participation in ranking priorities. External approaches are best if you have little existing data, are in the early stages of your product development lifecycle, or want to add the voice of the customer into a prioritization process that otherwise might favor short-term business goals. Be sure, however, that you don't have just a few key customers determining feature-level requirements.

Some prioritization techniques are far more time- and resource-intensive than others. For example, financial analysis and the Kano Method require extensive data-gathering—the former involves modeling; the latter, interviewing many customers. Simpler techniques such as weighted scorecards or theme-based frameworks, although inappropriate for making major investment decisions, can be quickly completed and frequently updated. Simpler techniques are also useful in getting alignment or revealing any misalignment. Here's why:

1. Within a stakeholder group, there tends to be more agreement than not on the critical priorities. (Although there may be disagreement on less critical priorities, these initiatives won't be worked on soon anyway.)

2. You will more quickly discover any dispute on overall goals and evaluation criteria—and without agreement on these, you cannot determine feature-level priorities anyway.

While there are hundreds of methods and adaptations, I've chosen a few to include here because they are particularly effective based on their structure and creativity and because they demonstrate the full spectrum of quantitative and qualitative prioritization techniques. Some are simple and useful in guiding you on the direction you should take; others are more complex (and therefore time-consuming) and robust enough to determine major investments.

Weighted Scorecards (Quantitative–Internal)

Weighted scorecards accelerate goal-driven prioritization as a counterbalance to purely intuitive decisions that might otherwise prevail when there's a lack of time, limited data, or a "loud voice" in the room. Scorecards align stakeholders on overall goals, their relative importance, and the features likely to be of more benefit than others. They make assessment criteria explicit—forcing a discussion on the criteria rather than a debate on pet features. While you generate the framework internally, you can validate scorecards with trusted customers for additional confidence.

1. **Agree on the scoring criteria to use**—First, establish a set of evaluation criteria to use to score your features. Here are examples of commonly considered criteria:

- Improve customer satisfaction (add features, improve user experience).

- Drive revenue (ARPU).

- Accelerate growth (increase market share, scale).

- Develop new markets (add segments, geographies).

- Enhance customer conversion or retention.

- Lower costs (enhance operational productivity).

Although scorecards have the benefit of being able to include everyone's suggestions, as a general rule, a few criteria are better than many. Avoid expressing criteria in terms of business benefits alone. You, as the voice of the customer, must advocate for purely customer-centric goals to be included as part of the overall criteria. Similarly, include operational criteria (such as productivity improvements achieved through evolving the tools to manage and support your product). Because these criteria are often not as visible to stakeholders, they can be overlooked or undervalued. Even if their weighting is low, there is a good chance a few key improvements will result in their scoring high enough for inclusion in the overall priorities list.

Once you have agreed with stakeholders on the proposed criteria, determine together the relative weight (in importance) of each. The sum of the weights of all criteria should equal 100 percent. For example, as illustrated by **Figure 4.2**, together with your stakeholders, you might determine criteria number one to be 40 percent of the overall importance, with another four goals ranking between 10 to 25 percent of the total weighting each.

2. **Identify feature candidates to evaluate against the criteria**—
   Create a list of ideas including your research, those you have gathered in brainstorming and by interviewing stakeholders. Stakeholders may wish to include 10 to 20 features *each*, but it is not possible to understand and evaluate so many items simultaneously. A too-long list may cause the process to get bogged down with debates over rankings of marginal project ideas that have too little data to inform a decision.

   You must balance efficiency with the desire to reassure stakeholders that their ideas have been considered. To do so, try asking stakeholders to provide you with a full list but to force-rank their top three for evaluation. Once this exercise is done a few times, you can slate the next tiers of priorities for later consideration.

You may choose to perform this exercise with stakeholders individually first (on their list only). Then, once individual consolidations are done, it should be easier to combine scorecards. If items appear multiple times, you can easily spot where stakeholders share a point of view (such as a project that is consistently ranked high by multiple stakeholders) and where there may be misalignment (such as the same project appearing in multiple lists but with wildly different scores for the criteria).

3. **Enter the features, along with the criteria and their weights, in a spreadsheet**—A simple spreadsheet will allow you to make and calculate scores and to rank and fine-tune results with decision-makers. To populate the spreadsheet, gather all of your feature candidates. You may need to add a brief two-sentence description of each feature to ensure a shared understanding of what each is to achieve. Then list your features in the rows and your criteria and weights in the columns.

4. **Score feature impact on each criterion**—Give each criterion a rank anywhere from 0 (no impact) to 100 (very high impact), using multiples of 10. Rankings need not be highly accurate but should be debated objectively, using rationale and data (if you have it), to surface disagreements.

You will unlikely reach a firm consensus on scores—look for those scores with the largest variance and difference of opinions that, if changed, might drive a different outcome in the ranks. Debate those more rigorously.

In **Figure 4.2**, feature 1 clearly improves revenue and growth, with less impact on other areas. The weighted impact is $(80 \times 40 \text{ percent}) + (0 \times 20 \text{ percent}) + (50 \times 10 \text{ percent}) + (80 \times 25 \text{ percent}) + (10 \times 15 \text{ percent}) = 59$.

5. **Estimate cost for each feature**—Costs come in three categories: implementation, operational cost, and risk. A simple "T-shirt size" evaluation (S, M, L, XL, XXL) is all you require at this point. Add this as another column next to your score, for an overall perspective of impact versus effort/risk. Draw a hard line, shading lower-priority features as out of scope, because higher priorities already exceed available resourcing.

CRITERIA	REVENUE	USER ENGAGEMENT	CUSTOMER REQUESTS	GROWTH	TEAM PRODUCTIVITY	SCORE	RANK	EFFORT
Weight	40%	20%	10%	25%	15%	100%		
Feature 1	80	0	50	80	10	59	1	XL
Feature 2	50	20	40	90	30	55	2	S
Feature 3	30	60	30	30	60	44	3	M
Feature 4	10	10	40	50	80	35	4	L

FIGURE 4.2 *Example weighted scorecard*

In **Figure 4.2,** you may notice that features 2 and 3 require lower effort than feature 1 and have a combined impact of 99. These may, therefore, be better candidates to work on before working on feature 1.

6. **Bring stakeholders together to discuss**—Rather than argue each feature's merits, debate the overall goals and the relative contribution of each initiative toward those goals. You are likely to uncover missing criteria, particularly those of less vocal stakeholders who (once they realize how projects become priorities) will now push for their objectives. Scorecards also show stakeholders that you are seriously considering their needs but that there may be competing priorities that take precedence.

Some issues with scorecards:

- Although they appear to be quantitative, weights and scores can be easily biased. Scorecards are not a useful tool in environments where priorities are primarily influenced through lobbying or for those who are not open to challenging their strongly-held opinions. It is too easy to game the scoring to get the outcomes they want.

Scorecards Can Be Easily Biased

My manager was in charge of prioritization for all the product initiatives across the company. He built a spreadsheet that allowed us to line up all the projects we could do inside the rows—about 50 in all. In each column, we placed the top-level business criteria, including revenue, customer satisfaction, cost reduction, and stability. Then using a scale of 1 to 5, we rated the impact we thought each project would make against each criterion.

We also added a "level of effort" (LOE), which told us roughly how many resources each project would take to be implemented. This scoring methodology allowed us to use business criteria to rank projects—the more impact across more business criteria, the higher a project would automatically rank. Projects that impacted only one measure, or those that impacted several measures but did so only weakly, naturally fell down the list.

Did it work? Well, almost. For the first time, we had a clearer understanding of which initiatives would be more likely to produce the desired business outcomes. And since, with limited resources, there were way too many projects on the list to possibly do them all, it made it easier to decide what not to do.

It also proved still too subjective to be used alone—just by changing a couple of the 1-to-5 rankings, you could force a project to rank higher on the list. Occasionally stakeholders pushed for a number to be higher as a way to get something done earlier.

- External customer perspectives and risks are not always fully considered.

- If you have too many criteria, you might end up with a product plan with many fragmented features that does not deliver a single coherent product vision.

Because of these significant limitations, do not "outsource" your prioritization solely to weighted scorecards—use them to anchor discussion and drive alignment. They are but one input in deciding prioritization.

Theme-Based Frameworks (Qualitative-Internal)

Focusing on themes rather than projects elevates prioritization discussions—they become more strategic with greater emphasis on the business outcomes. Among the benefits, *theme-based frameworks* do the following:

- Enable you to debate goals, results, and metrics rather than ideas.

- Substantially reduce the number of items to prioritize. It's easier to force-rank five themes than rank dozens of projects with wildly different benefits.

- Naturally align with resource allocations. For example, you can staff a team for each theme to ensure a dedicated and focused effort on each.

- Allow for concurrent work on several key themes. More important themes receive more of the available resources. However, some resources can be made available to less critical themes to allow them to make some progress rather than none.

- Empower teams and product managers with the flexibility to adjust prioritization decisions within a theme as they validate and learn—that way, they are always working on the priority most likely to advance that theme.

- Naturally lead to hold teams accountable to key performance indicators (KPIs), objectives-and-key-results (OKRs), and product performance metrics, and not just to project execution.

Theme-based prioritization is best when managing an overall product portfolio. If you are in charge of a smaller product area, you might be assigned a theme with goals that are more or less set. In that case, themes are helpful for putting your work in context so you can support overall company goals and understand resource constraints.

Identifying Themes

A theme can be any strategic imperative for your product. Here are some ways to come up with your own themes:

- See the overall criteria under weighted scorecards (above).

- Use the customer funnels outlined in **Chapter 11**. Each stage (acquisition, conversion, activation, retention, upsell) can be a theme.

- Overall product initiatives can be themes, each perhaps separately staffed. Examples include growth, onboarding, business tools, community development, internationalization, discovery and search, personalization, scale and speed, and technical debt removal. Each theme must also include a set of accountable business metrics.

- Customer segments can be themes (if you have different products for each). Include a set of priorities advancing each segments' needs, with resources allocated in proportion to potential growth and value.

- If you set quarterly business goals or use OKRs, the objectives (not key results) might provide a good set of themes if they don't change too frequently.

In the online resources at http://www.influentialpm.com, you will find a theme-based prioritization framework with an example.

McAllister's Framework

Perhaps the best-known, theme-based methodology for prioritization is that proposed by Ian McAllister, former head of product for Airbnb.[4] McAllister's framework is best used at a larger company where teams can be dedicated against individual themes:

1. **Identify and prioritize themes, not projects**—Create a list of themes and force-rank the top three. Rank them according to greatest need, given your product's lifecycle stage, and how they align with companywide goals.

2. **Sequence and resource your themes**—For the few themes you'll be focusing on now, roughly allocate resources, time, or both. Do this before you discuss features or specific initiatives. While you should provide a recommendation as a starting point, it is essential to get

buy-in from managers and stakeholders to reaffirm that these are the right themes and that time and resources are correctly allocated.

3. **Map projects to themes**—Take your potential project list and map each project as a candidate under one of the themes. (Even if a project impacts several themes, allocate it under the one with which it is primarily associated so as not to complicate the process.) Themes that have not had much previous attention are likely to have few associated projects so you may need to brainstorm to add more ideas.

4. **Estimate potential impact and cost**—For each project, assign an order of magnitude (0 through 10) or T-shirt size. Impact is the level at which you believe you will advance the theme; cost is a high-level estimate (SWAG) for development effort.

5. **Prioritize projects within each theme**—With your team, decide on which projects to tackle first, based on their impact and effort. Do not reconsolidate your projects into a single list but keep them separate under each theme. Allow teams to revisit their lists to ensure they are working on those projects presenting greatest opportunity.

When using McAllister's framework, I recommend you do the following:

- Define a quantifiable metric for each theme in step 1. That way, each theme can be described in terms of its business outcome, and you can measure team accountability.

- Draw a hard line to scope out projects under each theme that won't be worked on due to higher priorities and limited resources. Keep visibility on what you are saying no to. Should a higher-potential idea turn out to be less promising, you can always move another project up above the line.

- Measure how much of your allocated resources end up working on each theme (rather than on other priorities). Exclude overheads like meetings, but do include being pulled into other teams to help and working on projects or bugs not aligned with advancing the theme. Regularly (perhaps monthly) review results with stakeholders. You may find that the allocated resources are incorrect and need to be shifted or that more discipline is required to stick to the allocations. Without this step, you are in danger of making less progress on the theme than expected (and disappointing stakeholders through no fault of your own).

Making Engineering Effort Estimates

Few things can create friction more easily than asking a development team to estimate the required "effort" for a project with nothing more than a two-line description to go on. And who can blame them? You are essentially asking them to provide an estimate for a project entirely lacking in scope.

Some companies have successfully moved away from this practice, instead emphasizing time to discover and validate scope and using roadmaps with only vague timelines.

If you must ask engineering for estimates to help you prioritize work, here are some tips to make this process more successful:

- Keep estimation relative, perhaps by using T-shirt sizing, and avoid using developer months or dates.

- Pick the initiative with the best-known scope, or one that has already been delivered, and assign a size to it first. Then compare and score each additional initiative in relation to it.

- Add a risk column to your assessment, including cost risk, scope risk, and feasibility risk. This additional factor provides an outlet for engineering to express uncertainty. You can then choose to prioritize lower-risk choices or, better still, to prioritize discovery and research of high-risk items to uncover any surprises early.

- Never let estimates be used for any other purpose, especially to imply developer commitments. You'll never get them to engage with you again.

- Use "effort" estimates sparingly as the key determiner of priorities. If you focus on only the low-cost, low-risk initiatives, you will end up with a pretty mediocre product. Sometimes, you should prioritize exploration of a high-effort initiative. You are likely to drive the highest value by doing the hard stuff that others are not.

Feature Buckets

Adam Nash's *feature buckets*[5] is a favorite among startups and one of the most straightforward theme-based frameworks to use. Simply breakdown feature ideas into one of four buckets. Regularly including something from each bucket in releases leads to a well-rounded product and helps avoid focusing on customer requests to the exclusion of longer-term innovation.

Features don't have to fit into only one bucket—they may fit several. Here are some feature buckets recommended by Nash:

- **Metrics movers**—This bucket includes features that focus on stated business and product metrics. A prerequisite is that you have established a defined customer funnel and value-based metrics for evaluating features (**Chapter 11**).

- **Customer requests**—Includes features and incremental enhancements that customers are directly asking for. These may be gathered from customer feedback or requested by sales. Prioritization might be by revenue opportunity or whether they keep an important customer satisfied.

- **Delighters**—Innovations that are internally generated based on insights or differentiating ideas. Customers are not asking for them but will be pleasantly surprised if you deliver them.

- **Strategics**—Features related to learning or long-term future goals. Some teams combine this category with the former one, as Nash defines the strategic bucket as often the first step toward discovering innovations. If your company is poor at experimenting with new ideas, however, keep the two buckets separate.

To build on Nash's framework, one additional bucket I recommend is this:

- **Enhancers**—A constant set of improvements to the health of the underlying technology or to eliminate minor usability irritants. Gradually work down a list of reported bugs or design issues. Without this category, you may overlook the collective impact of a lot of small wins.

Although from one release to the next you may emphasize one bucket over another, track what you do from each bucket over time. This will help determine a rough "portfolio investment." If you see too little investment in any one bucket, it might be time to raise its profile.

Collaborative Voting (Qualitative–Blended)

Use collaborative voting techniques with internal stakeholders, customers, or both (but not at the same time). The premise is quite simple: the collective wisdom of a group of experts is likely to be a good indication of actual priorities. These techniques are best deployed to get consensus in a fast-paced, highly transparent organization where you must reach decisions quickly but can revisit them as needed and as more is learned.

Don't assign priorities strictly according to what players vote for (as this nullifies your role as product manager). Instead, use these collaborative methods to encourage participants to consider and explain their rationales for trade-offs. Their justifications will, in turn, inform your prioritization.

When running a collaborative process, be sure to avoid creating biases. For example, this can happen when junior employees just go along with the viewpoints of their seniors or stay silent rather than express a different point of view and risk conflict. Set the expectation that the process be democratic and safe. Consider, as well, staggering the voting to leave those most senior to vote last.

The KJ Method

The *KJ Method*, also known as an affinity diagram, was developed by Jiro Kawakita in the 1960s. It identifies and groups similar needs, building perspective as to where the best opportunities lie. The process starts with free subjective opinions from individual stakeholders and ends with objectivity and consensus through group voting and sharing of explicit rationale.

This method can be used for any level of prioritization, from high-level themes to granular priorities within a specific product area, and, as such, it is an excellent method for any level of product manager to reach consensus with their teams and stakeholders. It is also an excellent generative brainstorming framework. You should facilitate the process, as follows, being careful to move deliberately through each step to be confident of the outcome:

1. **Recruit a diverse group**—Bring together people from different parts of the organization, various informed advisors, or even disparate customer types. They don't all have to be senior stakeholders or experts but should have a wide variety of perspectives.

2. **Pose the focus question**—Depending on what you are trying to drive ideation and prioritization, write and communicate an overarching question to anchor the process. Here are a few examples:

   - "What are users coming to our product for?"

   - "Where are users struggling to use our product as it is today?"

   - "How could we increase user engagement?"

- "What tools and systems would make us a more efficient organization?"

Write your focus question at the top of a whiteboard.

3. **Have everyone put answers onto sticky notes**—Start with individual brainstorming where participants write ideas, opinions, and (if possible) rationale onto sticky notes. Have each member work alone and in silence to write as many as possible. Don't allow sharing, critique, or debate at this point.

4. **Share and place sticky notes**—Have each participant read out their answers and place them up on the whiteboard. Go around the room, with each participant selecting one answer to present on each turn until all responses are exhausted. Some details to consider:

   - Participants can place their answers anywhere on the whiteboard (but you'll start to notice they tend to put them near similar ideas).

   - If a participant has an idea that's identical to one already on the whiteboard, invite them to put it on the whiteboard immediately, next to the same idea, rather than discarding it.

   - As participants hear other suggestions, they will be prompted to come up with additional ideas. They can add to their list at any time (and put additional sticky notes up on the whiteboard when it is their turn again).

5. **Group and name similar items**—Have participants move around the sticky notes, placing them near others. They can move anybody's sticky note, not just their own. Ask them to explain their rationale for moving each note, using phrases such as the following:

   - "This is the same as. . . ."

   - "This achieves a similar goal to. . . ."

   - "I see a group of. . . ."

   Ask participants to suggest names for each group and add these names to the whiteboard, drawing a circle around each group of related sticky notes. Welcome disagreement, and combine or create new groups as needed. This is a valuable step, because everyone gets to hear what each stakeholder values and thinks.

6. **Vote for groups**—Have each participant vote for those groups of ideas (not individual ideas) that they believe are most important in addressing the focus question. You might give them a limit of around three to five votes, which they can cast in any way. A stakeholder may place all their votes in one area, excluding all others, showing that they feel the issue is critical in addressing the focus question. At other times, two stakeholders may disagree. At this stage of the process, critique is encouraged. Invite healthy, constructive conflict—have them debate the issues.

7. **Rank the groups**—Rank the groups by the number of votes. Participants can combine similar groups—provided groups remain granular enough to be useful to your later prioritization—adding their votes. If groups are excessively combined, stakeholders are likely trying to keep too much on the table and you will not be able to exclude enough ideas from scope. Keep going until several top-priority groups have emerged and lower priorities are clear or have been discarded.

8. **Communicate outcomes**—After the session, thank participants and send out a summary of the results. Develop a priority list that aligns as much as possible with the key groups that were identified. Some ideas may be flagged for "further discovery" (those that need customer validation and prototyping first); others may be flagged as impractical due to constraints such as resources and feasibility. Emphasize the groups that emerged, as this shows that you have integrated participant feedback.

Buy a Feature

Luke Hohmann (author of *Innovation Games*[6]) codified the *buy-a-feature* method that converts feature prioritization into "currency." It is played like a game, either individually or in small groups (of four to six). Players can spend on desired features and explain their reasoning. The game also helps emphasize that you can have only a limited number of priorities. This is useful if you are under pressure to commit to more than your team can reasonably work on. Follow these steps to use the buy-a-feature method:

1. **Create feature cards**—Name and describe the benefits of each feature on a separate card.

2. **Price features**—On each card, write a rough cost based on the feature's complexity, risk, and effort. A feature that is twice as complicated as another feature should be double the cost.

3. **Assign a total budget for each player to spend**—Use monopoly money or make your own.

   Each player's total budget should not allow an individual player to buy more than a third of the features (as you want them to make difficult decisions). Furthermore, one player should not be able to buy any one large feature. Players can spend all of their individual money on a couple of small items or pool their resources to purchase a larger feature.

4. **Describe the game**—Explain to players that they will use their budget to buy features important to them. Lay out the feature cards on a table and briefly review each, drawing attention to the cost.

5. **Take turns buying features**—As players buy features, take their money and ask them to explain why they're buying it. (Alternatively, have everyone place their money at once, and then discuss the overall results.)

Let players self-manage, with a moderator writing down comments, rationale, and arguments that each player made about why their items are most important to them.

Some features might be so costly that they will only be funded if several players negotiate with one another. Encourage such collaboration: stakeholders might reach a compromise that satisfies your needs without your needing to mediate.

One option to the game is to tie each feature's price to a rough estimate of the required development effort. The combined player budget becomes your total available development resources. While this option is not necessary to make the game work, it is useful if you are getting resistance to using false currency (as it may be considered too abstract).

You will find an excellent set of templates for this game online at *UX for the Masses* (http://www.uxforthemasses.com/). You may also want to research a similar method called the *hundred-dollar test*.

The Kano Method (Quantitative–External)

Developed in 1984 by Professor Noriaki Kano, the *Kano Method*[7] surveys and understands customer needs, and then ranks features by how much they will increase satisfaction. As illustrated in **Figure 4.3**, features are naturally grouped into five categories, according to levels of potential satisfaction and their current functionality:

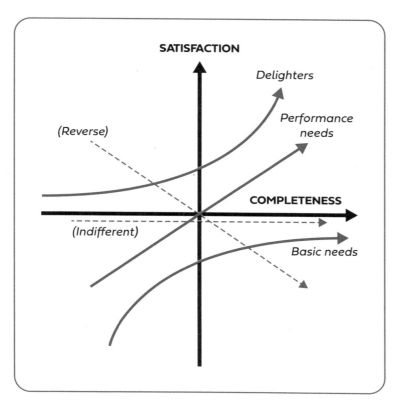

FIGURE 4.3 *The Kano Method groupings*

1. **Performance needs** (P)—These are the requirements customers more easily articulate; they are top-of-mind. They are what customers naturally always want more of and what competitors work to get ahead of your product on. Customers will use these needs to compare competitor options. The more you invest in making these features better, the more customer satisfaction increases *linearly*. Kano originally called these "one-dimensionals."

2. **Delighters** (D)—These are innovations that significantly improve customer satisfaction in a pleasantly unexpected way. It's rare that customers specifically request these features; instead, the features are derived by observing unsolved customer problems. Even a small investment in delighters can increase customer satisfaction *exponentially*. They are what sets a product apart, although their absence won't reduce customer satisfaction. Kano originally called these "attractives."

3. **Basic needs** (B)—These are requirements that customers expect and take for granted. Even when the features are done well, customers remain neutral about them, but when they're done poorly, customers become very dissatisfied. Overlooking sufficient investment in basic needs can destroy customer satisfaction. However, all that's required is *adequate* investment, as you'll never create satisfaction; you can only disappoint.

   Your product has to work, at least, at a minimum-quality level. Basic needs features are the price of entry—the greater the quality of competitors' alternatives, the higher the bar should go for basic needs. Kano originally called these features "must-bes." They are also known as "threshold features" (baseline features that have a binary effect on satisfaction—that is, if the features are not there, customers are not satisfied).

4. **Indifferent features** (I)—These are attributes that will neither improve nor decrease satisfaction. While customers may be indifferent to the investment, these requirements (such as automating business processes or improving back-end technologies) may still interest the company. A flaw in the Kano model is that it exclusively drives prioritization from the viewpoint of customer satisfaction. In practice, you must complement it with other prioritization techniques to capture initiatives that provide value to your business but not directly to customers.

5. **Reverse features** (R)—For completeness, Kano included a fifth category. Theoretically, a feature can have a high level of investment or achievement but result in customer dissatisfaction. Removal or reduction increases satisfaction. Typical examples include secondary features that interfere with the product's primary features (perhaps adding confusion and friction).

Over time, delighters will shift into the performance category, and performance needs will become basic needs. When you (or a competitor) wow the customer with an innovative feature, you set new expectations. The market gets used to a certain level of functionality and expects other alternatives to follow suit. Your innovation becomes commoditized.

There is plenty of literature on how to conduct a Kano analysis. Advanced Kano analysis requires you to carefully develop questions, survey customer segments separately, and take into account the variation in answers from customers. (For example, it can be challenging to reconcile why some customers rank a feature as a basic need and others as a performance need.)

The Kano Method does an excellent job in predicting what customers will value in your product and is especially useful when balancing your requirements portfolio between adding new features and improving existing functionality. However, note the following:

- It can be very time-consuming.

- It is based on emotionally biased responses, which are not always reliable because customers don't always know what they need.

- It can't tell you why a feature is considered "bad" or what you should change to make it better—it can only show you the areas to focus on.

At http://www.influentialpm.com, I provide a simplified "quick and dirty" Kano analysis approach and an example.

Customer-Assisted Methods (Qualitative-External)

Customer-assisted methods structure the gathering of priorities directly from customers. Unlike the Kano Method, these methods tend to be quicker in gauging customer preferences and their underlying rationale, but they are less accurate. They are excellent techniques to complement internal and quantitative analyses as they can be repeated frequently and used for prioritization decisions, right down to the feature level. They are frequently used in user experience research.

Bubble Sort

Provided your list of possible feature priorities is not extensive, list them in random order and have customers compare adjacent ideas in pairs, row by row. For each pair, they should decide which is more important. If the second option in the pair is more appealing, the order is swapped. Repeat the process until the user believes all priorities are correctly ranked.

In each step, only ever rank adjacent options—not those above or below the two under consideration. This reduces each prioritization decision to a binary "yes" or "no." As illustrated by the example in **Figure 4.4**, after many small decisions you will arrive at an overall priority across all options. The disadvantage is that the rationale behind each decision might not be apparent, so have the participant verbalize these as they go.

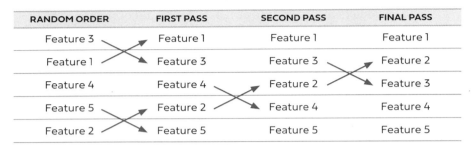

RANDOM ORDER	FIRST PASS	SECOND PASS	FINAL PASS
Feature 3	Feature 1	Feature 1	Feature 1
Feature 1	Feature 3	Feature 3	Feature 2
Feature 4	Feature 4	Feature 2	Feature 3
Feature 5	Feature 2	Feature 4	Feature 4
Feature 2	Feature 5	Feature 5	Feature 5

FIGURE 4.4 *Example bubble sort*

Innovation Games

These methodologies, from Luke Hohmann (author of *Innovation Games*), create a gamified environment to engage customers (but can also be used with stakeholders). The two games I have found most useful are *prune-the-product-tree* and *speedboat* (sometimes called *sailboat*). There are many resources describing these techniques and dozens of variations.

Speedboat is a particularly interesting approach since it focuses on what users don't like, rather than what users want, in a product. This game is useful if you are facing unsatisfied customers who are highly critical of your product's limitations. Their demands might even overwhelm you; asking them to provide feedback on priorities just creates a tirade of frustration, full of emotion and despair. (We've all been there.)

Although customers may have many complaints about a product, they're rarely out to destroy it or you. But asking for only what they want to change isn't helpful. By gamifying negative feedback, you can get a good sense of which issues are of most importance—namely, those that have customers considering abandoning your product. Speedboat forces customers to prioritize the least-liked features or most significant limitations of a product in a constructive, controlled way.

Ask customers: "What anchors do we need to remove to make the speedboat (product) go faster?"

1. **Draw a boat on a whiteboard or large piece of paper**—Tell your customers that, as a speedboat, it should be going much faster. It is currently doing 30 miles per hour. It could be doing 80 or more. The speedboat is your product. What are the anchors?

2. **Have customers write features or issues they're not happy with on sticky notes**—Make it clear that the issues have to be very specific. Ask them to expand on generic answers (for example, rather than just

saying the product isn't "intuitive," ask them to specify why and where in the product they have run into a lack of usability). Post their completed notes below the boat and draw a line from each note to the boat as an "anchor."

3. **Identify the heaviest anchors**—Ask customers to estimate how much faster you could be going by addressing each anchor (for example, 5mph, 10mph or 30mph). Place the heavier anchors, the ones slowing you down the most, lower down. Each anchor gives you a measure of customer "pain" for prioritization and improvement. Lighter anchors can be ignored; heavy anchors need attention.

4. **Put it in writing**—Record the outcomes, making sure to note the heaviest *and* the lightest anchors. By putting it in writing, you can avoid revisiting trivial issues and focus on the big issues. But you'd better do something about the issues you've noted if you are to maintain credibility.

An enhancement to the game is to add propellers (the positives in the product, also written on sticky notes). **Figure 4.5** shows a simple template you can use, also downloadable online at http://www.influentialpm.com.

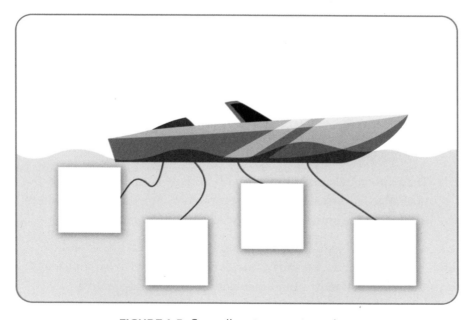

FIGURE 4.5 *Speedboat game template*

Five Whys

Customers and stakeholders often request specific features for reasons that are hard to determine. Use this technique to establish a root cause and its relative importance to other issues. Ask why—up to five times in succession:

- Why is this a problem? In what situations has this problem arisen?

- Why is this important to you (or whoever is requesting this)? What is the expected business outcome?

- Why is this an issue now? How have you worked around the problem before?

- What has shifted in your business priorities that makes addressing this goal important now, and why has that shift happened?

- Given we're working on X, why is it important we stop that work and pursue this instead?

Asking the five whys is also an excellent team retrospective technique. When something goes wrong internally—say, a product feature, a project, your processes, or communication fails—use it to get to the root cause issue and identify areas for future team and organizational improvement.

Optimizing on Customer and Business Outcomes

Many companies overemphasize new feature development as a way to continually deliver customers value. These companies tend to have the following characteristics:

- They have a backlog of hundreds of ideas they intend to get to eventually.

- After a product release, they start working on secondary, nice-to-have features that got cut from scope.

- They rarely revisit a feature once it's initially launched—tending instead to start working on the next project immediately—regardless of whether the launched feature is succeeding or not.

Yes, you should ensure delivery against the long-term vision of the product by adding new features or major enhancements to existing features. However, you must simultaneously ensure existing features are performing optimally. Striking the right balance between these competing demands (adding new features or optimizing existing features) can be challenging. If you fill up your schedule with new feature development, you will potentially miss generating impressive business results for relatively little effort by optimizing existing features. On an ongoing basis, endeavor to budget some portion of your team's time for optimization and quick-wins.

The prioritization techniques we've discussed so far in this chapter provide excellent ways to choose among substantially sized projects (those likely to take several development cycles and those demanding disciplined assessment and up-front validation). But they are less effective at surfacing the many micro-projects that may incrementally improve features already available to users.

A *prioritization methodology* should not be used alone to identify and rank such initiatives. Instead, use an *experimental methodology* to brainstorm ideas, quickly implement a lightweight solution, and test on a small

The Little Things Matter

Over the years, I have observed some outsized gains in improving outcomes from simple ideas and concepts. Here are notable examples:

- Investing in SEO, such as writing better copy on 10,000 "long-tail" pages of the website, resulted in a 30 percent increase in overall qualified traffic coming from search queries. Even though any one page didn't have the volume to be of interest, in aggregate, they generated a significant lift.

- Reducing the file size of assets (images and videos) and using a third-party service to deliver scaled-down levels of fidelity appropriate for the user's device and internet speed sped the site up and drove a 20 percent increase in the conversion rate (from free to paid user).

- The discovery rate of a new feature was low (less than 5 percent of users interacted with it). Rather than remove it, we brainstormed ways to make it more prominent in navigation—resulting in significant uptake and higher overall customer satisfaction.

- Sending an email with a discount to users who had an item in their cart but hadn't checked out (cart abandonment) resulted in a 10 percent increase in purchase completion.

- Of five possible calls-to-action (CTA) on a key page of the website, heatmap analysis revealed only one mattered. This was a link to "learn more." We realized we were trying to get users to purchase before they were ready. Counterintuitively, adding more information on the page and placing the purchase CTA later improved outcomes.

- A growth team ran 51 small tests in 90 days across an (admittedly highly unoptimized) online learning subscription-based website and drove the conversion rate up by 43 percent. Most tests failed, but the collective wins added up mightily.

scale against clearly defined metrics. If the outcomes are positive, you can roll out your improvement to your whole user base.

Incremental optimizations tend to exhibit one or more of the following traits:

- They can be implemented relatively quickly.

- On their own, they are each too small in effort to justify the overhead of extensive up-front research, prioritization, and debate.

- They are among many potential ideas to test, and it is unclear which will be winners.

- As a group, they require resourcing over time to gradually improve an existing product's performance (that is, they are not a "project" but a series of iterations).

- On their own, they may not make a large difference, but as a group, they can add up to a lot.

The most popular technique for finding which incremental changes work is *A/B* or *split testing*. It is well understood in concept but often misapplied. You can only use it once you have a baseline experience from which to iterate and test against and an active user base using your service to gather statistically significant data from.

To run A|B testing effectively, use the guidelines that follow.

1. Determine Your Desired and Measurable Outcomes

Don't try random ideas. Narrowly focus and align your team by declaring precisely what overall business or customer outcomes you are striving for. Here are some examples:

- A series of landing-page optimizations might each improve customer conversion by a small fraction of a percent; but collectively their impact may be hugely valuable.

- A page or feature in your product has a particularly alarming abandonment rate, and you want to see if you can reduce it.

- You have a hypothesis that increased sales might offset a discount on the current price.

- A recently launched feature has lower engagement than expected. You wish to improve its discovery by finding the most effective places to promote it.

- You wish to find which email content and subject lines drive the highest open rates and click-through rates back into your service.

Set a KPI/metric by which you will determine overall success. You will likely also have several secondary metrics, which are easier or quicker to measure and are leading indicators of movement toward your overall goal. Measure the existing experience to create a baseline. Ideally, you will hold back a group of users who don't receive any enhancements to compare against and determine a definitive overall result.

▶ In **Chapter 6** I introduce a specification template. Use it to thoroughly document an experiment note for each split test to capture your hypothesis and the precise metric (and existing baseline) you aim to move.

Also identify counter-metrics, which you don't want to see negatively affected. For example, if your overall goal is to increase your effectiveness to drive visitors to become paying customers, your primary metric is likely *conversion rate*. Counter-metrics (that you don't want to see get worse) might include average order value (AOV), customer satisfaction, and refunds.

2. Gather and Prioritize Ideas

With the goal in mind, develop ideas for testing and convert them into an ordered backlog. Here are two of the most effective techniques for doing this:

1. Identify companies that are good at achieving goals similar to yours (not just competitors). Research their products for ideas, taking careful note of small details and features that might be good tactics.

2. Using the KJ method, bring together a cross-functional group to brainstorm ideas that can be built within a short timeframe. Walk through your goals and share examples. As ideas are generated, anything that might be too much effort can be a candidate for your larger product roadmap; alternatively, encourage the team to break the idea down further.

Capture the hypothesis behind each idea—the "why" something might work, in addition to the "what" (such as a whiteboard, wireframe sketch). For example, a hypothesis might be, "If we invite users to submit their email addresses, they'll be more likely to transact later as we can market the service's value proposition to them through email."

▶ Refer to earlier in this chapter and to **Chapter 8** for tips on making high-level developer estimates.

Roughly prioritize ideas according to what you and your team believe are likely to have the highest impact for the least effort. One tool, which is popular with growth teams and will help you decide which optimization tests are likely to have the greatest impact prioritize, is called *RICE* (Reach, Impact, Confidence, Effort/Ease).

To score an idea, you must first assign a percent, ratio, or number to each of the four attributes based on available data or, if data is unavailable, your best guess or team consensus.

- **Reach**—How many users you would affect with the improvement idea in a given period. If you are optimizing a website, use the pageviews or visitors per month. Clearly, low-traffic parts of your site should receive a lower reach score.

- **Impact**—An estimate of how much the idea will improve your goal when a user encounters it. A 0-to-10 scale is fine. If you don't have definitive research or strong conviction (such as seeing the improvement idea already in use by other services), the collective opinion of the team will suffice.

- **Confidence**—Given the available data, intuition, and past experience, what is the percentage of confidence that the idea can be executed and will have the estimated impact. Agree not to be too conservative, so that ideas are not all rated low simply because you're working with such little information. Most ideas should spread across the 30 to 80 percent range.

- **Effort** (or **Ease**)—Another scale of your choosing that corresponds roughly to developer effort. If you use T-shirt sizing, convert sizes into numerals, or use a rough estimate of developer weeks, or you can use *story points* to estimate a score.

Each percent, ratio, or number is a *relative* measure comparing each idea to your other ideas. Precision is not required, just consistency.

Once you have assigned a number for each attribute, an idea's *RICE* score equals

$$\frac{\textbf{Reach} \times \textbf{Impact} \times \textbf{Confidence}}{\textbf{Effort}}$$

As illustrated in **Table 4.1**, the higher the *RICE* score, the greater the idea's overall contribution and, therefore, priority. For example, idea 1 is

TABLE 4.1 Example *RICE* prioritization matrix

	REACH ('000 VISITORS PER MONTH)	IMPACT (1-10)	CONFIDENCE (PERCENT)	EFFORT (STORY POINTS)	*RICE* SCORE	RANK
Idea 1	50	6	80	8	30	1
Idea 2	30	7	90	13	15	2
Idea 3	50	4	30	5	12	3
Idea 4	10	9	50	20	2	4

clearly a winner because it reaches a wide audience within your userbase, you are fairly confident it will work, and development effort is relatively low. Despite its high impact potential, idea 4's *RICE* score is much, much lower because it reaches a fraction of your audience and effort is substantive.

Encourage the generation and implementation of tweaks (low-impact, high-confidence, low-effort) and of bigger swings (high-impact, low-confidence, medium- to high-effort). Tweaks add up over time, each moving the dial by a tiny fraction, but collectively they produce material business outcomes. Simple changes such as calls to action, the positioning of buttons, and value-proposition messaging can have a powerful impact on metrics.

However, while bigger swings might have scores for lower confidence and higher effort, if they happen to work their overall impact can be dramatic. Many teams get stuck iterating around a local "optimum"—when a radical change can break open new possibilities for outsized, unexpected results. For example, eliminating entire steps or features in your product might mean simplifying functionality resulting in increased goal completion of your primary use case; or sending one richly personalized email per week might work better than sending a dozen basic templated emails.

3. Execute Your Experiments

Only one idea should be run on each "surface area" at a time. A surface area is each unique flow or section of your product. For example, if you are testing to improve conversion, you can run a different test for every entry point of your product (up to the checkout page, the point of conversion).

Randomly assign users to at least two test cells—a *control* and a *variant*—to allow for all other factors and to eliminate the risk of correlation appearing as causation. Your control is usually your existing baseline experience; whereas your variant is identical in every aspect except for the single change you are testing.

Seemingly small considerations can reduce the effectiveness of your test. For example, if you direct all users from a particular geography or channel into the new experience (a supposedly easy way to run an A|B test), you have not controlled for the fact that those users may exhibit different behaviors than your broader user base. Likewise, if the user can opt in or out of either experience, then your results may be skewed as more enthusiastic users may select to try your new offering.

You can run A|B testing on a concurrent basis (where users are randomly assigned to receive one of the two experiences.) You can also run tests using a time basis (where all users are sent to a new experience for a short period, after which the test ends). However, you must not do anything to change the mix of users during a time-based test (such as launching a marketing program that brings in many less-qualified visitors.)

If you don't have an A|B testing platform, invest in a third-party tool. To speed up your ability to test, you need to be able to swap out different user experiences easily and to track and reliably report on all the data necessary. If you are working on a multi-platform product, you will need to test mobile and desktop applications independently.

You must wait until you receive enough user interaction to declare the test either way with statistical significance. Depending on the reach and impact, tests can range from hours to weeks. *Frequentist* inference is more accurate but takes longer to reach high confidence. *Bayesian* inference is quicker and requires less time and volume but is directionally useful (for example, you may know your test resulted in a positive outcome even

- -

Rapid Testing of Call-to-Action Messaging

Viral growth was a critical part of our user-acquisition strategy for our mobile application. Users were prompted to send a SMS invitation to friends and family with a short default message and a download link. The conversion rate for signing up new members from these messages was about 5 percent.

We tested hundreds of variants in message text. The results were not obvious: the best-performing message—"Send Free SMS I Use **[URL]**"—had more than double the rate (9.9 percent) of the lowest performer—"FREE SMS **[URL]**"—at 4.4 percent.

Can you see any difference? Perhaps the capital letters seemed unnatural and too spammy to recipients. Maybe the word "I" turned the first invitation into a more personal one. Whatever the reason, only testing could have uncovered it, along with the tremendous difference in business outcomes.

- -

though you aren't able to determine the exact increase on your KPIs). Your data science teams can help you decide which is right for you.

A *multivariate* test allows you to run more variants concurrently, such as an A|B|C test. As you add more test cells, the number of users in each cell is reduced, which may increase the time you must test to get statistically significant results.

A 50/50 split test will be the fastest to run. However, to manage risk, you can easily limit the number of users who will be subjected to the new experience—depending on the speed at which you need to learn. This means you won't be putting your day-to-day business at risk if you adversely affect users. If an idea looks promising, you can gradually roll out the change to more users, to verify that the beneficial outcomes are sustained.

4. Use Cohort Analysis to Track Long-Term Impacts

While some metrics will be immediately measurable, others will require you to track users over a longer time. For example, while an increase in conversion might be immediately obvious, effects on customer retention take time to evaluate, as the changes are only measurable over time.

In **Figure 4.6**, Test #1 seemed immediately promising. But it was only later validated that the counter-metric (customer retention rate) was unaffected. It improved overall customer lifetime value (LTV) by 10 percent over the baseline.

Test #2 initially looked even more promising, but after a while, it became clear that the aggressive call to action possibly misled customers, which resulted in high churn in the first month. Test #3 was a surprise. After investigation, the discount proved a good way to get people to trial the product, but once pricing returned to previous levels, these users canceled (resulting in a net neutral effect overall).

5. Encourage a Culture of Experimentation

In baseball, the "batting average" is calculated by the number of hits a batter has divided by the number of "at-bats." Even the top 100 batting averages are between 0.309 and 0.366.[8] In A|B testing, just as in baseball, most of the time your tests will fail or make a seemingly marginal difference. If they are *not* failing, then you're not testing big enough ideas!

You need to be willing to implement multiple ideas that might be discarded. Some users might be unhappy with receiving a new experience.

	CONVERSION RATE (MONTH 0)	FIRST MONTH RETENTION	RETENTION AFTER 3 MONTHS	WEIGHTED CUSTOMER LIFETIME VALUE
Baseline	1.0%	80%	60%	$60
#1 Enhanced messaging on the homepage	1.1%	80%	60%	+10%
#2 An aggressive call to action	1.3%	50%	35%	-7%
#3 A substantial discount to try the product out	2.0%	80%	30%	~±0%

FIGURE 4.6 Example subscription product A/B tests across three test cells

If you become invested in a pet idea, you might keep trying to make it work long after it is clear it will not. Or maybe your team or management is intolerant of "mistakes."

But tests fail. This must not be perceived as an error of judgment; otherwise, you will try out only the safest ideas. If you are faced with this problem, start small, making basic, noncontroversial changes to the experience and sharing positive results to gain momentum and to encourage a culture of experimentation—then gradually try out bigger and bolder ideas.

Fear of Failure: Radical Tests vs. Tweaks

A product manager was assigned a team and the goal of optimizing conversion rates for our subscription education product.

Over the course of three months, she toiled away, running A|B tests on the homepage to drive up performance. The team tested different messaging, layouts, and even gave away some free content—but, unfortunately, each test generated only marginal results. Conversion rose from 1.00 percent to 1.05 percent—barely enough to justify the investment we were making in her engineering team.

The team had been trying only "safe" ideas—minimal tweaks and design changes. They worried that we would blame them if any idea had a strongly negative result, even though only a small percentage of users were ever exposed to an idea before it was proven effective. They felt we expected every idea to work.

I reset the expectations with the team and encouraged them to embrace potential failure. Either an idea should work spectacularly or fail miserably—either was fine so long as we learned from it.

After that point, they tried radically different ideas, including a longer service trial, highly personalized pages, sending more email in the first few days to educate users about the service, and changed pricing options. The results were much more promising.

CHAPTER 5

Discover and Validate Customer Needs

Test your assumptions and emergent product solutions through continuous customer feedback.

1 Why you must conduct product discovery and validation with customers both from the start of, and continuously throughout, the product lifecycle.

2 How to structure a routine and low-effort validation process to improve product decisions, building customer empathy.

3 How to get the most from user interviews, validating whether users value and can use your potential product solution to achieve their goals.

Are You Building the Right Product?

Product discovery is the gathering of customer insights and evidence in order to

- build empathy for your customers and understand their needs (their needs are your opportunities);

- inform the priorities and overall direction of your product roadmap—specifically, the function and design of your proposed product solution; and

- determine whether your proposed solution will (or will not) successfully solve your customer's needs better than their current solutions.

Discovery occurs at the start of an initiative—before you flesh out product requirements and start development—and continues throughout the product lifecycle. It requires you to invest design and development resources in creating and iterating on testing artifacts such as prototypes. You must identify, qualify, and interview potential customers. It requires discipline to slow down, carefully consider, and test your assumptions and to confirm you are creating a valuable, usable solution.

For these reasons, product discovery is often skipped. Feeling a sense of urgency and having firm conviction in their product roadmap and ideas, product managers and stakeholders tend to want to "get on with it." They may see product discovery as a waste of time. But consider this:

> The product manager's role is *not* to build the product right.
> The product manager's role is to **build the right product**.

No matter how good the execution, the wrong product solution for the wrong customer need is 100 percent waste.

Consider **Figure 5.1**. The following *external* validation needs for your product with customers are to ensure the following:

- **The product is valuable**—There must be evidence that the product solves a real problem for your target customer. You can get a sense of value by completing *customer observations and interviews*. Understand your customer's unmet needs and challenges in addressing the problem you aim to solve.

- **The product is usable**—The target user can complete the goals that your product enables in an intuitive, efficient, and enjoyable way.

Valuable?	The product solves a real problem as evidenced by customer interest
Usable?	Users can complete their goals in an intuitive, efficient, and enjoyable way
Functional?	The product meets specifications as determined by internal testing

FIGURE 5.1 *Three levels of product validation*

Through *usability testing*, you can recruit users to interact with a prototype of your proposed product. Then, as development gets underway, you can continue to test the product as it takes shape, as a means to keep learning and tweak the product's direction. You can observe users' perceptions and where they are struggling, noting issues to address.

Perform product discovery for any significant initiative—whether for new products or enhancements to existing products. While product discovery is most critical at the start, you must continue gathering data and validating your product throughout the execution phase, and even after launch, because of the following factors:

- Customers, markets, and products continue to evolve. What may have been correct at one point may no longer be applicable.

- Usability testing with a partially or fully working product is easier for users to comprehend than concepts, designs, or prototypes. (Although waiting until you have a finished product to show is too late to start!)

- Once a product is live, you can augment and focus your testing by analyzing user-interaction data alongside qualitative feedback.

In this chapter, I describe some of the challenges behind product discovery, along with techniques you can use to design an impactful interview process. At its core, if you validate early, validate often, and keep your process repeatable and simple, you will have a greater chance of creating a needed product that delights your customers and makes money for your company.

Product Discovery Is Challenging!

Customer-based validation is perceived to be challenging for a variety of (easily refuted) assumptions:

1. "Customers don't know what they want."

2. "Discovery and validation are complicated, costly, and time-consuming and often lead to inconclusive results."

3. "Our understanding of the customer and internal validation processes are sufficient."

1. "Customers Don't Know What They Want!"

You've probably heard the adage that great product companies don't ask their customers what they want because customers don't know what they want—and instead great product companies delight customers with solutions they never thought were possible. Well, that's partly true. However, customers often *do* understand their problems—or are at least aware of them, if not able to clearly articulate them. But they generally don't offer good solutions.

Customers are limited by their routines, habits, and familiarity with existing solutions. They rarely envision a world with a solution that doesn't exist yet. They cannot predict how they will change their behavior; they can only compare against their current frame of reference.

Another common scenario is when sales reps or other stakeholders tell you what the customer wants based on *their* interactions or discussions. These secondhand requests have been filtered through their own perceptions, organizational prerogatives, and interpretations of what the customer has said.

▶ You can use the five-whys technique from **Chapter 4**.

Your role is to tease apart the underlying problem from the customer's requested solutions. Do so in collaboration with your customer—unpack why they need the proposed solution until you feel you have surfaced the root cause. If a customer proposes a solution or feature, work back until you understand the underlying need, then work forward toward potential and possibly very different solutions than those prescribed.

Do not ask customers what features they want—even if the customer is adamant about what those features should be. Also do not ask them to prioritize your features—except indirectly and relatively (for example, asking to rank whether problem A is more important to solve than B, and having them explain why).

Instead, have them describe what they do to meet their goals today, identify poorly solved problems to which they feel motivated to explore alternatives, observe them in their environments, and look for common patterns across many customers. You must interact with customers to learn about them and their needs—but it is you, not them, who imagines, defines, and validates new solutions.

2. "Discovery and Validation Are Complicated, Costly, and Time-Consuming and Often Lead to Inconclusive Results."

Focus groups and large-scale consumer research projects have their place but can be expensive and time-intensive, and they can divert resources away from other priorities. Because of their complexity, they occur less frequently. Yet investing in consumer research to inform product priorities is critical. On the other hand, you do not want it to slow your progress in getting your product into customers' hands.

Similarly, conducting usability testing on your product is easier and more effective the more complete your product is. But you will want to invest in a fully-finished product only after you have sufficient testing. It's a chicken-and-egg situation. If you start usability testing late in the development cycle, you are too far down a set path, committed to a specific scope

- -

Focus Group Disadvantages

While focus groups remain popular, they are often (but not always) the wrong choice for solely evaluating technology products, particularly those you can iterate on quickly.

I participated in running a focus group that cost thousands of dollars to run and weeks of special preparation. We worked with a third-party company to set it up, developing special-purpose prototypes, recruiting users, and scripting the test.

We watched from another room via a video hookup, while the tester took them through our products. Her questions were excellent, and we learned a great deal. But for every question answered, we now had more new questions to explore. Because the focus group was a one-shot event, we wouldn't have a chance to fix and retest any of the issues raised, let alone make even the smallest tweaks to the prototypes, to see if these made a difference.

In one interview, one particular test subject had very strong opinions, and it became clear others in the group were being influenced by him. As they expressed similar opinions, it wasn't clear whether that was due to shared beliefs or simply groupthink. For all the effort, we didn't learn fast enough. We decided it was too expensive, intensive, distracting, and ineffective to do again.

- -

and schedule. Making significant adjustments at this late stage is much more difficult, so only minor tweaks are made to keep on schedule—risking product failure once the product is in the market.

To combat these challenges, consider decoupling long-lead market and user research projects and running them in parallel with execution. Complement execution with iterative, frequent customer interviews and testing. Learn in small increments and address insights immediately. If you test on three to five users each week (likely less for enterprise customers, but not a great deal less!), you'll have put your product in front of 150 users or more in a year. And your product and understanding of the customer will have evolved a little each time.

Keep each session simple and focused—agree on a lightweight testing goal such as validating *one* flow or feature, identifying a few usability irritants, or understanding more behind particular customer behavior.

Establish a hypothesis, design a rough interview script, and compile artifacts (whether that's ideas on paper, mock-ups, or a partially finished feature set). Leverage much of what you already have to reduce preparation time—anything and everything as you have it, in whatever state it is in.

Recognize that the resulting customer feedback will be inherently messy and sometimes contradictory. Despite your best attempts, you may find it

Messy, Contradictory Feedback

User testing can be a frustrating experience, as when we were testing enhancements to a mobile messaging product that had been on the market for about a year. We had flown over 20 hours to India to interview users. With each new person we spoke to, we discovered that everyone was struggling with entirely different challenges when using the product.

One had difficulty downloading the application, another navigating through menus, and another sending group messages. Others easily achieved each of the user goals but brought up previously unidentified reliability issues that they said stopped them from using the product more frequently.

We didn't know what to do next and despaired that perhaps the product was a complete failure.

But we weren't going to give up: instead, we devised additional lean testing strategies to explore each problem in more detail. Each round of subsequent testing focused on a single hypothesis, revealing actionable improvements, which we added in new releases. Gradually the product improved and user satisfaction increased—but only after many rounds of testing that were more focused and cost-effective than our original approach.

hard to make testing quantifiable and statistically relevant when interviewing customers. You can introduce variations in your interview candidate selection and qualification process, in how test subjects interpret your questions, in the quality of your test artifacts, and in your ability to draw accurate conclusions from user observations. Also, your product and customer needs can evolve quickly.

As such, customer feedback should be considered directional, not conclusive. You are collecting data points and must balance them with your perceptions and actual product usage or other market analysis. When deciding actions based on your last round of customer validation, choose one or two small course corrections in your plan. It would be a mistake to make a significant pivot in response to the opinions of a handful of people.

More than that isn't necessary—so what if a few tests fail? There will be another chance shortly. While each insight collected is not likely to be applicable across your entire customer set, with each iteration you will learn, adapt, and increase your confidence in the fact that you are building a product of value.

3. "Our Understanding of the Customer and Internal Validation Processes Are Sufficient."

Don't make the mistake of thinking you have a valuable, usable, working product just because you have stakeholder support or have met internal milestones.

Creating a product that will make your customers happy is the key. It's easy to focus on making your stakeholders, particularly senior management, happy; however, neither you nor your stakeholders are the customer. Stakeholders can be biased by their own experiences, reputation, resource contentions, incentives, and goals. In particular, guard against their (and your own) recency bias—overresponding to what the last customer or prospect said about the product.

Inexperienced product managers might view passing internal approval "gates" as validation. They work hard to put together their research, proposed solution, business case, and a presentation to pitch. They utilize buy-in techniques (**Chapter 2**) to build stakeholder support. Once given the thumbs-up, they don't realize that now is when the hard validation work really begins. You must remain vigilant to ensure you are spending scarce time and resources on the right priorities.

A common internal validation technique is "dogfooding," where you and others in your organization use your own product to test out functionality. While helpful to detect usability issues and increase your empathy with customers, it is no substitute for observing real users interact with it.

Finally, referring back to **Figure 5.1** again, you may be familiar with the testing required to validate that the product is functional: *internal* testing that ensures that the product works as intended, meets visual and interactive design specifications, and operates stably (continuing to perform under load and with minimal bugs). Often referred to as *quality assurance* (QA), this testing generally occurs in parallel with, and at the end of, building a product.

Internal testing to confirm a product meets specifications is essential—but insufficient. At worst, checking the boxes that your product works as *you* specified gives you a false sense that you have created something of value.

Engage Firsthand with Customers

Your user experience team is an indispensable partner for validation and should lead usability testing. You may also have a dedicated consumer insights group whose role it is to build a deep understanding of customer needs and behaviors. Or perhaps, in your company, incoming market data has historically been managed by a product marketing or sales group. You should collaborate and leverage these highly talented professionals for conducting well-designed tests, as you will learn from their keen insights.

Validation Occurs outside the Building

Early in my career, I focused on demonstrating product updates to executives, managers, and peers. I sought approvals for prioritization decisions, gathered extensive product requirements, and worked with QA to ensure we passed functionality tests. Each step felt like I'd jumped a hurdle.

Overly confident, I quickly learned with my first product failure (named "Smart-Links") that customers don't care how clever your ideas are or how well-executed your implementation. They just want the product to solve a problem. I discovered the product didn't serve as critical a need as we thought and, with too many features, I had overly complicated the user interface. All that time spent inside the building would have been better spent outside with customers—I would have discovered these issues earlier.

Do not wholly rely on these groups, however. You must also have firsthand experience observing and talking to customers for the following reasons:

- **To prioritize hypotheses**—As a product manager, you must know the most pressing business and customer questions that will influence your product direction. Directly participating in customer validation allows you to establish and prioritize the hypotheses for testing—those that are most critical to your decisions.

- **To develop customer empathy**—By watching customers engage with your product, you develop a firsthand understanding of your customer and your product's limitations.

- **To discover new needs**—While observing customers in their environment, as product manager, you are uniquely positioned to identify new customer opportunities and possible technology solutions.

- **For exposure to primary observations**—Third-party studies generate summarized insights and conclusions, which are helpful when

Fail Fast and Pivot

During validation, you may discover the initial product direction is flawed. There is no use continuing down the same path; instead, you must reevaluate possible new approaches.

Despite their popularity, "fail fast" and "pivot" can be misleading concepts. They may lead to having a cowboy culture, trying random ideas, perhaps wildly thrashing between priorities, or skipping planning and product-discovery entirely.

I prefer "learn fast." Enter each iteration with a hypothesis based on your understanding of the customer's needs. Know how you will measure success or failure and explicitly discuss what you learned so you can incorporate those lessons into the next cycle. If it turns out you were wrong, there was still a good outcome because you learned something new.

Similarly, pivot *to* a promising new idea, not *from* a bad idea. Use insights gathered from your previous attempts to decide a new direction. Hold true to your overall strategic goal—a pivot should help redefine a workable solution but rarely redefine your strategy to tackle a wholly different problem space.

communicating high-level outcomes but lack details. You need raw data: to make your own interpretations, to catch subtle signs and clues from customer behavior, and to see patterns that may emerge only over time.

- **To accelerate follow-up**—Research and testing can generate more unanswered questions. If you're meeting a customer in person, you can find out more about the issue on the spot, rather than having to wait to run the next study.

Product managers must own and drive research around problem definition, customer value and market validation, and priority of features. You cannot delegate this work—summaries of what others have learned are insufficient.

Generally, user experience designers and researchers own and drive usability testing, including workflows, functionality, and user interaction. However, you must also participate in testing sessions to glean firsthand

Customer Advisory Boards

Enterprise companies often establish a customer advisory board (CAB), inviting the highest-ranking executives or buyers at the company's largest customers to periodic events.

Product managers will often participate in these events, giving presentations or fielding questions, efforts that often include discussing emerging market needs and receiving product and roadmap feedback.

Recognize these as sales events and not opportunities for serious product research. They are for salespeople to build relationships with their most important customers. You must still conduct your own research and discovery outside of these events.

The companies that represent your most important customers are not representative of the overall customer base, especially not of segments you are underserving or customers who have chosen a competitor's product over yours.

As economic buyers and executives, customer attendees likely have little day-to-day interaction with the product or with actual end users. They may request unique features that may be of little value to the broader market. Anticipate being "put on the spot" in front of customer executives and avoid inadvertently committing to address an issue or add functionality.

insights. Given you and your team's different roles and backgrounds, you will look for and learn different things from the same conversations.

You must guide decisions about what is covered in interviews, both during preparation and "live" as they are being run—do not just sit and watch. Otherwise, good usability testing may result in poor concept, product, or value/economics validation.

Also, don't underestimate the power of including your engineering team in interview sessions (not all at once—rotate through team members so you don't overwhelm your interview subject). When they have been in front of customers struggling with an issue, they are much more likely to support taking decisive action.

Make Product Discovery and Validation Continuous and Low-Cost

Integrate low-effort, routine, iterative user-centric interviewing and testing into a regular schedule for you and your team. Then you can refine the product constantly, building confidence, eliminating risks, and tweaking designs and feature priorities.

A simple framework to help you conceptualize this process of continuous validation is the *scope-design-test-learn* cycle (**Figure 5.2**). To illustrate the framework in action, imagine a hypothetical online skills development service, *Photo-Pro*, targeting aspiring amateur photographers. *Photo-Pro* is looking to grow its online presence through increased awareness and membership. Assume you are the product manager and you plan to add a community feature for members to receive feedback on their work.

- **Scope**—During product discovery, you are describing a *hypothesis*, not a set of requirements. You are proposing that building the product, functionality, or feature *may* (but *may not*) contribute to solving customers' needs.

  For example, for *Photo-Pro*'s community feedback feature, start with a high-level hypothesis:

  "We know that many aspiring photographers enjoy collaboration with others as they learn new skills, and we believe that we could enable their virtual interaction within the product. In providing a mechanism for existing members to upload their work and receive feedback from other members, we expect to drive more frequent and stickier engagement."

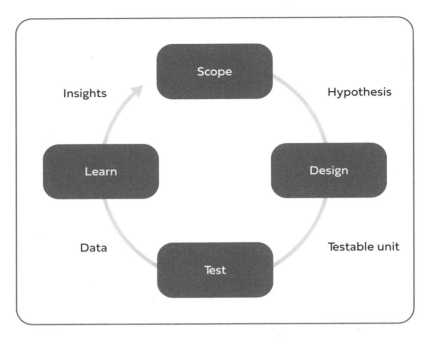

FIGURE 5.2 *Continuous discovery and validation conceptual framework*

In your first set of interviews you might focus on validating and understanding aspiring photographers' true needs: Do they indeed enjoy collaboration? Do they value feedback? From whom? In what form?

As you learn more, you can adapt and test variants in later interviews. For example, perhaps aspiring photographers *do* value feedback but see a difference in specific versus high-level feedback and in artistic critique versus tips on technique. You may have interviewees walk through examples of providing feedback on others' work or using existing online tools.

In later cycles, after understanding more about the customer need, you might then test a design or prototype. A prototype is simply the embodiment of your proposed solution. Prototypes are useful in testing, because the best time to identify that a feature isn't valuable is before you build it.

Don't test anything that you can't or won't take action on if the results are unexpected. And test early those hypotheses that represent the greatest assumptions and the greatest risks to the success of your product.

- **Design**—Plan your experiment and complete the minimum increment of work (a *testable unit*) to validate your hypothesis.

  For example, you may create these artifacts to test *Photo-Pro*'s community feedback feature:

  - a series of photos for test subjects to voice feedback on,

  - existing competitor tools for you to observe test subjects using,

  - a survey of your existing users with multiple-choice and open-ended questions,

  - a slide deck of your problem statement and value propositions,

  - a draft website and messaging to explore test subjects' interest in and understanding of the proposed feature,

  - early designs and sketches of two or more proposed solutions,

  - a clickable mock-up (a high-fidelity design) for your product flow,

  - the output of a feed algorithm selecting photos for the test subject to provide feedback on (to test that the data is consumable),

  - a prototype of your proposed product enhancement in which users can upload a photo and provide feedback on others (and in which the "back end" is not real and the data is not saved),

  - a rudimentary feature added to a version of your current product (which, if testing proves successful, will be further fleshed out), and

  - a partially working product already under development.

  (Note how the categories above start out being broad and exploratory and easier to prepare, then progressively become more detailed, requiring a high amount of effort.)

  What you build at this stage does not require bells and whistles. It does not even have to work. Leverage anything you have already put together or are currently building before you consider creating artifacts purely for testing. However, set expectations with your team that you are learning what works and what doesn't and that you will "change your mind." While some of what you create won't be throwaway material, you are not yet aiming to create fully functioning, reusable code. Be ready to discard or make changes based on your interview results.

▶ Later in **this chapter**, I cover how to prepare and conduct basic interviews. A sample interview script for *Photo-Pro* is available online at **http://www .influentialpm.com**.

- **Test**—Using your testable unit, put it in front of users, customers, and internal stakeholders. Collect qualitative and, if possible, quantitative *data*. Adaptability is more important than preparedness. Don't be afraid to change your interview questions or update your testable unit in real time if your testing isn't producing useful outcomes.

- **Learn**—Tease out *insights* from the data that support or, importantly, call into question your hypothesis. Develop thoughtful, objective, potential actions and agree on those few you will pursue. One to three recommendations at a time is all you need. Note the others and plan to come back later to test further. Your insights might point to problems, suggesting that you need to try a different path—or perhaps you have affirmation that you're on the right track.

Implement your recommendations, refine the scope, and decide on your next hypothesis to test. Now you can enter the next cycle with more confidence. And even if your test results were inconclusive, you'll have another chance to learn shortly.

Validation must continue throughout the various stages of your product-implementation lifecycle. Here's what that looks like at each stage:

- **Needs exploration** (divergent)—At the start of an initiative, you primarily understand customer needs and explore potential solutions. Investigation starts with high-level items such as testing value propositions, validating user goals, and comparing functionality options.

- **Product execution** (convergent)—As you and your team move into execution mode, do not assume product discovery is complete. Validation becomes easier at this stage because you can move beyond concepts or prototypes onto working features. As each part of the product is further refined and details are added, you must confirm that the product you are implementing will satisfy the customer's goals and be easy to use. As such, be ready to adapt, perhaps redoing some development work.

▶ In **Chapter 4**, I introduce techniques for optimization through brainstorming, *RICE* prioritization and split-testing.

- **Post-launch** (optimization)—Some of the best learning occurs once users are actively using your now functional product. You will be generating plenty of quantitative and qualitative user data (such as product tracking and customer support email). Unfortunately, this is when many teams wrap up a project. Instead, continue to test existing products and features and prioritize development work to optimize performance or address lingering usability issues.

Repeat the cycle as often as practical, given your development schedule and access to customers. For consumer applications, I recommend interviewing and testing with five users every one to two weeks—spending about two hours interviewing users and about two hours on overall preparation and wrap-up (assuming you are using simple testing artifacts). This equates to only 5 to 10 percent of your work week (though that percentage should be higher during periods of intense product discovery). Creating the right product for your customers deserves at least that amount of time—I am consistently amazed at how often I meet product managers who have *never* spoken to customers.

You may decide to bring users into your office or visit them in their surrounds. If you have an existing product and a sizeable user base within your locale, it should be relatively straightforward to recruit users. Often a customer service representative or an office assistant is open to managing the process. Expect many invitations to users to go unanswered; some will also back out of a scheduled interview at the last minute. Usually, a simple reward, such as a gift card, is sufficient motivation and, to ensure an

Test Early, Test Often, Keep It Simple

Six months into building a new mobile application, the client was still gathering input on design preferences and feature priorities. The problem? All the input came from weekly internal reviews, and changes were made based only on what stakeholders wanted. External testing had been infrequent, as well, limited to a couple of surveys and walk-throughs of design options for feedback.

The mistake was to think that, for effective user testing, they'd need to wait for a mostly functioning product. Moreover, they had confused reaching internal consensus with getting market validation.

We agreed to move to a lean, frequent external-testing model. We set up a weekly half-day testing session, inviting three to five users into the office. We limited testing to just a couple of essential hypotheses each session, based on the decisions or choices we were about to make and the current state of the product. We'd first ask each user about their lives and their needs. Then we'd share our latest product ideas and last week's designs, or try out the partially finished product.

After three months, we'd talked to 50 users. Not enough to have statistical "proof" of product success, but the rich, qualitative data gave us useful input on needs, features, and designs. We could move faster then, more confident in our decisions.

authentic interview, is preferable to paying them. Always give the user the incentive before you commence the interview so as not to make them feel they need to "work for it" by giving you positive feedback.

If you are looking to interview users outside of your current user base or locale, you may need more creative recruitment methods. This might include visiting places they frequent (such as stores or coffee shops), posting interview requests on web forums, or conducting tests via a video call. Remote interviews are also possible to reach a global audience, if necessary—at some loss of establishing rapport and detecting subtle clues.

For enterprise applications, I recommend visiting at least one customer's office every two weeks to understand your product in their context. More preparation and time to schedule is generally required than consumer applications. Given the time commitment upon yourself and on your busy customer, you might consider attending as a small cross-functional group to achieve a couple of goals during a single visit. Identify and interview a representative cross-section including end users, their team leads and managers, your product's internal administrator, your product's internal champion, your IT/security personnel, buyers, and executives. Interview them separately so as not to risk groupthink or their unwillingness to contradict their seniors. If there are specific areas requiring their thoughtful consideration, send a brief ahead of time to increase the chance they are prepared.

You may need to negotiate access to customers with the sales team. It is essential that you agree with sales that you are not conducting a sales call, that you script your discussion carefully, and that you decide ahead of time off-limits subjects. Until you build trust, sales team members may want to attend or otherwise be involved; welcome that but explicitly agree on your mutual roles and be adamant that you will not make any roadmap commitments to the client.

Structuring and Conducting User Interviews

A well-structured interview can provide you with insights into each of your hypotheses. As discussed, your user interviews should cover both exploration of the customer and their needs (*value*) and testing of specific functionality (*usability*)—you do not have to make every interview about both, but you do need to strike a balance. You should take the lead in the former, whereas your user experience partner usually takes it in the latter.

Perfecting user interviews takes practice—so engage your user experience group in helping you structure and design user interviews to ensure you are applying industry-best practices. If you are following the recommended continuous-validation model, you will have many opportunities to develop your skills.

1. Carefully Script Your Interview—Capture What Is Said and Observe What Is Not Said

You have only a short time with each user, so make the most of it. Without a script, it is easy to get off track, inadvertently reword questions and bias the user's answer, or be inconsistent in your questioning across multiple interviews. If you start asking different questions, wording questions differently, or asking them in a different order, it becomes difficult to see patterns and draw conclusions over multiple user interviews.

Stick to your hypothesis. When you go on a "fishing expedition" without a clear outcome in mind, you'll discover little useful information or actionable feedback. Write down known issues ahead of time (so you're less likely to dismiss feedback as something you already knew); however, use the script as a general guide. Every interview and interviewee is slightly different. Let the user take you on their journey and do not be too rigid. It is okay to go off-script and explore further if a user says or does something interesting and unexpected.

In the interview, write down everything you see and hear in response to your questions, especially direct user quotes. Resist drawing conclusions in your notes; stick to documenting the facts and interpreting them later. Nonverbal clues are sometimes more telling than what the user says. Perhaps they seem not particularly interested in what you offer but are being polite. If you wish to tape the conversation or take photos or video, ask permission first.

Pairing up will be more efficient: one person can ask the questions and build rapport with your test subject; the other can document what is said and capture nonverbal observations. Ideally, the product manager and designer pair up, with a developer listening in. Practice the script live with your partner before you go into your first interview and, to improve your skills, ask them to observe how you conduct the interview and to give you feedback immediately after. The more interviews you do, the more comfortable you will be with it.

2. Give Control to the User—Probe to Understand Rather Than Draw Your Own Conclusions

Never run a controlled user demo, where you walk through each step. After all, you're unlikely to be physically present when every user of your product needs help. Create a real-world environment by designing interviews around a user goal and the product in the state they would find it if they had interacted with it for the very first time. Do not give them step-by-step instructions.

Resist answering their questions, solving their problems, or helping them when they get stuck. If they ask "What does this do?" or "What should I do next?" turn that around by asking "What do you think it does?" or "What are you thinking of doing next?" Listen for silences—wait at least 10 seconds before asking what they are thinking. And still, don't help! There is nothing more painful than to see a user struggle while you sit there watching—but you learn valuable lessons.

Remember that you are not selling your idea; you are validating it. Maintain objectiveness and be open to the possibility that you might hear or see something counter to your assumptions. Stay neutral during the

Letting the User Take Control Can Be Challenging

To create a comfortable and realistic environment for our photo-sharing product user testing, we arranged to conduct testing of our website at our users' houses. We arranged to meet with a typical user—very friendly, eager to help us, her computer outdated, her internet connection slow, and her technical capabilities limited.

We asked her to complete a goal using our service—to share some photos with her friends. At first, she couldn't even find the browser's desktop icon (she'd accidentally hidden it), and then she couldn't figure out where the Share feature was on our homepage (which we thought we had clearly labeled). Flustered and frustrated with herself, she struggled through the process of sharing photos. Finally, as she uploaded photos from her desktop, it took so long, her cat seized the opportunity to leap up on her lap and distract her from the task. She barely completed this single goal.

My colleagues and I were stressed and desperate to help her navigate through the site, but we knew we had to remain detached. And all the time she apologized and blamed herself for her technical and "feline" challenges. Perhaps concerned she'd hurt our feelings, she insisted we'd done a lovely job with the product.

Despite our assurances, with several people watching her every move, it must have felt like we were evaluating her, and not our product. (Don't underestimate how daunting user testing is for users and design around it accordingly.)

Nonetheless, the highly authentic, nail-biting experience drove home our need to simplify our service for our target market.

interview—don't show surprise, judgment, or disappointment. Seek to understand users' struggles with your product—do not dismiss something you don't like or that doesn't fit with your view.

Keep your users talking while you do as little as possible—ask them to verbalize their thinking, have them explain what they are doing or what they expect to happen. Give them neutral feedback and encouragement (such as "Okay, please go on . . ."). Be aware that your user can become frustrated or disengage. Sometimes it is better to get fewer things done but get much more detail.

Don't settle for generalizations or half the story—get to the "why" and uncover specifics. Ask probing questions to understand what they are thinking and what concerns they have. Then ask for concrete examples. If they give you subjective feedback (colors, visual design, opinions on feature priorities), push them to explain their underlying reasoning.

3. Carefully Phrase and Order Your Questions to Eliminate Bias and Build Rapport

There are many user testing methodologies and expert approaches to user-interview issues. I outline here a "quick-and-dirty" approach to an interview that you can readily apply in most situations.

Example Probing Questions

Try this short list of useful probing questions:

- Can you tell me more about…?
- Can you give me an example of…?
- Can you explain…in more detail?
- What do you mean by…?
- What would…look like?
- What motivated you to…?
- Why do you think you noticed…?
- Why is…important to you?
- How would you go about…?
- How do you feel about…?

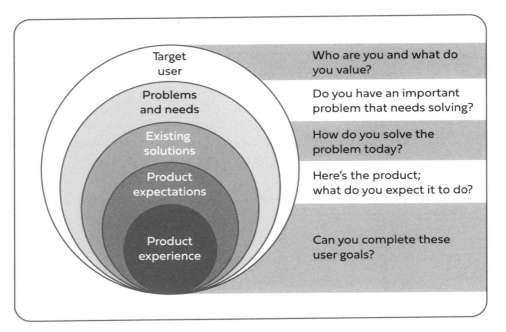

FIGURE 5.3 *Onion model for sequencing interview questions*

Imagine structuring your interview like you would peel an onion (**Figure 5.3**): start with broad, open-ended questions and gradually narrow in to ask about specific product tasks and functionality. In this way, you will learn valuable information about your target users, how they think about the problem, and how important the problem is to address *before* they learn about your solution.

Keep them in the dark as long as possible. Avoid giving away too much context early on—such as explaining what your product does or showing the product designs to them before they hear the big picture. Give away too much information too soon, and you will bias your results. You will lose the opportunity to gather useful information about the user's real needs and "first-time" impressions.

Ask questions about these topics, in this order:

1. **Target user**—You want to understand more about the target user, what they value, and how they think. If you have personas, use them to drill into specifics and to further qualify your test subject as a bona fide target for interview.

   For example, after engaging in small talk to warm up the interviewee, the product manager for *Photo-Pro* might start by asking the following:

- How did you get interested in photography?

- Describe to me your process. What excites you most? What challenges you?

2. **Problem and needs**—Explore how important it is to solve the problem they aim to solve and what does (and does not) motivate them to address it. Have them describe the value of addressing the problem. Ask neutral and indirect questions, so you aren't biasing their answers.

   For example, ask the following:

- Here's a list of 10 statements. Please rank from least to most true/ important. ("Getting feedback on my work" is only one need on the list.)

- Specifically, what are your goals for improving your photographic skills?

3. **Existing solutions**—Ask the user how they solve the problem today. Do they use a different (competitive) product? If so, what is it? If not, why don't they care to solve the problem today (and would that change once your product is available)?

   For example, ask the following:

- What do you currently do to learn new photography skills to improve?

- What/who do you use to receive feedback on your work?

4. **Product expectations**—Show the user your product and, without prompting, ask them to describe what they expect your product to do. Give them your product in the state they would find it "out of the box" (without you there). Do not tell them what it is or what it does. Ask why the product appeals to them (and, if it doesn't, why not). This will help you determine whether your product "speaks for itself" and helps you evaluate your product value and messaging.

   For example, give prompts such as the following:

- Spend a few minutes exploring *Photo-Pro*. Please verbalize what you are thinking as you go.

- Explain to me what you think the "get feedback" feature does. (Probe to surface misunderstandings or concerns.)

5. **Product experience**—Ask them to perform a few specific tasks and observe them doing so to understand product usability and

effectiveness. Rather than instructing them to use a feature, ask them to achieve a user goal.

For example, assuming you have an artifact to allow the interviewee to simulate using the new feature, you might say the following:

- Please go ahead and get feedback for one of your photos and talk out loud while you're doing it.

- What do you like most and least about this feature?

Design your interview in a way that will allow you to quickly build trust and rapport with your end user and allow you to extract details and insights. Then plan to close with a debrief, to confirm your conclusions with the user.

Begin the interview by setting expectations such as the following:

- How long the interview will take (and make sure you honor the time commitment).

- That you're not looking to sell anything.

- Whom you work for (don't mislead them).

- That there'll be two or three of you (if you have multiple attendees).

- That you're looking for an honest critique.

Also, ask for permission to video or record them, if you plan to do this. And give them any incentive (such as a gift card) *before* you start.

As you ask about the target user, build trust by asking softer questions to get them to engage by talking about themselves. You also have the opportunity to qualify your test subject further (what it is they do and if they fit your target).

Be sure to guide the user as you transition from one stage to the next (for instance, say, "Now let's talk about your experiences with the mobile interface").

Toward the end, wind things down by letting them know there are just a few more questions to go, and reinforce the value of their feedback and insights. Ask them if they have any further thoughts or opinions, saying something like, "Is there anything we didn't ask that we should have?" An informal chat toward the end, when the interviewee is deeply engaged and relaxed, can reveal surprising additional insights.

Finally, thank them for their time, inviting them to contact you if they have anything to add later. And before you interview another user, note any questions that didn't work very well and adjust your script accordingly.

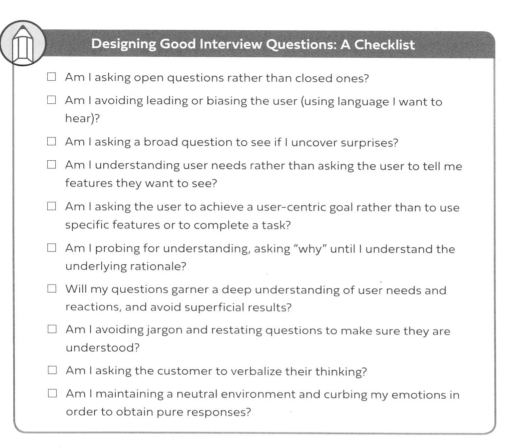

Designing Good Interview Questions: A Checklist

☐ Am I asking open questions rather than closed ones?

☐ Am I avoiding leading or biasing the user (using language I want to hear)?

☐ Am I asking a broad question to see if I uncover surprises?

☐ Am I understanding user needs rather than asking the user to tell me features they want to see?

☐ Am I asking the user to achieve a user-centric goal rather than to use specific features or to complete a task?

☐ Am I probing for understanding, asking "why" until I understand the underlying rationale?

☐ Will my questions garner a deep understanding of user needs and reactions, and avoid superficial results?

☐ Am I avoiding jargon and restating questions to make sure they are understood?

☐ Am I asking the customer to verbalize their thinking?

☐ Am I maintaining a neutral environment and curbing my emotions in order to obtain pure responses?

At http://www.influentialpm.com, you will find an example interview template for *Photo-Pro*'s community feedback feature.

Testing with Wireframes, Mock-Ups, and Prototypes

User experience visualizations let you rapidly design and test different potential solutions before you have a fully working product. They are also an excellent way to communicate your concept to stakeholders and to illustrate customer-facing interaction and visual design requirements to your engineering team.

Visualizations show how the product will operate without the expense of building a fully functioning back end. They save time: you can iterate on the visualization long before writing code (code which might need substantial changes as you learn more about the actual needs of users).

Find the right balance between *fidelity*, to enable robust validation of your current assumptions and proposed solutions balanced with the speed and cost to create the required testing artifacts. Early in discovery, when you may have several concepts to test and only a vague idea of the user interface, use low-fidelity methods. You can rapidly iterate on different ideas for little cost. As you converge on your solution, you can become increasingly detailed in the representation of your product for robust usability testing. Higher fidelity is costlier in design and engineering time but is needed only once your product is well understood, and you can often reuse the work product during development.

Each of the three following types of visualizations (**Figure 5.4**) can be used for testing and communication at different levels of fidelity:

- **Wireframes**—Use them to represent the overall content architecture, roughly sketching out

  - features and functionality (*what*),

  - the structure and layout of the page (*where*),

  - the fundamental user interface/interaction, such as consistent menus and how the user will flow between pages or states (*how*).

  Wireframes quickly illustrate high-level concepts to get customer and stakeholder reactions and to gather opinions in order to compare different options. They are low-cost, ideal for fast iteration where you throw away concepts that don't work. You can hand-draw features, flows, and functionality with a pen, paper, cardboard, and scissors—or use software illustration tools. You typically create a sketch using just a few colors and replace images and layout with basic lines and shapes. Text is also limited to the main directions and buttons.

- **Mock-ups**—A static, visual representation detailing the layout and structure of information, content, interactive responses to user actions, and core functionality. Unlike wireframes, mock-ups are complete with images, draft text, menus, buttons, and forms.

  Use mock-ups to validate more detailed user interactions and to test user understandings of menus, flows, and calls to action. Unlike wireframes, they start to represent the end-user experience accurately. They are also helpful for capturing "look and feel" guidelines, such as branding, fonts, and colors.

  To mock-up tools or reports, something as simple as a spreadsheet can serve as a mock-up or a prototype. The user can see numeric insights, and you can even simulate interaction through filters and toggles.

WIREFRAME	MOCK-UP	PROTOTYPE
Conceptual functionality, layout, and interactions between states (pages)	Static, visual design detailing functionality, layout and interactions	Simulation of the full user interface of the planned product

Increasing fidelity →

	WIREFRAME	MOCK-UP	PROTOTYPE
Artifact	High-level sketches (paper or virtual)	Linked (clickable) image, PDF, Photoshop, Excel, or Word files	Semi-functional front-end (design + HTML)
Cost	Cheap, highly iterative, "throwaway"	UX-level designs with rough images and copy	"10%" of the code: no back-end or business logic
Validates	Concepts and flow options	Interaction and visual design	Usability as if product is built
Communicates	Alternatives	Direction	Requirements

FIGURE 5.4 *Differences between wireframes, mock-ups, and prototypes*

Advanced mock-ups—which provide an excellent set of "visual requirements"—also include the following:

- Details on animations or states (such as elements that might change emphasis upon mouse-over or an item that moves or rotates).

- Error responses for incorrectly entered information, such as wrong passwords or illegal values in forms.

- Edge cases, such as "X returned no search results."

- Offline mode behavior (in the case of mobile applications).

- Nonvisual input and output, such as voice instructions or sounds.

A *clickable mock-up* enables you to link multiple mock-ups together (through a technique called "hot-spotting"), so you can simulate what happens when users click on parts of the page. Individual pages are linked to simulate basic navigation flow in canned scenarios: users won't enter data but can navigate through each screen as if they are achieving a goal.

- **Prototypes**—Prototypes are a highly accurate representation of the user-facing "front-end." A high-fidelity prototype allows a user to experience content and interactions with the interface in a way that realistically shows how the final product will function. From a testing perspective, the user might not even know they are interacting with anything other than the completed product.

  A prototype is the most efficient way to iterate on a final design and is the gold standard in outcomes from a well-run product-discovery process. You can be confident the product meets usability goals before detailed development begins. The level of clarity a high-fidelity prototype can give engineering, copywriters, marketing, and business teams is better than any written specifications.

  Prototypes need little to no connection to any back-end services—allowing the user experience to be validated before you invest in these systems. For example, if your prototype is a website, you may produce static HTML/CSS to be rendered in the user's browser. A mobile application prototype might contain screens run in an emulator but no link from the client to a server system. In both cases, you invest minimally in any of the back-end features such as algorithms, services (APIs), business logic, error handling, or data management. You can use canned data for testing.

  Prototyping is a more expensive and time-consuming process than creating wireframes and mock-ups, but the final version can be reused in development as it contains assets, copy, and some front-end code.

In addition to design software tools from Adobe and Microsoft, online prototyping tools and user testing platforms help you efficiently build high-quality artifacts and complete user validation.

- **Wireframing**—Create "drawings" or a storyboard of your key screens and functionality, to describe the user interaction and overall flow.

- **Clickable mock-ups**—Upload PDFs, images, or Photoshop files, and hotspot areas of each page to link them. They often include collaboration areas to make notes and discuss improvements quickly.

- **Interactive prototyping**—Convert wireframes and other assets into a prototype that feels close to the front-end user experience of a final product.

- **Virtual user testing**—Test almost anything, from a concept to a working product, to help you recruit, conduct, record, and share user tests virtually (online and remotely).

There are dozens of online tools and services—free and paid (some with a free trial)—that can help you create artifacts and conduct user research with ease. With the emergence of these tools, there is no excuse not to make product discovery and user research an ongoing part of your product management process. You will find a list of tools in the online supporting materials at http://www.influentialpm.com.

Modern Tools Make Usability Testing a Breeze

A meeting to review and decide between two design options for a subscription service landing and conversion experience was scheduled after much back and forth over email.

A senior stakeholder preferred the first option as it contained more information about the service and provided additional pricing choices for users to select from. The second option was simpler, with a strong call to action (CTA) and a single path to sign-up.

The stakeholder was concerned that the second option would lead to user confusion about the service's value proposition and that conversion would be lower without multiple price options. He also worried the second option's call to action was too aggressive and that users might react negatively toward the brand. However, the product and marketing team believed the second—because of its clarity and simplicity—was more powerful and that the stakeholder's concerns were unwarranted.

These were complex issues to resolve between two groups of internal stakeholders with very strong points of view.

Just before the meeting, I asked the design team to put both options up on Usertesting.com. In only a few hours we received multiple user test results, complete with videos of users interacting with each of the designs and expressing their thoughts out loud.

Incontrovertibly, the first option had failed. Far from being helpful, the extra information caused users to get quickly lost. In addition, each user reacted positively with the second option's CTA, voicing no negative feelings toward the brand.

We walked into the meeting armed with supporting data and the confidence that the second choice was the right one—which was duly adopted.

CHAPTER 6

Define the Right Product

Use hypothesis-driven specifications to get your team exploring solutions and delivering on outcomes.

1 How to deliver hypothesis-driven and contextually relevant product specifications for any initiative, aligning stakeholders and allowing you and your team to focus.

2 The principles and benefits behind tightly constraining a product initiative's goals and scope to speed time-to-market, reduce risk, and avoid overinvestment.

3 How to apply a five-step top-down framework and a powerful, yet concise, product-specification template.

What Makes a Great Product Specification?

Before a prioritized initiative moves into the delivery phase—where design and engineering will formally start to execute against it—it is customary for a product manager to produce a specification document.

To be clear on terminology, I use the term *product specification* as a high-level document (as short as a few pages) intended to capture enough detail to

- communicate context—goals, measurable outcomes, and constraints—to stakeholders and team members;

- determine the high-level scope (the primary features and functions) of the product undertaking;

- serve as a platform to kick off the design and development process; and

- start the process of breaking down the initiative into a detailed set of feature requirements, such as user stories.

It is essential to separate the specification—which you create up front and before an initiative is kicked off—from a set of detailed product requirements. The spec includes descriptions and even conceptual designs of the desired scope and features but leaves room to flesh out the specifics. Separating them has several advantages:

- It keeps the specification readable and comprehensible for all. Context and overview are not lost in pages and pages of uninspiring details.

- It allows requirement specifics to emerge and be refined with further customer validation and collaboration with your team.

- It reduces up-front investment in discussion and documentation. You can avoid wasting effort on scoping functionality that will later be cut or preemptively making decisions that are better taken later.

▶ **Chapter 7** introduces user stories and product backlogs as a means for building upon the high-level scope in a specification. These tools enable detailed requirements and feature-level priorities to emerge through close collaboration with your team.

Unfortunately, many product specifications tend to be of poor quality. They fail to provide sufficient business or customer context and leap straight into dictating a laundry list of desired features. They often neglect to include major functionality needs (initially overlooked by the product manager), which appear later as scope creep. Alternatively, they include functionality that is superfluous to meeting the initiative's goals and will therefore be waste.

Poor specs are a common point of conflict between product managers and engineers. Product blames engineering for a perceived lack of timely delivery or for failing to deliver what was expected. Engineering blames product for lacking context, prioritizing low-impact initiatives, or shifting scope (perceived as "changing their mind") during development.

Excellent specifications establish a defined goal, contain context for why tackling the goal is important, and include only that scope that delivers upon those needs and no more.

1. Establish a Defined Goal with Measurable Outcomes

Set a clear objective limiting you to one or few business and customer goals. Focus is powerful—providing clarity, decoupling dependencies, and motivating your team. When you attempt to deliver against too many competing goals simultaneously, you struggle with confusion, misalignment, complexity, and feature prioritization.

Write your goal as a testable hypothesis for why the functionality is needed—starting by articulating the problem to be solved from the customer's viewpoint. It must be supported with quantitative and qualitative data and what more you seek to learn.

Include metrics that define success. Ideally, you will quantify the current baseline and set a target. This demonstrates accountability—moving your mindset from the tactical (one of executing and delivering projects) to the strategic (delivering value to customers and driving outcomes for the business).

A clear and common goal establishes a framework for including or excluding functionality into or from scope. It helps you identify and prioritize a narrow set of functionality initially and manage scope creep later. When stakeholders request additional features or changes, you can refer back to the goal to decide whether it justifies inclusion and provide a rationale for declining out-of-scope requests.

Stakeholders are far more willing to approve new initiatives that clearly articulate the business benefit when they are supported with data. It also helps to break the cycle of launching new capabilities but never returning to improve on them. Rarely do first product releases completely address a problem—if you haven't hit your goal, that's your ready-made business case for additional investment for further development and optimization.

2. Determine the Narrowest Set of Scope Needed to Deliver on the Goal—and No More

Attempting to build a feature-rich "perfect solution" the first time, with many unproven and potentially wasteful features, burns through company resources. This can be particularly deadly for startups. It is best avoided for two reasons:

1. You are assuming your customers need all the features you propose. In reality, historically, as few as 20 percent of features built are required to serve 80 percent of customer needs. Building secondary features wastes valuable time and resources.

2. No matter how well-researched and validated, any product may initially fail to address customer needs, requiring substantial rework to fix what you didn't get right. Better to get something to market earlier, gather feedback, and start iterating instead.

In addition to direct waste, the opportunity cost can be high. Instead of delivering secondary features, you could have used your development team to deliver something else of greater value. When you allow this to occur, you are failing in one of your key responsibilities as a product manager—what you decide *not to* work on is often more valuable than what you do decide *to* work on. You don't have to deliver on the big picture all at once.

Scoping can be a subjective process, but with a clear goal, defined metrics, and useful constraints in place, it becomes easier to scrutinize every single feature as being necessary or not.

Don't make the mistake of brainstorming all the functionality you'd like to build and then cutting everything back until it feels like you can deliver the product within a specific timeframe. If you do, you'll end up with a large number of questionable features, often labeled as "must-haves," "should-haves," or "nice-to-haves."

Select only must-haves to meet your goal. Try to pare down to a couple of core-use cases and scope just those components necessary. Focus on them and do them exceptionally well, at the expense of having more features. Pay attention to the details such as first-use experience, discovery, and edge cases (recovering well from extreme errors or conditions). Do not take shortcuts in design and testing to fit in more scope. Customers expect products to be intuitive and aesthetically pleasing. Build a product that does a couple of things very well.

If you find yourself scoping out what seems like a colossal product initiative, perhaps your goals are too high-level and all-encompassing—for example "increase revenue" could justify almost anything. Return to your goals to sharpen them and plan on delivering a smaller product increment first. That will set you up to learn where additional product investments should (and shouldn't) be made, based on customer feedback and behavior data.

> ▶ Refer to **Chapter 9** for more on making intelligent scope tradeoffs.

If you apply this principle correctly, later cuts to scope risks disabling the product from delivering real value to the end customer. Do not cut scope that was important enough to be considered necessary in the first place, unless assumptions have changed after customer validation. If you find yourself reducing scope late in the development process, then perhaps you didn't constrain scope tightly enough up front. If, however, you are cutting critical functionality just to hit a launch date, then it might be best to delay launch.

How Goal-Driven Specs Can Accelerate Time-to-Market

The client's mobile dating application was simple to use and popular, with a loyal customer following. In two years, they had delivered no major upgrades and only minor tweaks.

A new 3.0 version was in development but had become a mammoth undertaking. After such a long time without significant product updates, there was pent-up demand for new features and infrastructure improvements. Each time a product release was nearly ready, new must-have requirements were added to an already complex upgrade.

Using the outlined principles in this chapter, we first set about identifying and prioritizing a few key goals for the upgrade. These included addressing the top 10 usability irritants and improving underlying application stability. With fewer goals bundled into one release, we could more easily decide what was (and, importantly, what wasn't) in scope. Secondary features would be reviewed later.

Next, we carefully reviewed usage figures for all features in the existing version. About 20 percent of the existing features weren't often used—so we determined we could put these out of scope for the rebuild.

Finally, as new needs came up, we managed scope by filtering all requests against the original stated goals. Anything that wasn't deemed essential to meeting those goals went on hold.

Within six months, the team was transformed. No longer was it struggling to make progress; rather, it was confidently shipping regular product enhancements that delivered new value to customers.

The single greatest advantage of limiting the project to the essential scope is to get to market earlier. In turn, this allows you to establish a customer feedback loop and observe actual user behavior so that you can prioritize additional functionality or improvements with hard data. The sooner you engage your target customer, the more confident you can become that you are making the right investment decisions for your scarce resources.

3. Set the Context to Align Your Stakeholders around Rationale and Expected Scope

You, your team, and your stakeholders likely have different ideas as to what the product will do and for whom it will do it. It is common for stakeholders to have preconceived notions about what outcomes and functionalities will be delivered within an initiative. Upon seeing the product take shape, they may become disappointed or query why components they had assumed would be included are missing. If the desired outcomes are unclear, they may be dissatisfied with the results even if you consider those results to be a success.

A clear specification helps avoid later conflict and misunderstandings, stating from the outset what the key business goals are (and are not) and what high-level functionalities are (and are not) in scope. Include a list of useful constraints that deliberately call out parameters, such as the customers to be served (and not served), the geographies or markets of initial focus, and the included and excluded platforms or legacy technologies.

There is now a higher chance that you have a shared understanding of what success will look like. However, keep careful track of trade-offs and

Avoid One-and-Done Product Initiatives

When an organization has a culture of launching new product capabilities, and rarely revisits later to evaluate and improve upon them, product specifications tend to be overly ambitious from the start. Stakeholders (correctly) worry that this will be their "last chance" to get all the scope they want included in the specification for a new capability, and so tend to push to pile on lower-value features at the beginning of the project. A good spec will increase the chances for a productive conversation, perhaps resulting in splitting out a large spec into several smaller increments, each with a compelling case to justify ongoing investment. Goal-driven specifications intend for products to evolve after launch, not to be forgotten about.

agreed-upon constraints so that you are not later surprised by demands for everything to be done sooner. Explicitly document the functionality agreed upon as being out of scope and ensure your stakeholders have committed to living with the decisions.

Providing context and clarity is a great motivator for your design and development team too. They understand how their work fits into the business. They feel empowered to own and strive toward solutions—and you give them permission to push back on those components that don't seem aligned with the goal.

Steps to Create a "Top-Down" Specification

Let's use a five-step framework to define your hypothesis and your customer and business goals, with useful constraints for scoping a limited set of functionality. Use the framework whether you are delivering an entirely new product or a set of functionalities for an existing product or to create an experiment note for conducting a split-test to drive incremental improvements.

I will use the framework to create two example specifications—one an experiment and one a more substantive feature—for our hypothetical online skills-development service *Photo-Pro*. Introduced in **Chapter 5**, *Photo-Pro* wishes to raise awareness of its products and services among amateur photographers and increase membership. It makes money today by advertising photographic gear but desires to become a marketplace, matching photographers to paid opportunities.

The final specifications for each example are available at http://www.influentialpm.com.

Step 1—Articulate Your Hypothesis, Your Learning Goal

The hypothesis is a short statement of

- what you know,

- what you believe to be the underlying need or issue,

- what you plan to do and for whom, *and*

- the desired results.

A simple template you can use is:

> We know that [data or observation] and believe that [need or issue]. Through delivering/testing [concept] for [target user] we expect [measurable outcome].

You generate your *data or observation* from available quantitative analysis and the results of your qualitative research (**Chapter 5**). A high-level, top-line (but inconvertible) fact is all that is required—if there is substantial disagreement on this part of your hypothesis, then you are unlikely to get much further. You do not need to list all your data in the hypothesis, just the top-line—include details and additional data for further color later, in your specification document.

The *need or issue* is what you believe is the desire or cause. Describe your *concept*—avoid jargon and keep it descriptive and easily understood by outsiders. Include a *target user* from your subset of user types. If you find yourself just writing "user," then perhaps you are trying to do too much for too many or you aren't challenging yourself to be specific enough.

Your *measurable outcome* is your desired user or business result—you do not need to list precise metrics in your hypothesis, but what you will select in step 2 must align with this goal.

Here are example hypotheses for *Photo-Pro*:

Example A (a user-registration experiment): "We know that 50 percent of visitors to the *Photo-Pro* website do not create an account and believe that the registration process is asking the user to make too much of a commitment before they are ready. Through an improved registration experience for first-time visitors, we expect increased sign-ups."

Example B (a community-feedback feature): "We know that many aspiring photographers enjoy collaboration with others as they learn new skills, and we believe we can enable their virtual interaction within the product. In providing a mechanism for existing members to upload their work and receive feedback from other members, we expect to drive stickier and more frequent engagement."

Your hypothesis in hand, you should find that your stakeholders and team members have greater appreciation of the overall context. Your hypothesis is an anchor: everyone can ask relevant questions, challenge assumptions, and brainstorm ideas. In the later stages of development, it helps keep everyone on track.

Step 2—Pick a Measurable Business Goal

Picking a single business goal brings focus to your efforts and defines success for your initiative. Do not confuse a *user goal* with your *business goal*. While your initiative must deliver value to users as defined by its value proposition, you must also decide what you most want as a business.

You need to make your choice of goal appropriate to the stage of your business. If you are in the early stages of your product lifecycle, don't invest in building a large user base but in acquiring your first customers and delivering value to them. If, however, your business already has scale, then perhaps your goal might be to increase your average revenue per customer from your existing customer base or to expand your service into new markets. An even more mature business might focus on managing risks, building new partnerships, and protecting its customer franchise.

Table 6.1 has example business goals, roughly ordered by product maturity. (Although this is not at all a strict grouping. You may, for

TABLE 6.1 Example business goals by stage of product maturity

Early stage (demonstrate product–market fit)

- Acquire first users/customers (early adopters)
- Gain new customer insights (test a concept)
- Increase user-engagement time or repeat usage
- Eliminate key usability irritants (friction points in your service)
- Move from early adopters to mainstream customer segments
- Optimize customer conversion rates

Growth stage (product is scaling up)

- Drive customer acquisition volume
- Generate sustainable revenue streams
- Improve your marketing and CRM outreach
- Streamline onboarding of new customers
- Build and integrate a strategic partnership
- Expand into a new market (geography/segment)
- Improve retention/renewal rates
- Improve upsell and cross-sell rates

Mature stage (protect and optimize the business)

- Reduce cost of customer acquisition (CAC)
- Reduce a key business cost
- Automate a business process for efficiency
- Improve product reliability/uptime
- Eliminate technical debt (improve infrastructure) for future scale
- Reduce security risks
- Modernize brand image (for example, product UX redesign)

example, need a product-development initiative to "reduce a key business cost" even in the early stage.)

Make your goal measurable, by establishing what metric you will use to gauge success, and, ideally, include a performance target. Your metric should be aligned closely with the stated measurable outcome in your hypothesis as illustrated for *Photo-Pro* in **Table 6.2**.

It is often also helpful to include secondary metrics—correlating or leading indicators you expect to improve as a consequence of pursuing your primary metric. These metrics might be easier and quicker to measure. Secondary metrics allow you to highlight multiple performance indicators while retaining the ability to describe and focus on *one* primary one.

Likewise, if you might negatively affect a key business metric, include that as a counter-metric. For example, for *Photo-Pro*'s hypothesis A, additional sign-ups are of little benefit if they soon churn, because that means driving a less-qualified user base into your service. For hypothesis B, you may find adding the feedback feature a success when considered in isolation; however, you may have inadvertently reduced user engagement in other core features (as every feature you add can compete for customer attention, clutter your product, or increase cognitive load).

TABLE 6.2 Metrics for validating *Photo-Pro*'s hypotheses

HYPOTHESIS EXAMPLE	PRIMARY METRIC	SECONDARY INDICATORS	COUNTER-METRICS
A	% sign-ups of all new visitors	• Time to complete sign-up • Drop-off at each stage of the sign-up flow • Enhanced recall of value proposition by visitors (qualitative)	• Month 1 churn rate
B	Repeat usage per active user	• Stickiness DAU/WAU • % photos uploaded per active user • % photos with at least one piece of feedback	• Discovery/ engagement with other parts of the product • Customer satisfaction (NPS)

Step 3—Identify Useful Constraints
to Lower Scope and Simplify the Problem

Deliberately adding constraints can drastically reduce complexity, dependencies, and timeline. Limit your initial product delivery to a few dimensions or segments of your market, such as:

- **Customer type**—Can you focus on a couple of key user types, personas, or clients? You can address the others at a later date.

- **Industry vertical**—Is there an enterprise industry segment more receptive to your product for your initial launch?

- **User lifecycle**—Can you focus first on one part of the user journey, such as first-time visitors or loyal users?

- **Function**—If you are optimizing business processes or introducing new tools for an enterprise, can you do so with a particular department or function first and scale from there?

- **Geography**—Is one market or region, or perhaps even a couple of test locations, initially sufficient?

- **Channel**—Is your product distributed through many partners and marketing channels or integrated into many third-party platforms? Can you perhaps tackle fewer players first?

- **Device platform**—If your product is intended to be available across many platforms (such as iOS, Android, web, SmartTV), can you build for one first, rather than trying to master all simultaneously?

- **Product "surface area"**—If you are implementing features that cut across your entire product, such as in a site redesign, can you do one section first? To gather accurate success data on either experiments or new features, it is best to add one to each surface area at a time. Otherwise, you will not definitively know what changes drive the most benefit.

Ensure that no single constraint or combination of constraints reduces your volume of user interactions below that required for a statistically confident evaluation within a short timeframe. If you have too few interactions, you'll need longer to gather enough data before you can declare a test or feature successful.

Table 6.3 illustrates applying these categories of constraints for *Photo-Pro*'s two example initiatives.

TABLE 6.3 Constraints added for *Photo-Pro*'s initiatives

EXAMPLE A	EXAMPLE B
• First-time visitors. Run as 50/50 split test.	• Amateur landscape photographers (reduces copyright and image-review risk and complexity).
• Test in Canada. Roll out rest of world if successful.	• Active, logged-in members (who currently visit at least once a month).
• Desktop web only.	• English-language countries.
• Homepage. Channel-specific landing pages out of scope.	• iOS and Safari. Most of our users are Apple fans.
	• Initial features only added to member profile pages.

Step 4—Identify and Prioritize a Few High-Level User Stories That Encapsulate the Overall User Benefit Delivered

As explained in **Chapter 7**, high-level (or epic-level) *user stories* are short, simple descriptions of the desired functionality from the perspective of the end user in the format:

> As a [type of user], I want [to do something]
> so that [benefit or value].

A few epic-level user stories can encapsulate an entire initiative. For example, a simple job-search website might have just two:

As a prospective employee, I want to be able to apply to advertised positions so that I can find a job.

As an employer, I want to list available positions so that I can fill them with qualified candidates.

Select a few user stories that you believe will make the most impact on your customers. User stories drive discussion around intended customer-centric outcomes rather than around features, functionality, or design. You must ensure they also are within the constraints of previous steps (for example, if you decide to constrain your customer segment on your job-search site to "computer programmer," change it from "prospective employee" accordingly).

▶ In **Chapter 7**, I will go through the process of breaking down your epic-level user stories into smaller components to create a product backlog.

High-level stories form the basis of a much more detailed breakdown when you kick off the development process, and they are further refined throughout

TABLE 6.4 High-level user stories for *Photo-Pro*'s initiatives

EXAMPLE A	EXAMPLE B
As a new visitor, I want richer information about the *Photo-Pro* service offering so that I know what to expect once I sign up.	As a landscape photographer member, I want to be able to upload and manage a portfolio of work, so that I can showcase and receive feedback.
As a new visitor, I want fewer sign-up steps, so that I can complete registration quickly.	As a landscape photographer member, I want to be able to view other members' work, so that I can get inspiration for my own.
As a new visitor, I want to be asked for fewer sensitive personal attributes, so that I feel more comfortable completing registration.	As a landscape photographer member, I want to receive and manage comments on my work from other members, so that I can improve my skills.
As a new visitor, I want to receive feedback and derive immediate value, so that I can see how completing registration will benefit me.	

implementation. Reviewing **Table 6.4,** in example A's case, these stories might already be small enough; but each should run as a different test. In example B's case, the feature is still very high-level and requires more refinement.

Step 5—Now, and Only Now, Scope Functionality

You have now developed criteria with which you can scope out potential high-level functionality.

Your process here is to evaluate each candidate and determine the following:

- **From step 1**—Is it essential (or a necessary precondition) to test my hypothesis?

- **From step 2**—Will it further my business goal? Will it help me hit my metrics?

- **From step 3**—Does it meet the tight set of constraints I've established?

- **From step 4**—Is it *required* to deliver on my high-level user stories?

Scoping can be highly subjective and will depend on your specific business, customer needs, and product maturity. This usually requires negotiation with stakeholders. The value of the top-down process, though, is you have now established an evaluation framework to manage your discussions in a structured, goal-oriented way.

Cross-Business Considerations: A Checklist

Capture early cross-functional issues and requirements. Here is a short list of common, easily overlooked items I've run into over my history as a product manager.

SALES AND MARKETING

- ☐ Go-to-market plans, dependencies, and timing
- ☐ Customer acquisition, outreach, and CRM/email
- ☐ Pricing and positioning relative to existing company or competitor offerings
- ☐ Messaging (copy) and assets production, and brand approvals

DATA ANALYTICS AND BUSINESS OPERATIONS

- ☐ Definition of new-event tracking, data definitions, and reports, and thorough data QA
- ☐ Financial analysis: R&D investment (sometimes amortized), budgeting/vendor payments, impacts to customer acquisition cost (CAC), or lifetime value (LTV)
- ☐ Planning and accounting: forecasting, revenue recognition, taxation, and refunds
- ☐ Unintended consequences to data systems from which reports are generated

LEGAL AND COMPLIANCE

- ☐ Protracted contract negotiations or changes to existing contractual obligations
- ☐ Regulatory compliance, such as personally identifiable user data, disclosures, policy and service terms, unique international market considerations
- ☐ Copy and asset approvals
- ☐ Security audits

VENDORS AND PARTNERSHIPS

- ☐ Adding or changing the use of third-party infrastructure and tools
- ☐ Negotiating (and timing) distribution and strategic partnerships
- ☐ Specific requirements in partnership or customer contracts (best avoided)

CUSTOMER SUPPORT AND SUCCESS

- ☐ Training and resourcing to support new products
- ☐ Provision of tools and knowledge-base items to manage customer inquiries

Consider that your desired specification exists within a "gray zone," somewhere between a bare-bones and fully mature product. Your job is to use judgment (based on your understanding of customers) and negotiate with stakeholders to decide which features are in or out of scope.

For simplicity, bucket potential functionality into one of three types:

1. *Table stakes* includes the functionality you must build in order for your product to be considered operative by your customers.

2. *Potentially in-scope* is functionality that you believe you need to build to deliver on the goal and fall within the filters you set out in steps 1 through 4. You may find yourself returning to steps 1 through 4 to add to, clarify, or change your initial assumptions if candidates don't fit.

3. *Likely out-of-scope* contains all the desirable functions and capabilities that you want but that are not required to reach the goal. Anything that fails the tests laid out in steps 1 through 4 is likely in this bucket. Pet features or sophisticated technologies required to perform "at scale" are also in this bucket.

Table stakes includes all the basics that will make the product functional but does not, of itself, deliver on the stated goal:

- **Supporting functionality**—Any baseline features and foundational technologies required to make your product work. If you have a mobile product, for example, this would include the ability to download, install, and log into your product. Baseline features also include internal business requirements for marketing, tracking, and reporting; customer service; or enabling other business functions.

- **Hygiene factors**—This includes security and data integrity, a lack of significant bugs, and compliance with legal and regulatory requirements. A lack of usability "irritants" also fits this category—you don't want critical usability issues that will stop users from achieving their goals with your product. For web- and mobile-based products, speed (or responsiveness) is also of paramount importance.

- **"Reasonable" market parity**—You don't need to have every feature your competitors do. However, your customers are likely used to certain levels of user experience, performance, functionality, and service. All the products and services launched over the years have set the bar—and their innovations eventually become table stakes. You need to be a match for any viable alternative and on par with other commonly used products. Your users will overlook a lack of secondary features they rarely use but not core capabilities or experiences they have come to expect.

In addition to identifying functionality that your user and customer will need, capture edge cases and high-level nonfunctional business requirements (such as legal, financial, analytics, and marketing requirements). The latter forces you to meet with cross-functional stakeholders (who will make clear their overall needs or concerns early on). It is critical you capture this information during the specification phase; an unexpected internal business need can derail an initiative entirely if you only learn of it during implementation.

A Specification Template

In very small teams, informal, short specs might be okay. Even for large teams, it's best to keep written specs to a few pages (some companies like to call their specs "one-pagers"). Regardless, following a disciplined process for tightly constraining your scope around a clear business/customer goal is essential.

At http://www.influentialpm.com, you will find a real-world spec template used in a company of about 200 people. Even at this scale—relatively small by most comparisons—the level of stakeholder buy-in can be quite complex and the number of customer and platform considerations quite extensive.

You can download and adapt the template to suit your needs. You will also find a completed spec for each of the *Photo-Pro* examples (hypotheses A and B).

More generally, specifications are only useful if generated collaboratively—read by and contributed to by team members. Stakeholders must be asked to consider and challenge assumptions and agree to the goals and scope—you may need to walk them through your spec or a summary presentation of it to ensure you have their buy-in. You want to build commitment and support.

Similarly, avoid turning a spec into a lengthy, detailed requirements document. Focus on capturing the key high-level needs and issues. The details can be fleshed out later into user stories and a flexible product backlog (as discussed in **Chapter 7**). Otherwise, your specification quickly becomes unmanageable, and no one will read it.

A specification is also a living document, updated as you learn more. As you develop artifacts such as wireframes, detailed designs, and technical plans, keep linking to your supporting materials. Don't let your specification atrophy.

Capture User-Centric Requirements

Frame desired functionality from your user's point of view and remain adaptable to new learning.

1 How to collaborate with a broad range of stakeholders to define powerful customer and business-centric requirements.

2 What methodologies to use to capture product-requirement details and the expected outcomes in a way that is flexible and time-efficient.

3 How to create and regularly groom a product backlog, ensuring you execute the most critical, timely needs.

Collaborate on—Do *Not* Collect—Requirements

Now that you have completed high-level specifications for your initiative's goals and functionality (**Chapter 6**) and have stakeholder support, your prioritized project moves into execution mode. Next, you need to define detailed requirements so that your team can determine the set of experiences, technologies, and systems it must build. In turn, this will ascertain the resourcing requirements, dependencies, and timing.

When compiled, a set of requirements will cover the following:

- How specific customer and user segments will benefit from using the product in unique and different ways.

- The functional needs of each user segment on all supported platforms (if your product is user-facing, these needs will also require interaction and visual designs).

- The set of inputs and outputs, as well as outcomes, the system must support.

- What you need to support a product (marketing, sales, operations, tracking, and reporting) and required integrations with partner or company systems.

- Nonfunctional constraints and considerations (such as those of authentication, legal, security, or throughput/scale).

- Edge cases, error handling, and exception management.

There are many ways to specify product requirements; companies and teams adapt how and when they define and document them to suit their needs. They collectively decide how much clarity is needed to prioritize initiatives and to make go/no go decisions, as well as how much detail engineering needs to deliver the technology.

Reach an agreement with your team on the best requirements definition, approach, and tools. Keep the end goal in mind—you want a high-performing team that knows what's expected and has the necessary details to deliver value to your customers and organization. Your agreed approach must provide a mutual understanding of what items are required, why, and in what priority. The resulting processes, on the surface, may not look much like those of other companies or even teams within the same company.

Specifically, great product requirements:

- Explicitly express needs in terms of the business and customer value they will deliver. (Don't just list a set of features or tasks.)

- Invite engagement and negotiation with implementation teams and stakeholders and enable flexibility with learning through "just-in-time" elaboration.

- Avoid wasteful discussion and documentation by not introducing detail too early that might potentially be wrong or need to be discarded.

- Keep estimation simple and high-level but allow for a predictable project timeline to emerge over time. (You might start, for example, with a rough "level of effort" [LOE] and become more exact as more details surface.)

- Prevent premature commitment to design options or solutions and leave technical decisions to the architects, engineers, and testers.

- Provide clarity on acceptance criteria so all involved know what the definition of "done" is.

- Organize needs such that their relative priority to *one another* is clear.

Your job is *not* to collect requirements. Don't ask customers or managers for what features they want in the product, for you to add to your backlog. Also, do not define your own set of requirements in isolation—don't just specify what *you* think should be in the product and how *you* think it should function, while preempting the clarification questions that *you* think your team might ask.

At its core, capturing requirements is a collaborative exercise, not a gathering exercise. You will collaborate with four key groups:

- **Product development teams**—Your user experience group has access to consumer insights and specializes in exploring alternative solutions. Your engineering team is immersed in the product and can guide you toward feasible technical solutions and identify possible tradeoffs.

- **Peers and colleagues**—Your peer product managers can provide a second opinion on scope and priorities, and identify dependencies with their own products.

- **Cross-functional business teams**—Often overlooked, other departments can also inform your requirements needs. Some must support your new product once it's in the market and, therefore, they may require operational processes, tools, data, and tracking and reporting to be defined. In addition, marketing, sales, and customer support are excellent sources for identifying market trends, pinpointing existing problems, and providing input on prioritizing product features. Likewise, consumer insights and analytics teams can help you gather or access data to drive your decision-making.

- **Customers**—Don't ask customers to tell you what they want, but do observe them. It will help you to prioritize their pain points and new needs and to validate improvements to your solutions. Avoid selection bias—talk with not only current customers but also potential customers, lapsed customers, and customers using competitors' products.

This chapter is intended to be a starting point—outlining principles and techniques you can adapt to your unique environment. I'll focus on user stories and product backlogs since, when used well, these frameworks

Avoid Introducing Wasteful Requirements Detail Too Early

Early in my career, I worked at an organization with a culture common to older enterprise companies. Decision-makers wanted all the details up front to help them manage the approvals process, set deadlines, identify risks, and confirm resource allocations. The engineering team needed highly specific requirements before it could engage in this process.

I was to create a mobile application for enterprise users—an automated travel assistant for employees' travel, accommodations, and dining needs.

The four documents required before the project could be approved took two months to draft:

- Market requirements (MRD)—20 pages
- Product requirements (PRD)—32 pages
- UI flow specification—18 pages
- Detailed UI functional specification—56 pages

Engineering had limited availability, and I knew of only one engineer who ever read all the documentation. By the time implementation could kick off, many features needed removal from the first version of the product due to feasibility and resourcing constraints. There were many rewrites of the PRD and frequent updates to the UI specifications.

The team recommended alternatives and helped to prioritize features requiring less effort—those that were more achievable but still important. The resulting application changed substantially over the course of the project. The version outlined in my detailed documentation was barely recognizable in the final working version. We realized only a fraction of the full product I'd spent so much time defining and designing.

embody all the best practices outlined. *User stories* capture the needs of the customer and business, and you can enlarge or refine them as you learn more details. A *product backlog* is a loosely prioritized collection of requirements at different levels of completeness, detail, and size, which you can add to or change at any time.

To illustrate user stories in action, I'll use examples for a fictitious financial literacy application (*Centsible*). This mobile-only application targets millennials—in particular, recent college graduates—who wish to improve their management of personal finances.

Users validate their knowledge by taking quizzes, and their answers are used to recommend the video content or articles they need to improve their financial literacy. They can link credit cards to track their spending and receive personalized recommendations. The product makes money through affiliate commissions received from recommending financial products, such as credit cards or loans, and through online advertising. You can view an introduction to the product (and a short demo) and a link to a set of partially completed user stories for the application in the product backlog at http://www.influentialpm.com. (You'll find the stories under "Current/ backlog" and "Epics" in the linked backlog.)

Overview of User Stories

There are many ways to structure your requirements, but however you do it, ensure you follow industry standard practices. A popular approach is the *user story*. Even if you do not use user stories in your environment, understanding the overall design and applying the underlying methodology can help you write and manage better requirements.

As illustrated in **Figure 7.1**, the user-story template comprises three components:

1. **The card**—This is the most familiar element of a user story. Don't mistake the card *as* the user story—as we will see, it is just the starting point.

2. **The conversation**—This component comprises the details and specifications for the requirement generated through questions and clarifications with stakeholders and team members (it is not written in isolation).

3. **The confirmation**—Also known as *acceptance criteria*, this element includes the tests that the user story must pass for you to consider it done ("potentially deployable code" as in functionally complete with a requisite level of proven quality).

Card	A brief statement encompassing what, for whom, and why
Conversation	Details and decisions captured throughout collaboration
Confirmation	The acceptance criteria by which a story is declared "done"

FIGURE 7.1 *User story components*

1. The Card

The *card* syntax can be any useful description of the contents of the user story. However, the most common format uses the following statement (which captures the user-centric intent of the story):

> As a **[type of user]**, I want **[to do something]**
> so that **[benefit or value]**.

The card encapsulates these questions:

- *Who* are we building this for? (Which target user or stakeholder?)

- *What* are we building? (As described by the target user's intention.)

- *Why* are we building it? (What is its value to the target user?)

This format has the advantage of anchoring product development in terms of value to the customer and business, rather than as a feature request or systems specification. It enables you and your team to understand why you are working on a requirement and the intended end result, so you can collaborate to find the best solution to get there. Nothing in the statement dictates precisely how you must build your product or solution.

User stories—or any requirement format—can exist at any level of specificity. You can capture a user story whether it is vague and high-level or detailed and at an incremental feature level. Here are some examples of typical user stories:

> *"As a recent college graduate, I want to learn about responsible personal finance so that I can confidently manage my money."*—A high-level user story for the finance application *Centsible*.

Within this high-level story exist smaller, constituent user stories such as this one:

> *"As a user, I can take a multiple-choice quiz consisting of 10 questions that are relevant to the lesson."*

But this is a poor user story: the word "user" is too generic, the solution is prescribed, and no user value (the why) is given.

So a better variant might be,

> *"As a newly registered user, I want a formative assessment of my current knowledge so that I can be guided toward relevant lessons and improve my skills efficiently."*

You might break down this smaller story into highly specific user stories detailing individual components. Consider the following stories, for example:

> *"As a test taker, I want to receive a score at the end of the quiz so that I know my level of mastery."*

> *"As a test taker, I want to receive hints during the quiz so that I learn even when I get stuck."*

> *"As a test taker, I can quit a quiz and save my progress so that I can return later and pick up where I left off."*

> *"As a content production employee, I want to be able to write new questions and answers so that I can keep available tests relevant and engaging for users."*

User stories can be for any kind of user, not just end users. In the last story above, the user is an internal stakeholder—the content production employee who is writing tests for users. This requirement captures the need for an administration tool to create and manage the tests offered to end users, which will be used by personnel within the company.

The cards capture the intent for the development of discrete business value. They are a reminder to discuss with your team the goal and the best way to implement it.

2. The Conversation

The *conversation* is where you answer questions, clarify intent, specify functionality and implementation details, and record the decisions made along the way. Do not confuse this with documenting specifics in isolation, without input from the team—conversation is intended to be precisely that; a dialog you have with the team to elaborate *needed* information.

A product manager and team will find that some stories require a lot of detail while others need very little. Avoid wasting your time and energy on the low-detail stories—a short few minutes chatting or commenting on a ticket might satisfy the team's need for guidance. Focus your energies, instead, on those user stories requiring more detail. These may require substantive elaboration—such as breaking down larger stories into smaller ones, answering team questions, and linking to supporting materials. Efficiency in communication over the completeness of the documentation is preferable.

Capture the outcomes of conversations as notes inside the user story to serve as a record of the decisions you have taken. Consider the user story *"As a test taker, I want to receive a score at the end of the quiz, so I know my level of mastery."* Here's an example of the type of conversation details that you might add to this story, after discussion and clarification with your team:

1. Why should the user care about getting a score? What is the intended outcome?

2. How is the score calculated?

3. What would a final score look like? (The number of correct answers out of 10 or a letter grade?)

4. Where and when is the score shown? (Progressively or only upon completion?)

5. Can the user retake the test? What happens to the previous score?

6. What happens after the user takes the test, and under what conditions? (Various conditions might include if the user fails, passes, or achieves a perfect score.)

7. What device platforms, markets, and languages are supported?

8. Under what conditions might a score not be able to be shown? What happens then? (These are also known as edge cases.)

To see the resulting conversation details for this user story, visit the *Centsible* backlog and open the top story and scroll down to the "Activity" section.

Don't let conversations disappear into the air. Capture them from emails and briefly comment, recording conclusions from meetings at the appropriate points within the user story—enough so a new team member (or someone reading the user story for the first time) can follow it. Keep your conversations organized and readable.

Don't, however, add every little detail; stick to the outcomes relevant to challenges with the current implementation. Similarly, do not write anything that you can more easily show in a picture. Diagrams, photos of whiteboards, and simple mock-ups can illustrate a decision, containing much useful information regarding how a system or interface should look and work. Cross-reference with links to useful secondary documentation or notes inside your user story.

Sometimes you won't be able to answer a question. In these instances, you can do one of the following:

1. explicitly leave it to the team's discretion to decide the best course of action;

2. delay the story for a future development cycle, so you can gather more data, seek input from stakeholders, or explore options; or

3. prioritize a research task (called a *spike*) to discover the answer.

3. The Confirmation

The *confirmation* contains the acceptance criteria your solution must meet to be considered complete and working. Acceptance criteria flow naturally from the conversation and define the minimum expectations for functionality, visual design, performance, and robustness (such as error and edge-case handling).

Acceptance criteria adhere to the following guidelines:

- **They are deterministic and testable**—They usually consist of a single statement with a clearly stated desired outcome (including a target if required).

- **They are established before you work on a user story**—New criteria should not emerge during development, since this makes it hard for developers to predict the amount of work a user story will take. New criteria identified during development become a separate

"My Engineering Team Expects Too Much Detail"

Some development teams might expect to receive highly specific and detailed specifications before any work starts. They may view the user-story approach to requirements definition as being too vague. They may think the product manager doesn't know exactly what he or she wants. And they may not want to give up time to meet, discuss the conversational details, and ask clarifying questions.

To address this situation, before you meet with the team add *some* questions to the conversation that you would expect them to have. You allow your team to react and probe, clarifying details as they go, instead of working from a blank slate. In this way, you can ease your team into becoming more comfortable with user stories and other collaborative processes.

Working with your team, identify which stories need the most elaboration and why. Then ask which stories already have too much detail. What might emerge are patterns or types of stories where more detail is generally needed. For example, certain stories may require the team to work on a complex system with many user states and edge cases. Recognizing this, you know that future stories involving the same system will require more detail.

Another approach is to ask the team to put a level-of-effort (LOE) estimate against each story. Once asked, they will naturally start to ask clarifying questions, so they understand more about the scope and can make an accurate estimate.

user story. (However, you can give your engineering team discretion to make changes to acceptance criteria in a user story that they are currently implementing, if they can easily address them. You may also do so if it means you avoid having to complete work you know isn't going to be valuable given new information.)

- **User stories are either "done" or "not done"**—There is no "percent" done. If just one test fails, you cannot finish the user story. While any team member can write acceptance criteria, you, as product manager, are the ultimate arbiter of whether criteria are met or not. Developers shouldn't determine whether their own code meets expectations.

One key benefit of well-written acceptance criteria is to allow the engineering team to build automated tests in parallel with development. This allows for continual debugging of code, increasing the likelihood that the user story will pass. You can avoid last-minute testing of an entire development cycle at the end, overwhelming quality assurance (QA) with a rush of code submissions that must be tested to make a deadline. Furthermore, these tests can be rerun at any time in the future to ensure later user stories did not break earlier user stories.

To see the acceptance criteria for the user story *"As a test taker, I want to receive a score at the end of the quiz, so I know my level of mastery,"* open the top story in the *Centsible* backlog.

"As a User"—Not All Users Are the Same

To avoid confusion as to the intended outcome of a user story, always specify precisely whom the story aims to serve.

For example, consider the story *"As a newly registered user, I want a formative assessment of my current knowledge, so that I can be guided toward relevant lessons and improve my skills efficiently."*

If the story had begun, instead, with just "As a user" the team may have assumed the story was for all users of *Centsible* and not have optimized the feature around the needs of newly registered users.

Here are common classifications for different types of users:

- **A target-user segment**—While the product needs for many users might be identical (in which case, "As a user" suffices), each user segment may have some unique needs. If any product functionality is specifically designed to serve the needs of one persona and not another, make that explicit. Doing so is especially helpful if you are prioritizing work to deliver functionality to one user segment over another, since you can more easily group requirements and increase their priority.

- **Lifecycle stages**—Your users will be at different stages in their lifecycle with you. Some will be visiting your product for the first time, while others will be highly loyal repeat users. Feature development that targets new users may be irrelevant to repeat users. Similarly, subscription or freemium products commonly offer trial or limited free offerings, while reserving premium services for paid users. You must explicitly define user stories for each.

- **Complementary customer types**—Multiple user types deriving different benefits from the same product require their own user stories. For example, media offerings require stories to serve content

▶ Refer to **Chapter 3** to review target-user segments and personas, common lifecycle segments, and complementary customer types. Each may be a source for a unique set of user stories.

to consumers, but also require stories to target advertisers' needs (yes, ads are a product!). For enterprise offerings, the economic decision-maker, managers, and employees all need your product for different reasons. They are rarely the same individual, so you must use separate stories for each, such as "As a sales executive . . . ," "As a system admin . . . ," or "As a trainer of new employees . . . ."

- **Business stakeholders**—You can also write stories for internal users of your system. These stakeholders require the product to meet their needs in specific ways that might not be obvious or important to your end users. Here are some typical examples:

  - Your *marketing* team may want tools to segment users and personalize messaging throughout customer touch-points.

  - Your *sales* and *account management* teams need tools to support sales, customer onboarding, and relationship management.

  - Your *finance* team needs stories to describe how revenue is realized, collected, and reported, along with many other metrics.

  - Your *legal* team may need stringent security or compliance stories.

  - Your *technical operations* team requires stories for how they monitor your product and what they do when something goes wrong.

  - You and your *data analytics* team need stories to define the type of data to be captured by your systems, so that you can track your KPIs and other product metrics.

How to Make Large User Stories Smaller

High-level stories are useful for defining an overarching user goal based on a set of product functionalities. Even if the high-level requirements are apparent, most details become clear only as you develop a system. As illustrated in **Figure 7.2**, for user stories to be a useful implementation tool, you must progressively break the large, vague stories into smaller, specific stories. These smaller stories have the detail necessary to enable your developers to deliver discrete pieces of functionality in a short timeframe.

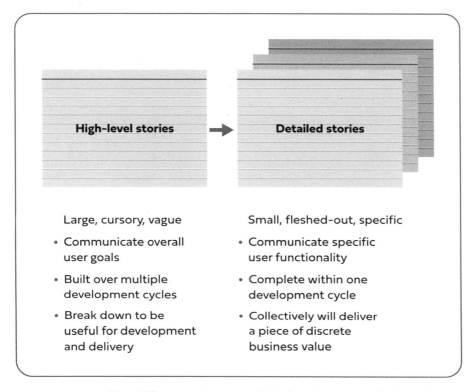

FIGURE 7.2 *The difference between high-level and detailed stories*

User stories start with just the right level of detail to enable planning, letting you flesh out specifics as you go, in a "just-in-time" manner. High-priority detailed stories enable focus on what matters right now and with the best information available. Lower-priority, high-level stories remind you of future work without requiring you to invest in adding details until necessary. User stories are naturally easy to adapt, remove, add, or reprioritize, given new information and learning. You make decisions when they are pertinent and only once you have sufficient information to make a confident choice.

There is no canonical distinction between a high-level user story and a detailed user story. The team gets to decide which stories are too big (or too small). Your team might use development criteria, deciding that stories are too big when they take more than a couple days' work or, if using Scrum, when they exceed a story-points threshold. The intent is to enable a high-performing team to complete quality work that contributes to your business and company goals. Keep breaking down your stories until they feel they can meet their goals.

You will break down stories both in preparation for your team (when grooming your backlog, as described later in this chapter) and, importantly, in collaboration with your team during the conversation and estimation process.

Mike Cohn, in his book *User Stories Applied* (2004),[9] outlines seven questions to answer to help identify where larger stories can be broken down into smaller ones:

1. **What are the component user workflow steps?** Map out a customer journey or a conceptual wireframe of your solution. Break out each of the workflow steps into smaller stories—every separate action a user can take in each workflow could be a different story.

2. **Are there multiple user types?** A story that has multiple target-user types might be better broken down, one version for each of the target users. The first story will be more focused, while the second story will leverage the work of the first story and, as a result, be smaller—the "delta" required to add support for the second user type.

3. **Are there multiple user operations?** This is a typical scenario when manipulating data. Rather than write a single story covering multiple operations on the data, pick one operation first and include the others in subsequent stories. For example, if a user can add, edit, delete, update, filter, sort, or restore data, you can make each operation a different story.

4. **Are there many data attributes?** This is common when presenting structured data to the user—for example, when providing search results or multicolumn reports. Start with delivering one or two attributes to simplify your story, allowing the development team to focus on the work to get a basic case in place. Once the core work is complete, lower-priority stories might contain all the other data attributes.

5. **Is the user interface complex?** If there are complex interactions or tricky design components, make a simple version first and refine it later. For example, your first story for the user interface might merely be a basic form or even a command-line entry, with little or no visuals. Obviously, you'd not launch this to the end user without some visual design, so later stories can capture the implementation of detailed designs around a basic interface.

6. **Can we defer complexities?** Typically, functionality has three components:

   - *Core functionality*, also called the "happy path," works 99 percent or more of the time users interact with it.

"As a User...So That..." Fatigue

As stories become highly granular and specific, it may become tedious to write the user type and articulate the benefit when the target user and outcome are obvious or trivial. Provided your team can avoid confusion and everyone fully appreciates the context for each story, you can simply focus on the desired functionality, and drop the user and benefit reference when writing smaller stories.

- *Edge and error cases* are how you handle situations when things go wrong—such as when users enter data incorrectly or do something unexpected.

- *Performance* is the ability, at launch, to operate smoothly at the required scale.

   You can separate each component into distinct user stories, with complexities left for later. Complete core functionality first and then edge cases, with performance hardening last (and perhaps much later after you complete the initial story).

7. **Do we need a spike?** You add discovery stories or "spikes" when you must make a critical decision before you can address your user story. If there are too many open questions remaining, run a proof-of-concept, build a prototype, experiment, or conduct additional research to get answers. Create and prioritize a separate spike user story and return to the original user story only after the spike is complete and new learning can be usefully applied.

   At http://www.influentialpm.com, you will find a detailed breakdown applying each of these seven techniques to the high-level *Centsible* story *"As a recent college graduate, I want to learn about responsible personal finances so that I can confidently manage my money."*

How to Define Acceptance Criteria

If you and your team have been carefully documenting details in the conversation component of the user story, you can easily define acceptance criteria. These details will suggest tests you might run. You do not usually need to identify every single use case or scenario. Look to write tests that will demonstrate a robust system but not place undue burden on the development or testing team. Passing all of these critical tests means the user story can be declared done.

Encapsulate acceptance criteria in a simple statement describing what the test will be. Complement it with a target outcome if the intended result is not apparent. For example, in the *Centsible* application, you will likely allow users to use popular credit cards (like Visa, MasterCard, and maybe American Express) and mandate their usage in acceptance criteria. Don't just validate that functionality works as expected but include unexpected user or system behavior that may lead to an undesirable outcome. For *Centsible*, you might also add a test against linking debit cards but require this case to fail (if you do not support tracking activity on debit cards).

Pay attention to the following areas in your validation process:

- **Functionality**—Ensure that features work for all of the agreed-upon cases (such as credit cards) and don't work for the defined counter cases (debit cards, for instance).

- **Design**—Assuming your product has a user interface, include visual inspection of the service as validated against the provided design specs. State the platforms you will support but consider whether you should split stories for features across multiple platforms into separate stories (for example, supporting both iOS and Android may not be in a single user story).

- **Performance**—Validate nonfunctional specifications and constraints to ensure the application will work at the expected scale. Possible acceptance criteria might include:
  - response time (speed)
  - data tracking, accuracy
  - testability (coverage)
  - availability (uptime)
  - security
  - throughput (capacity)

  Usually, performance criteria are determined in collaboration with your technical teams and are not necessary for stories very early in the product-development process—or they may be separated into their own set of stories to prioritize later. Do not set unreasonable levels but do test at your expected "peaks" (not averages). Too many performance criteria burden development, so be judicious.

- **Stress tests**—Think about all the things that could go wrong, either through user error or unexpected system responses. Common examples include:

  - incomplete, incorrect, or skipped user data entry;

  - corrupted data;

  - a sudden loss of connectivity or a sudden switch to "offline" mode (on mobile phones);

  - security or DOS attacks (hackers are happily intent on stress-testing your applications—better you find the holes before they do).

Table 7.1 illustrates the four types of criteria, with four examples each, for the "link credit card" feature in *Centsible*.

TABLE 7.1 Acceptance criteria for a *Centsible* user story

Card: *"As a recent college graduate, I want to link my credit card to my account so that I can receive spending-activity reports."*

TYPE OF CRITERIA	DESCRIPTION	EXAMPLE ACCEPTANCE CRITERIA
Functionality	The user features work for all the agreed-upon cases.	• Test with Visa, MasterCard, AMEX • Test with debit cards (fails) • Test that past purchases appear accurately • Test confirm, cancel, or add additional cards
Design	The product accords to interactive and visual design on supported platforms.	• Test user flows against designs • Test pages visually against designs • Test support on iOS, Android • Test that CVV is obscured with (***)
Performance	The application works securely and stably under the expected load.	• Test 90% of cards linked within 5 seconds • Test 100 linked cards per second • Test data-transmission uses PCI DSS • Capture test data in database
Stress-Testing	The application gracefully handles extreme, edge, and error cases.	• Test a card with no past purchases • Test if a duplicate card is already in the system • Test an invalid and an expired credit card • Test a DOS attack

The Product Backlog

The *product backlog* is a flexible master list of all the requirements for your active product initiative. It is a forced-rank prioritized list of requirements put roughly in the order you'd like them to be implemented. It will likely be a mixture of smaller, detailed, high-priority requirements (those that you will implement soon) and more substantial, vague, lower-priority requirements (describing future functionality) as illustrated in **Figure 7.3**.

You refine and change your backlog as you learn more about your product and customer needs. Sweat the details at the top of the backlog. Since you will work on requirements closer to the top before those that are lower down, concentrate on adding details and accurate estimates and carefully prioritize the most important. For immediate priorities, you must have broken the stories down and ensured there is sufficient detail in the conversation for development to proceed. Your team needs clarity for anything likely to be considered in the next few iterations. Beyond that, approximations are okay.

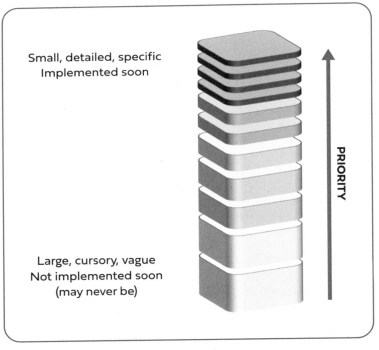

FIGURE 7.3 *A conceptual product backlog*

Types of Backlogs and Tools

Your product backlog contains requirements that relate to currently priori-tized and committed initiatives—whether active or soon-to-be active.

Other kinds of backlogs are the idea backlog and the icebox. In the idea backlog, you place potential future initiatives—any ideas you've gathered from stakeholders, projects you would like to get to eventually, and antici-pated but (as of yet) uncommitted items on your roadmap.

In the icebox, place any old or low-priority items (anything you are not likely to work on anytime soon). That way, you don't pollute your product backlog with random entries.

Whether you combine these backlogs into one area within a single tool or split them is up to you and your team. For an idea backlog, you might use a simple spreadsheet: include brief descriptions of each idea and use columns to rank overall priorities (see **Chapter 4**). For a product backlog, you might use a ticket-based project management tool, so the team can quickly move requirements through development phases.

Alternatively, you may combine your product, ideas, and icebox backlogs into one location to make management easier, eliminate content duplication, and avoid arguments with stakeholders over when an idea will be "promoted" into the product backlog. Label the different backlogs clearly—say, as different tabs—to avoid confusion. Developers will usually be assigned to work on single items in the product backlog, while product managers will be assigned to explore or prioritize multiple ideas.

At http://www.influentialpm.com, you'll find recommended tools for product roadmaps and backlogs.

Have a single product backlog for your team to draw from, even if you are working on several initiatives concurrently. Since you must allocate the available work for the same team, you want visibility. Keep track of which stories belong to which epic or initiative—most tools have tagging tools that make this easy.

1. Build Your Product Backlog

Some product managers tend to add requirements into a backlog only when they have all the details—sometimes just days before development will commence. Unfortunately, this leaves the team blind to possible future work and makes it impossible to get a sense of when a project will be delivered.

Instead, establish a backlog for any new product initiative as early as possible—even when product discovery is still underway to define the scope. Start with a first pass, capturing and breaking down requirements. Create just the cards, as placeholders, and then add, rewrite, or delete as you learn more.

Here are the benefits of establishing your backlog early:

- You have a bird's eye view of the known scope, making it easier to recognize the full extent of the project. It's easier to make early prioritization and descoping decisions or to revisit timeline or other goals that may seem unreasonable, once you have an understanding of known scope.

- You can have more productive, fact-based conversations about dates (the time to market) and resources with the team and stakeholders.

- You have a plan on record for stakeholders to react to, where they can flag missing scope and provide other input.

- When preparing for each new development iteration, you have an incremental amount of work to do (breaking down stories, filling in details, grooming the backlog) rather than having to create entirely new stories.

2. Prioritize Your Product Backlog

Prioritizing requirements is an art more than a science; it is highly situational to your product, company, team, and business priorities and to how well you understand your customers' needs.

Fortunately, product backlogs make prioritization easier, simply because they allow you to change your mind at (almost) any time. You can move requirements up and down in priority as the product takes shape and as you learn more about customer and business needs. You don't have to be right the first time.

Force-rank requirements from most important to least. Do not label groups (for example, as High, Medium, and Low; as 1 through 5; or as Must-have, Should-have, and Nice-to-have.) Instead, carefully sequence the more fleshed-out priorities at the top of your backlog—then you need only to roughly order the rest.

You should not, however, reprioritize a requirement once the team has started implementing it—at least, not without a great reason. Also, your

Getting a Product Backlog Started

1. Take high-level requirements and write a card or ticket for each.

   • Add each requirement as a separate entry in your backlog tool.

   • Don't fill in many details (conversations or confirmation) yet.

2. Roughly prioritize the requirements.

3. Break down the essential requirements (which will now be at the top of your backlog) using the approach outlined previously in "Making Large User Stories Smaller." It is particularly useful at this early stage to sketch out the customer journey or a conceptual wireframe. List what the user wants to do at each step; this will help you generate feature-level requirements.

4. Brainstorm with your team using a story-writing workshop. Taking each high-level requirement in turn, identify smaller increments, and add missing requirements.

   • Stop when requirements feel small enough to do in a single iteration or when you don't have enough information yet to break them down further.

   • Do not debate details or priorities (go for breadth over depth), as you can progressively fill in details and priorities over time.

   • Make sure every added story is relevant to your original goals.

5. Conduct interviews with select stakeholders to surface internal requirements, such as tools or reports—expect them to focus on their own needs so be careful of what you promise.

6. Prioritize and roughly estimate everything with a T-shirt size (see "Estimating Your Product Backlog" later in this chapter).

   • Your first pass through all priorities and estimates helps establish a sense of the time-to-market and a rough plan of action.

   • Keep in mind that anything at this early stage is just a hypothesis, not an established project plan.

force-ranked list of priorities may not be the order that requirements actually get worked on. For example, engineering often alters sequencing to accommodate technical needs, to optimize resource allocation, or to wait until a requirement has enough detail to start.

To prioritize your requirements, use these practices and roughly order according to the following steps (from highest to lowest priority):

1. **Prioritize requirements with the highest learning or complexity**— Certain requirements can have a significant impact on the scope and priority of other requirements or even on the project as a whole. It makes sense to place these at the top of your backlog and deliver these earlier, so you don't have major dependencies, long-lead items, or critical information surfacing late in development. **Table 7.2** illustrates these types of stories to surface and rank higher in the backlog.

2. **Identify key customer and business goals to move relevant stories higher**—Show progress toward key project goals or "hot buttons" earlier by ranking those below your highest priority stories from step 1. For example, if your project will include the addition of new revenue-generating features and this is a key project goal, deliver them before non-revenue-generating items. Or if there is a feature or tool that stakeholders are particularly excited about, build confidence, support, and momentum by showing progress in that feature or tool. Stakeholders will be more excited to see progress against a single key area rather than piecemeal components. With this approach, you are also more likely to demonstrate early delivery of larger discrete contributions to business value.

3. **Group together related requirements**—To prioritize the remaining scope, group related requirements together. In addition to making grooming much easier (you can review, add to, and move them around together), it allows your team to focus longer and more completely on one area without too much context-switching.

   Look for and group requirements that

   - came from the same high-level requirement (user story),

   - serve the same user-type, or

   - are part of the same flow.

   For example, for our hypothetical application *Centsible*, it is better to complete all the "link my credit card" stories over one or two iterations and deliver them together than to provide, say, one story for login, one feature for credit cards, and another story for viewing video.

TABLE 7.2 Highest-priority stories to complete earlier

REQUIREMENT TYPE	DESCRIPTION	LOOK FOR...
Risky	Requirements where the outcome can potentially dramatically change the direction of your project; critical to eliminate these risks earlier in the development cycle	• advanced new-user functionality • innovations where the user value isn't proven • invention and proof-of-concept of new technology
Long-lead	A group of interdependent requirements that will take the longest time to do (known as "the long pole"—these dictate your earliest possible deployment time)	• new platform-level technology infrastructure • integration with legacy systems • negotiation and implementation of external partnerships • gathering of baseline data to inform decisions
Discovery	Activities that might lead to the identification of additional scope or new lessons that could change your direction	Anything that can help you test with real users earlier: • research or spikes • prototyping • design explorations
Differentiating	Usually those requirements that build distinctiveness into your offering, not available through competitors, also come with many assumptions and a steep learning curve	Any features that support delivery of your core-value proposition, especially your differentiation factors or USP
Dependencies	Requirements that might slow the pace of development or limit your ability to work on other requirements before it	• foundational engineering (such as architecture or database work) • requirements containing technology or design components reusable by other stories • any requirement that requires completion before other requirements can start

3. Estimate Your Product Backlog

Each requirement in the backlog should have a preliminary estimate, whether or not it will be worked on soon. There are three key advantages to having such estimates:

- **They encourage elaboration on details for the conversation**— Estimation starts a process for exploring how to tackle each requirement. Asking your team for an estimate for the level of effort (LOE) forces more than a cursory discussion—it gets them to ask clarifying questions, to debate design and engineering options, and to identify the most significant risks.

- **They surface stories that need further work**—If a story estimate is too high, the team has a wide variance in opinion, or the team cannot estimate it at all, that suggests you may need to break the story down further. Or it may have too many unknowns (and need further research). Alternatively, you may decide it is less important than once thought, as it appears too costly or challenging to implement—in that case, drop it into the icebox.

- **They size the overall project and bound timelines**—Estimating your backlog will help size the overall project and provide a range of completion dates, challenging you to reduce the scope to what's absolutely necessary. Rather than asking your development team to provide a delivery date based on a high-level project description, you can build it bottom-up by estimating each requirement and comparing it to the cumulative amount of work on past projects of similar size and scope.

Once a specific requirement is about to be worked on, your team might complete preliminary designs and technical specifications—understanding and breaking down tasks sufficiently enough to provide precise estimates. However, before that detail is available, it is unwise to expect your team to make anything other than high-level estimates.

Use a T-shirt-size methodology to strike a balance. Assign a relative size—from S to XXL (or a number, say from 1 to 5)—to each requirement in your backlog. Do this in collaboration with your team, allowing them to seek scope clarification and collectively vote on the size to assign each. Put estimates clearly on the requirement description (for example, on the card or as an easily viewed tag within the ticket). That way, you'll always be able to see the LOE involved, which will help you and your team prioritize quickly, and identify requirements that need further work.

Larger stories might span several development cycles, making them incompatible with iterative development methods (since it may be many weeks before you see any results). Break these down more, especially the stories toward the top of your backlog (because you will work on them sooner rather than later).

TABLE 7.3 Example of historical throughput for a hypothetical team

SIZE	HISTORICAL THROUGHPUT
S	10 per week*
M	4 per week*
L	2 per week*
XL	2–3 weeks—break down further
XXL	3+ weeks—break down further

(* or a hybrid of sizes: for example, this team could complete five S stories and two M stories per week)

While each estimate might have a low level of confidence, when taken in aggregate, they are usually a good indication of how long it will take you to finish the known scope. Based on your experience, and with your team's input, you can now roughly estimate how long completing all of the known scope might take you (see the example in **Table 7.3**). If you have the data, do this by counting all the S, M, L, and other sizes and multiplying them by historical averages for throughput. If you do not have enough historical data, you will have a much better idea once you start development and can see how fast you are burning through the backlog.

Recognize (as discussed in **Chapter 9**) that you will discover new requirements along the way and that, as you add details to existing requirements, estimates will almost always increase.

Finally, note that T-shirt sizing is all right for rough backlog-level estimation. But once you add detailed scope and conversation, and once the team chooses to start working on it, you will need to reestimate the requirement. For example, if you are using Scrum methodologies, you may replace the T-shirt size estimate with a *story points* estimate.

4. Regularly Groom Your Product Backlog

A backlog is emergent. You are continually adding, removing, and moving requirements based on business, market, and customer information. Project priorities change. You learn new things from your customers. You discover new scope or alternative solutions as your product takes shape. Be flexible and responsive.

Even if the high-level requirements are apparent, most details become clear only as you develop a system. Start with just the right level of detail to enable planning, fleshing out details as you go, in a "just-in-time" manner. Adapt, remove, add, or reprioritize given new information and learning—

make decisions when they are pertinent and only after you have sufficient information to make a confident choice.

High-priority, detailed stories enable focus on what matters right now and with the best information available. Lower-priority, high-level stories remind you of future work without requiring you to invest in adding the details until necessary.

While any member of the team or any stakeholder can identify new requirements or suggest changes to existing requirements in the backlog, it is your responsibility to own the backlog and *groom* it frequently. Grooming is a process in which you do the following (see **Figure 7.4**):

- **Close completed requirements**—Once requirements have passed their acceptance criteria, archive them. Do not delete them entirely. (This will keep them accessible should you need to revisit them later.) Discard old entries and cruft.

- **Add new requirements**—Additional requirements can be added based on new learnings. They can be inserted anywhere in the priority order.

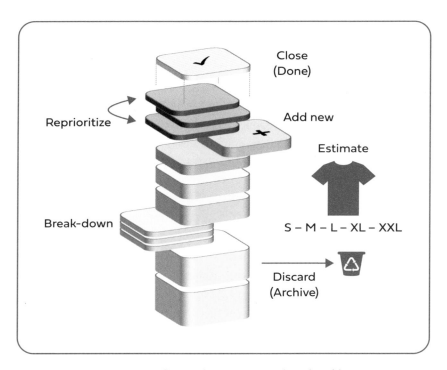

FIGURE 7.4 *Grooming your product backlog*

Any completed requirement that passed the acceptance criteria but that you received feedback or requested changes for, or that you later identified as needing additional acceptance criteria, is *still closed*. If you simply add these to an existing requirement, you risk creating a perception of scope creep, frustrating your team and stakeholders from seeing progress and disrupting any tracking of the team's throughput. Instead, add a new requirement or task (as a new ticket) to capture the new functionality or acceptance criteria.

- **Break down high-level requirements**—Any larger item eventually needs to be broken down. Do so long before it becomes a priority for development. Make sure the smaller requirements are, collectively, a complete replacement for the larger requirement and can be independently prioritized.

    When you break down a larger requirement, do not lose track of the original. For example, if you are using a ticket-based, requirement-management tool, it helps to cross-reference the original ticket from which the new requirements came. You can do so by adding a link to or tagging new tickets or by making a new ticket a "child" of the original.

- **Add details**—Any requirement closer to the top of the priority list must be fleshed out with conversation and acceptance criteria before you can start work on it.

- **Reprioritize the backlog**—Backlog items can be prioritized at any time, except once the team has started work on them. Always make sure the next-most-important work is at the top, so that you focus your efforts on discussing and adding details where it matters most.

- **Estimate new or changed stories**—Estimate any new stories, broken-down stories, or stories with substantive scope additions. Don't waste time reestimating existing stories unless they have substantially changed.

Set aside a regular time to complete grooming. You must complete grooming before asking development to start work. In Scrum, for example, you must groom the backlog before sprint planning, so that you are ready to go with a precise list of the next set of priorities and documented details.

CHAPTER 8

Partner with Engineering

Build trusted relationships and execute smoothly in collaboration with your primary stakeholder.

What you'll learn in this chapter

1 The mutually supportive roles and responsibilities that product managers and engineers have in the development process.

2 Techniques to build and maintain strong relationships with engineers and to overcome common challenges.

3 Ways to engage engineering effectively to facilitate and advance the product through implementation phases.

Product Managers and Engineers Work as One Team

Do not see it as your role to *drive* engineering to execute against a given product plan. Your role is to *partner* with engineering. You effectively work as one team with complementary goals, collaborating on and having influence over each other's areas of responsibility to produce the best results.

In your partner role, it will be beneficial to do the following:

- **Communicate the overall goals and vision**—Help the team understand and be motivated to achieve the product's goals. Provide supporting business and customer context to show why something is important.

- **Encourage ownership**—Welcome the team to contribute ideas, solutions, or viable trade-offs. Let engineering take responsibility for making commitments. You should support investment in quality and process improvement, and invite input on the product direction.

- **Define, clarify, and prioritize requirements**—Ensure the team is "unblocked," knows what the most critical needs are, and has all the information required to do the necessary work.

- **Own stakeholder feedback and communication**—Provide air cover and identify and prepare for changes or potential disruptions. Enable focus by owning the resolution of issues. And don't become a source of ever-changing requests yourself.

Achieving these outcomes is a group effort, variously involving engineering management, Scrum masters or project managers, and experienced lead engineers. You should understand the structure of the engineering team and the product development process, and determine how and at what points you can play a role in empowering engineering.

In this chapter, I don't intend to provide detailed definitions of the different development processes used in modern software organizations. Some of the principles discussed are drawn from a set of methodologies known as Agile, and Scrum in particular. These are interesting both because of their popularity within modern technology organizations and because they imbue the values of collaboration, openness, and flexibility essential to the success of any high-performing team. Additionally, they can generally be applied in almost any environment.

For further reading on the mechanics of common development models such as Waterfall or iterative development methods (and notably Scrum), refer to the online supporting materials at http://www.influentialpm.com.

Understanding Roles and Responsibilities

It is critical to establish and understand what you are responsible for and which responsibilities fall on your engineering team. You must also know what the engineering team is dependent on you for and which engineering decisions require your consultation, which ones you need only be informed about, and which ones you should rarely be involved in.

> Product managers own the problems (the "why" and "what"), and engineers own the solutions (the "how" and "when")—but it is only by collaborating that you can develop and build the best ideas.

Failure to clearly understand responsibilities leads to two undesirable situations:

1. You frustrate your team by becoming overly involved in technical decisions, being prescriptive on features but lacking in context, interfering in execution details, or driving them toward deadlines.

2. Gaps emerge. Your engineering team does not receive what is expected from you (such as context, data, specifications, stakeholder buy-in, and quick trade-off decisions).

Engineering organizations come in many configurations and specialized roles. Names of roles or job positions that you hear thrown around might include front-end engineer, web developer, full-stack engineer, quality assurance, data scientist or analyst, and project manager. Rather than attempt to define each role, which would be a challenge given the variance across the industry, in addition to the product manager, I will identify two general roles and their primary responsibilities:

- **The project manager**—Sometimes also called the Scrum master, execution lead, or program manager. While this is often a separate role, project execution is sometimes managed by an experienced senior engineering leader instead (but not the product manager).

- **The development team**—Brings collective technical expertise to tackle difficult and meaningful customer and business challenges.

Table 8.1 contains examples of the key responsibilities for each role during the implementation/execution phase—which are subject to change given your unique environment and culture. As you review each responsibility line by line, you may notice how each is interdependent and essential to the success of the other team members.

A product manager must not double-hat as project manager for two primary reasons:

1. **Conflict of interest**—A product manager's incentive is to deliver maximum business value. He or she will encourage teams to be aggressive on commitments and have strong points of view about how to implement feature specifics. There is nothing inherently wrong with that, but, conversely, the project manager and engineering lead need to protect the team from an assertive product manager. When product managers attempt to perform both roles simultaneously, they may steamroll everyone into agreeing to a plan they do not believe in, disempowering and discouraging them. Negotiating with oneself is hard to do.

2. **Strategy versus execution**—The product manager owns the customer understanding, identification, and scoping of new needs, along with prioritization of the product backlog. He or she must think ahead of the team to plan, prepare, and validate future work. If too caught up in the day-to-day management, the product manager won't spend enough time with customers or stakeholders and won't prepare for the future with enough rigor. When the time for the next initiative arrives, the product manager can be left scrambling to define sufficient work for the team to complete or provide only vaguely thought-through requirements.

In summary, allocated responsibilities establish a deliberately healthy tension between engineering and product management. Product managers are responsible for identifying, defining, and facilitating new opportunities for the business. They want to deliver on more of these opportunities and do so quickly. Engineers need both to build new systems and maintain existing ones within real-world technical constraints. They want to do so efficiently and in a high-quality way—which may slow delivery initially but will provide greater flexibility and scalability in the long run. Engineers hate coding things twice.

TABLE 8.1 Three roles and their respective responsibilities

PRODUCT MANAGER	PROJECT MANAGER (OR SCRUM MASTER)	DEVELOPMENT TEAM
Owns product goals and vision.	Facilitates the process for smooth execution.	Builds the solutions to deliver against priorities.
Communicates context and desired outcomes (the "why").	Determines and negotiates appropriate resources (the "who").	Breaks down scope into engineering tasks and a plan (the "how").
Defines and prioritizes projects and requirements (the "what").	Tracks progress and manages the timeline (the "when").	Commits to what can be reasonably delivered (the "when").
Clarifies and elaborates scope.	Manages scope and technical dependencies.	Understands and seeks clarification about scope.
Seeks customer and stakeholder validation.	Removes impediments to team productivity.	Evaluates feasibility and the technology approach.
Updates stakeholders and ensures air cover for the team.	Runs team planning, execution, and review forums.	Provides high-level estimates initially and detailed estimates later.
Encourages and celebrates team achievements.	Coaches and motivates the team toward the goal.	Executes against the plan—providing frequent updates.
Provides feedback—without frequently changing scope.	Provides progress updates and cross-team communication.	Escalates issues and concerns quickly—with recommendations.
Triages bugs and determines trade-offs on scope against timeline.	Triages and negotiates resource and timeline-scope trade-offs.	Recommends trade-offs to accelerate the timeline while maintaining quality.
Stays ahead of the team with validated, detailed, prioritized requirements to work on next .	Holds the retrospective and communicates process improvements.	Ensures robust testing, high quality, and scalability.

You can't remove the inherent tension between these different roles and incentives. You can, however, negotiate the tension from a position of shared understanding and mutual trust and respect.

How to Build (or Lose) Strong Engineering Relationships

Your relationship with engineering is the most crucial to your success. In **Chapter 2,** I discussed techniques for leading through influence.

Extensively use the approaches outlined there to be an effective team member. Engineering will often know the product, business, and customer needs as well as you do, and it deserves a say in product direction, priorities, and solutions.

Engineers, as a rule, are incredibly rational, intelligent, and outcome-oriented. They demand efficient use of their time and talents. They want to have an impact on the business and expect you to provide the data to justify your recommendations and measure the success of initiatives objectively.

You'll lose credibility by wasting their time on a project that never sees the light of day or fails due to lack of customer validation and internal collaboration. However, if you involve them on each step of the journey, they will help you create better solutions and mitigate risks, and they will be your advocates—even if a project does not succeed from time to time.

Build strong relationships and maintain respect with your engineering partners by employing the following techniques.

1. Embrace Five Core Teamwork Values

It is essential as a product manager that you see yourself and engineering as "one team," where you frequently collaborate with designers and developers. Operating as one team breaks down silos and creates a feeling of joint accountability—reducing the likelihood of finger-pointing when things don't go as well as hoped. Don't merely deliver requirements and ask for a set of designs, a plan, and a timeline. This is known as "throwing over the wall," and that's just what your team will want to do to you.

To make cross-functional teams effective, you need to embrace five powerful teamwork values. While these values are explicitly stated as part of Scrum, I have found them to be essential values in any environment. Exhibit these behaviors and lead by example.

1. **Courage**—Work through challenges together so that the team can achieve the right goals. Constructive conflict is essential to finding the optimal compromise and best outcome that balances customer needs, simplicity and efficiency, and technical and resourcing constraints. Differences in opinion must be embraced and objectively debated. Keep discussion grounded in fact and rationale, and never get personal.

2. **Focus**—Strive toward a single (or few) goals at a time, to produce excellent work and deliver value sooner. Context-switching kills productivity, frustrates the team, and puts commitments at risk. This

is particularly true for engineers as they solve intricate technical issues that require deep concentration. While you may not be able to control all distractions, don't make a habit of becoming one yourself.

3. **Commitment**—Autonomously, collectively, and universally commit to scope and timelines, and strive to achieve them. Doing so, even for well-understood scope, is uncomfortable—there are always the unpredictable disruptions you could not foresee. Nonetheless, strive to deliver, even if that means working a little longer or harder.

4. **Respect**—Have trust and belief in team members, knowing that you are all technically and intellectually capable, and working with good intent. There should be no blame, no politics, no judging, and no undermining. Team members will double their efforts when working alongside someone they trust and enjoy being around. You don't need to be
best of friends; but mutual respect for others' contributions goes a long way.

5. **Openness**—Be transparent with stakeholders and each other about the status, timeliness, and quality of the work. No one likes to disap-

. . . .

Encouraging Openness When Someone Needs Help

I was the product manager for a client's engineering team charged with creating on-boarding tools for new customers.

I noticed that the tasks in the engineering backlog weren't being marked as complete at the same rate they had in the past. I was concerned we weren't making enough progress toward the deliverable—especially because the team had made a commitment to a key customer.

At our daily stand-up meeting, no team member expressed any blockers—so I kept quiet and trusted that the team was on top of it.

Unfortunately, a few days later, one of the engineers admitted he had been trying to solve a content-import failure for several days—well in excess of the amount of effort we had estimated coming into the sprint. Each time he thought he'd solved the problem, something else would come up. He got so enthralled and caught up in overcoming the challenge, by the time he told the team about it, he'd already spent three days on the task.

It turned out that one of the other engineers knew exactly what the issue might be. Within a few hours, the two engineers had worked together to solve the problem.

Had the engineer spoken up earlier, we'd have been able to help him. However, the delay meant we were now unable to hit our goal.

. . . .

Your Core Teamwork Values

Use this checklist to honestly evaluate how you and your team are living the team-work values. Reflect back on recent collaborations and highlight those that you seem to have mastered as a team and those that you could work together on more. (Perhaps score each item on a 1–3 scale.)

A powerful exercise is to take this checklist and ask each member to fill it out concurrently. Differences in opinion are very illuminating and could spark open discourse on specific areas where you collectively need to improve.

COURAGE

- ☐ Be willing to disagree and accept if you are wrong.
- ☐ Get with the program, after you have said your piece, even if the decision isn't what you advocated (don't continue pushing back).
- ☐ Stretch yourself by learning new skills or going beyond your role description if it helps get the team's tasks done.
- ☐ Commit to something without all the details or certainty you desire, to get there in the time available.
- ☐ Deliver bad news honestly. Avoid communicating with spin, skipping over inconvenient details, or leading with justifications or excuses.

FOCUS

- ☐ Anyone on the team can state the current goal at any time and explain how their work adds business value.
- ☐ Pull in work from only a predefined backlog. Allow for prearranged tasks such as scheduled company meetings, emails, and high-priority emergencies.
- ☐ Gently push back and alert your team if your manager or others task you with other work (even if it is deemed urgent). Ask team members to do the same.
- ☐ Do not let yourself procrastinate on completing your commitments just because you find them challenging or uncomfortable or because you find something else more interesting to do. Instead, see if you can complete them early and beat your deadlines.
- ☐ Continually evaluate how to work more efficiently and eliminate waste. Hold regular retrospectives to explicitly assess process improvements.

COMMITMENT

- ☐ Encourage your team to embrace challenges and provide believable (not padded) estimates for scope. Push yourselves out of your comfort zones.

- ☐ Believe in your goal and make it one that it is both audacious yet obtainable (neither too much of a stretch nor easily mailed in).

- ☐ If the goal is at risk, work harder and collaboratively to achieve it (with a sense of urgency and some friendly peer pressure).

- ☐ Be honest and seek self-improvement if you don't hit the goal or complete the committed scope.

- ☐ Meet all standards for quality, testing, documentation, and working functionality.

RESPECT

- ☐ Listen to and support each other—speak up if you notice someone needs help.

- ☐ After saying your piece, embrace decisions made by the responsible role (for example, priorities are decided by product managers; technology decisions by engineering).

- ☐ Operate as peer equals regardless of seniority (with no exercising authority or power over others).

- ☐ Drop the ego and heroism (as you will succeed or fail as a team, regardless of individual contribution).

- ☐ Avoid defensiveness, taking things personally, or reacting emotionally.

OPENNESS

- ☐ Immediately highlight challenges or difficulties that are slowing you down (and don't be afraid to ask for help).

- ☐ Explain trade-offs and decisions, and embrace critique and feedback on the work product.

- ☐ Be willing to report publicly on tracking metrics such as team velocity and progress toward goals.

- ☐ Encourage quieter members of your team to speak up by inviting and welcoming them into the conversation.

- ☐ Share perspective on what in the process is working and what needs improvement, and seek and adopt feedback.

point, but communicating issues early on increases the chance you'll receive help. Likewise, when things are going well, openly celebrate each other's contribution.

2. Start Off Right and Spend Time Together

When the team is first constituted (or when new team members join) explicitly discuss ways of working together. Topics to cover include the following:

- **Roles and responsibilities**—In **Table 8.1**, I summarize high-level responsibilities for product managers, project managers, and the development team.

    Explicitly discuss, adapt and adopt these frameworks to establish soft boundaries that welcome contribution yet clearly define the responsible party. Without accountability, certain activities can fall through the gaps, or you may step on each other's toes. It can lead to confusion, mistrust, and scapegoating.

- **Managing distractions and interruptions**—Engineers require extensive unbroken time to work on challenging problems and avoid context-switching. Find out what time periods they feel they work most effectively in and minimize disruptions during those times so they can focus. Also agree on what constitutes a necessary disruption and what doesn't. Answering non-blocking questions may not qualify but dealing with a high-priority emergency clearly would.

- **Meetings**—Understandably, engineers loathe poorly run, ineffective meetings especially if they are scheduled with little notice or interrupt a productive problem-solving session.

    Do not calendar a meeting to solve every issue or to extract status updates from the team. Instead, win their trust by limiting their involvement to a few high-impact forums, held regularly (the same time each day or each week). Plan your meetings well and run them efficiently to produce meaningful and clear-cut decisions.

- **Communication preferences**—In general, since engineers spend much of their time on computers, they may prefer to use email, instant or group messaging (such as Slack), wikis, and ticket-management systems (such as JIRA) to pose and receive answers to questions from you.

Agree upon minimum turnaround times for inquiries among team members. A courteous reply within 24 hours, even if an issue will require longer to address, signals that the receiver is working on it.

Nonetheless, do not forget that in-person interaction in addition to electronic communication is essential to tackle more complex issues, to avoid back-and-forth, and to build deeper personal relationships.

- **Feedback**—Discuss how to give each other feedback (there are many frameworks you can find online). Always ask first if the other person is receptive to the feedback ("Can I give you some feedback?") and focus on specific facts and behaviors, not the person. The very act of highlighting a norm for feedback is permission to give and—importantly—receive feedback openly.

  When conflict gets heated, give each other time to disengage but do not leave interpersonal issues brewing for long.

- **One-on-ones**—Schedule some time weekly with key engineering leads and engineering managers. Discuss work but don't make it all about work or a status update. Also schedule time (less frequently) with each of your team contributors, regardless of whether they are leads. Perhaps meet over lunch to keep it informal.

  When meeting a team member one on one for the first time, ask genuine questions about them—ask about their background and family, professional history, what brought them to the company, and personal interests. And share something about yourself. Not all people are forthcoming with personal stories (so don't interrogate), but the act of showing interest in others is a powerful trust builder.

  ▶ In **Chapter 2**, I suggest questions you can ask stakeholders the first time you meet them, which are appropriate for engineers too.

- **Collocation**—Have product, design, and engineering located in close physical proximity if possible. Informal interactions are critical to building trust. Relying on tickets, documentation, and email—punctuated with your regular meetings—might get the job done, but it can slow the pace of iteration and lose opportunities to build trust. When you don't work closely with your team on a daily basis, assumptions take the place of explicit communication. Conflict can develop, with each team erring on the side of "bad intent." The "us" versus "them" mentality takes root. Team members not part of recent

Build Trust by Spending Time with Each Other

Below are some fun ideas I've tried, and I have found they build close bonds among technology team members who work together regularly. Most companies are more than happy to invest a modest budget for these items:

- Games, trivia, or karaoke nights.

- A sports, book, or movie club.

- Any event where you make something together (such as sushi, home-brew, or painting).

- White elephant gift-giving during the holiday season.

- Volunteering for a day at a charity or environmental clean-up event.

- A "product camp"—bring kids in from a local school to the office to learn more about product management, design, and coding.

- Hackathons—effective to elicit ideas and prototype solutions they'd love to see in the product, or tools to help the team work better.

- Lunch-and-learn sessions—discuss the latest technology trends (not just the work at hand) or tackle a fun topic (like "the history of pirates").

- Quarterly offsite and regular brainstorming sessions to engage product and engineering leadership in the product's strategic direction.

discussions fall behind in having a shared understanding of current challenges and their status.

In today's technology environment, however, collocation can often be an unreasonable expectation. Commonly, teams are now partially co-located, with some remote members or outsourced third-party development providers. Some companies are 100 percent remote or work-from-home. Hiring large numbers of engineers in one location may be a recruitment and retention challenge. Costs may be prohibitive when hiring talent in competitive markets. And companies that can tap into a vast array of skills, cultures, industry backgrounds, and problem-solving approaches have significant advantages.

Differences in time zone, language, work styles, comfort with conflict, and a lack of face-to-face time (needed to help create trust) all undermine team effectiveness. To compensate, you may need to apply extra structure and put more effort into communication.

3. Involve Engineering Early—Appropriately, Not Excessively

Find a balance between collaborating with and distracting engineering. There is a huge difference between asking them to "do your job for you" and involving them early and sufficiently to understand the priorities and contribute solutions. Engage them too late and you risk ending up with a less-than-satisfactory solution that is also difficult to engineer.

Consider it your role to create the environment in which a team can start to solve a well-understood problem. Essentially, you must do the following:

Working with Remote Teams

Working with remote teams is never easy, but the lower cost and extra capacity can be very advantageous.

One client I worked with had several engineering teams with members in the United States, Argentina, and India. While some work could be independently assigned, projects generally required collaboration across all locations.

What did we do to make collaboration easier?:

- We established virtual chat rooms and all-day video hook-up between locations, encouraging face-to-face meetings and virtual water-cooler conversations.
- We paired remote and local developers, so remote developers had a single person responsible for responding quickly to issues.
- Product managers developed more specific and detailed documentation around context, data, and requirement definitions.
- Initially, the more-predictable, less-time-sensitive tasks were assigned to remote teams until they felt more at ease.
- To overcome cultural barriers and fear of conflict, we explicitly asked each team member for a status update during the stand-up and then probed deeper, rather than waiting for information to be volunteered proactively.
- When commitments were made, the responsible parties were expected to send a detailed email to make the obligations clear and transparent and to ensure shared understanding.
- The staff in India shifted their daily work schedule to late afternoon and evening to improve working-time overlap.

While not perfect, these strategies worked well enough to reduce communication gaps and overheads—while encouraging collaboration, a sense of purpose, and a unified team.

- **Establish shared goals**—Establish goals that drive customer and business outcomes. Without these, your team will be rudderless (perhaps even resistant) and confused as to whether their work is a valuable contribution.

- **Set context**—Complete necessary data analysis, specifications, and customer validation, so that you know all you need to know to justify why the problem is worth solving at this time.

- **Prioritize the work**—Break down requirements, elaborating on details where useful—but not excessively so—and have a point of view on the order of execution (ideally as a groomed, force-ranked product backlog [see **Chapter 7**]).

- **Align stakeholders**—Ensure your project has broad support and that stakeholders' concerns are addressed so you can preempt later distractions.

You must do some of this heavy lifting *before* involving much of engineering's time. However, never leave it till the end. Instead, do this:

- Openly discuss business and customer goals early and frequently. Talk about the high-level business metrics for the project as well as the metrics for which you and your team will be accountable.

- Share early drafts of hypotheses, data, specifications, conceptual designs, and potential solutions. The more context, the better.

- Invite engineers to customer interviews and share summaries of what you've discovered so they can understand the issues firsthand.

- Generate ideas together—with regular jointly held brainstorms, for instance—and support their sharing of technical concerns and limitations.

- Encourage the review of initial designs and requirements. You should start making trade-offs early so that development is easier and user experience remains of high quality.

Be open to your engineering team challenging you at all stages of the product lifecycle: the validity of your data and hypotheses, your planning and strategy, and the content and priority of detailed requirements. Do not dismiss their ideas just because you already have something in mind or have already invested much time going down a certain path. And never

Yes, Involve Engineering in Product Discovery

Engineering talent is expensive and in short supply. In many companies, any "distraction" from hammering out code is seen to be wasteful and inefficient. Perhaps the engineers on your team have had little exposure to customers and are reluctant to visit and talk to them. Unfortunately, keeping engineers doing just coding, while it may be an "efficient use of time," can be ineffective at delivering value to your customer and business. Here's why:

1. Engineers who understand the customer and experience their challenges first-hand are more driven to come up with creative solutions—perhaps ones you never dreamed of. They will have more context for what the priorities are and challenge work that doesn't seem to be necessary.

2. Engineers understand technical limitations and can see trade-offs that will make implementation easier and faster. Without their early involvement during discovery, the product might well be validated with customers but not be feasible to build.

3. Engineers, unlike most product managers, have the skills needed to build high-fidelity prototypes—the most effective testing artifact and lifelike product simulation. Without them, you may not uncover the optimal solution for customers.

present engineering with rigid, detailed product designs as "your" vision for implementation.

Proactively seek their involvement. Capture and document their input and demonstrate your interest in addressing and incorporating their recommendations. If none are forthcoming, do not assume there are no problems—you may need to be doing more to get busy engineers to engage.

With a firm grasp of the goals and supporting data, engineers are particularly interested in ideation and solution generation. In addition to having whole new ideas, they can spot opportunities to offer useful functionality by leveraging existing technologies that save engineering effort. They can research and find new technologies to integrate into the technology stack, not only to solve a specific issue but also, perhaps, to add new functionality.

Engineers also need to start thinking about the feasibility of solutions well in advance. Often, you'll ask them to build capabilities that push the limits of the stack or provide new core functionality. Engineers are good at abstracting the underlying systems required from user interfaces and high-level requirements, spotting patterns for efficiencies and opportunities to reuse existing code, perhaps avoiding some steps completely.

Share designs and emerging requirements early to allow them to start thinking about these opportunities. Encourage them to suggest new approaches to problems that will be more feasible—this speeds time-to-market while making the system easier to maintain and the team happier.

Mutually determine when deliverables are sufficiently fleshed out to start development work. A lack of alignment on the completeness and depth required for specifications documents, product backlogs, user stories (especially acceptance criteria), and analysis is a frequent point of contention between engineering and product. What you later assume to be refining and adding detail, engineering may claim to be scope creep.

Finally, be cautious not to overstate your expected outcomes in superfluous terms, in the hope that you will motivate them. You will quickly lose credibility if the promised benefits do not materialize. Instead, discuss the business goals, show them your data, and talk honestly about the risks. Engineers are problem-solvers at heart and enjoy a challenge.

4. Engineering Doesn't Work for You

One of the greatest, yet entirely avoidable, reasons for unproductive conflict is your attitude (whether intended or not) toward the role of engineering. You will quickly earn their ire if you see them as a service organization or as "order-takers," who must execute on your predefined plan.

Context is everything. Share your analysis and rationale openly. Engineering wants to understand and influence the reasoning behind why the project is a priority right now and how it will further the business and customer's goals. They have every right to know why their hard-spent hours will contribute. Sometimes a project's scope or deadline is non-negotiable, highly-constrained, or urgent for valid business reasons. In these instances, you must still help engineers understand what's driving the need and give them any possible opportunity for a say in the direction.

▶ In **Chapter 4** and **Chapter 7**, I include alternative strategies to approach estimation and to collaborate with stakeholders, including engineering, to set priorities.

Establishing estimates is a particularly sensitive subject. Focusing only on setting a deadline, especially with scant scope definition, drives an engineering team nuts—and before too long, they will expect you to deliver highly detailed, "locked-down" specifications before they even consider estimation. Early in a project stick to high-level T-shirt-sizing or relative-estimation methods.

Once a project is underway and the scope is better understood, though, it is reasonable to ask for and expect engineering tasks to be specified and estimated—but know that these can change for reasons outside everyone's control. Understand the root causes for a change and seek to support the team in revising estimates—and if these have high visibility, communicate the changes widely.

Understand the construction of your technology system, at least abstractly. Ask your team to map out the overall architecture, especially the more challenging areas to engineer. By increasing your knowledge of how things work, you will get a feel for the complexity of your requests. You will build empathy and become better positioned to inform trade-offs in implementation. It can also help you hold your own when engineering tells you that something is impossible—you will appreciate their constraints yet also be able to critique their approaches and suggest workarounds.

However, be judicious in setting your priorities based purely on how hard you think it will be to build the product. While this is a factor to consider in prioritization, doing the most valuable things first will usually deliver more benefit to your organization than focusing on many smaller, incremental features of marginal benefit, simply because they are deemed "easier." Engineers like a challenge, and they like their efforts to have an impact!

Micromanagement is an unpleasant trait in a product manager—following up on tasks repeatedly ("When will they be ready?") or asking for too much detail about implementation ("How are things being built?"). Driving accountability and predictability are key, but it is essential you have a strong project or engineering lead to manage and track execution tasks. Then you can then dedicate your time "outward"—on ensuring stakeholder buy-in, collaborating on trade-offs, and thinking strategically about what comes next—rather than "inward," on the day-to-day running of the implementation team.

Occasionally you might need to push engineering, such as when you need them to hit an original high-stakes deadline or when the team is repeatedly missing targets. If you have invested in your relationships up front, then holding engineering to a deadline is easier. But seek to understand the complexities before pushing—if a significant issue has arisen, it makes no sense to expect the impossible. If it's within reach, however, gently push and remind the team of the goal.

5. Hold Yourselves Mutually Accountable— and Admit Your Mistakes

It happens. Requirements change. Features fail. You miss something. Your customers and business needs must come first—and this may require fast-tracking, redoing, or abandoning a project. Changes can seem simple to you, but they may require a wholesale overhaul for the developers. If you do not own up to your mistakes—regardless of how well-intentioned you were or whether the changes were outside your control—you will frustrate your team and quickly lose their respect. Apologize sincerely and don't blame others or make excuses.

Be decisive—if you're not, your engineers can't make progress, and they may end up having to make less-efficient technology choices. It is often better to make a call and move on, acknowledging the risk, and then admit a mistake later.

Engineers love working with other high performers. Laziness; failure to follow through (saying what you'll do and when, but not delivering); or the tendency to give incomplete or inconsistent specifications, to leave assumptions unchallenged, and to politick—all are anathemas to most developers.

Having high standards for your own work earns you the right to challenge engineers when their work isn't up to expected quality. Work with your technical leads when a team member appears to have an attitude problem or is missing commitments (perhaps refusing to make them). Engineering management will respond by getting that person help or setting specific expectations. And, in time, with strong enough relationships, you should be able to provide (and receive) feedback directly.

When something goes wrong in execution, encourage the team to continually learn from their mistakes—through regular retrospectives or five-whys. Missed deadlines, quality issues, misaligned scope expectations—all are common and best seen as opportunities to learn and grow.

You can find a five-whys template and example online at http://www.influentialpm.com.

Key Execution Phases—and How You Can Contribute to Make These a Success

Generally—regardless of your specific development process—any initiative moves through four broad steps to completion (as illustrated in **Figure 8.1**):

PLANNING AND KICK-OFF	IMPLEMENTATION AND CHECK-INS	PRODUCT REVIEW	RETROSPECTIVE OR POST-MORTEM
• Align around an overall goal • Commit to a set of scope from the backlog	• Make quick decisions and trade-offs • Identify and communicate blockers and action plans	• Review/demo *product* • Get feedback from stake-holders and validate "done"	• Review *process* • Decide plan to adapt, and improve collaboration

FIGURE 8.1 *Key execution phases*

1. **Planning and kick-off**—Establish the context, supporting data, and goal. Introduce the scope, requirements, and known issues. Determine the engineering plan, resourcing, timeline, and next steps.

2. **Implementation and check-in**—You will spend most of your time in this phase. The project is taking shape at this point, and you are facing and addressing challenges. The team frequently checks in on progress, helps remove blockers, and shares information. Otherwise, the project could stall or head off in an undesirable direction.

3. **Product review**—You can demonstrate partially or fully working features, and inspect how complete the *product* is to specifications. You can validate whether it meets the needs of your target market and give stakeholders the opportunity to provide feedback.

4. **Retrospective or post-mortem**—Each cycle provides an opportunity for the team to identify what went well and what they can do better. Regularly review your *process* to determine ways to work more productively, avoiding unresolved issues that may become contentious.

Using iterative development methods, you can continuously cycle through these steps (in Scrum, a two-week cycle is not uncommon).

While more traditional projects may take months to complete and include formal gates or milestones along the way, the principles remain the same.

1. Planning and Kick-Off

As product manager, it is your responsibility to own the following:

- **Prepare and share**—Before kick-off begins, you must have completed customer research, data collection and analysis, and prioritization and justification, and you must have gotten stakeholder buy-in. You will have a detailed, fleshed-out specification (**Chapter 6**) and a groomed backlog (**Chapter 7**)—and if you don't, do not expect to get much further.

  Encourage engineering to actively review upcoming specifications and draft designs and to ask questions. Initiate the process with some one-on-ones with key developers, to preview the plan and unearth their concerns in advance.

- **Hold a kick-off meeting**—Getting the whole team around a new initiative together can be immensely energizing. A kick-off allows you and your team to start strong—with a common understanding of the "why"—and to identify issues and dissenting opinions early. Your goal is to ensure everyone is on the same page, in agreement that the proposed initiative is the right one for right now.

  Prepare a brief kick-off document that includes the following:

  - A refresher of your product vision, roadmap and key metrics;

  - The project goal and hypothesis of desired outcomes;

  - Quantitative and qualitative supporting data, especially of the customers' needs;

  - An explanation of how the project will map back to company priorities and KPIs;

  - An explanation of how it was prioritized over other potential initiatives;

  - Known issues, risks, and constraints;

  - Highlights from your product specification. Address emerging comments and questions, and encourage more.

  An example kick-off template is included at http://www.influentialpm.com.

Don't just present information to your team—facilitate a conversation. Listen and allow them to raise concerns. An excellent technique to make sure your kick-off stays on track is the "parking lot"—a whiteboard list of items you commit to coming back to resolve at a later date. At the end of the kick-off, create an action plan and immediately follow up on any blocking items to keep up the momentum.

- **Support the engineering planning process**—Whether you use Scrum to break down user stories into tasks for rough estimates, or a formal analysis for technical specification and timelines, it is essential the team has a sense of ownership and control over their commitments.

  Your role is to answer questions, or find answers, rapidly. Understand the technology challenges and encourage the team to suggest solution alternatives if this might accelerate the timeline, improve quality, or reduce complexity.

▶ See **Chapter 7** for more tips on managing the "conversation" component of requirements definition.

You share so much information during planning. Capture the details—summarize conversations, decisions, and outstanding issues in the appropri-

Product Managers Shouldn't Drive Engineering

I once sat in on a scope-planning meeting with a junior product manager. He led the meeting, and without first setting a goal for context, he immediately jumped into a walk-through of his user stories. He paused only briefly at each one—no one had any comments or questions. He then led them through the estimation process—each time they bid an estimate, he'd push them to select the lowest. Everyone in the room, except him, eventually fell silent.

After a while, realizing it didn't make any difference, the team became disengaged and resigned to defaulting their bids to the same estimate for every story regardless of actual complexity.

The product manager, sensing the disengagement and feeling frustrated said, "Look, I don't like this either but the CEO is telling us to deliver this." They finished the meeting and trudged out of the room.

The mistake? Well, many! Rather than *supporting* a team of self-organizing, motivated individuals, the product manager was *driving* the team and seeking to put the team on the hook for as much as he could.

The team members clearly felt disempowered. They weren't provided context for why or what they were being asked to do. And the product manager made a fatal mistake—using the positional power of the CEO to get them to fall into line.

Fortunately, he responded well to coaching.

ate place within the product backlog, specification document, or team wiki. If you observe team members taking notes, ask them to incorporate them or to send them to you to add them.

A common problem during planning is to underestimate the work required for full testing and validation. Ensure the team is considering sufficient time to write unit tests, validate, and debug code.

- **Respect but push on commitments**—Product managers are in a tight spot. They are accountable for shipping product of value to customers, yet they rely on the development team to deliver it. However, if they try to push too hard, morale drops and teams lose their sense of ownership. You may well find less being achieved, not more.

  You should, though, encourage the team to work outside its comfort zone—to practice courage and commit to more than they know how to deliver (or even despite whether they can deliver). In a high-functioning team, everyone understands the desire to achieve more and take greater risks. They're working hard and will push back when enough is enough.

2. Implementation and Check-In

Once an initiative is underway, your engineering team will take the lead. You will make yourself available to respond quickly to questions as they arise and keep them on track by blocking and tackling issues.

- **Overcommunicate**—You want to know the state of implementation without always checking in on status. Mature organizations will have a well-documented development process and formal meetings in which information is shared and artifacts (such as timeline and resources) are reviewed. You should actively participate in established forums but also augment these discussions with informal channels to deal with smaller issues.

  At the other extreme, if your team is small and co-located and you are in a high-trust environment, you might share information informally more often. This can be the broadest and quickest way to resolve issues, but it is usually insufficient as decisions are often made in silos that omit some stakeholders.

  In either case, err on the side of overcommunication:

  - For decisions made in informal interactions, capture a note and place it in your backlog, tickets, or team wiki. Follow up with an email to a broader audience if necessary.

Easily Overlooked!

Proactively keep tabs on public holidays, vacations, sick days, and other absences (such as in training, conferences, and off-sites) that may impact team velocity and project timelines. Shared resources are of particular concern as they split their time between multiple commitments. A universal calendar might help. Unexpected bottlenecks can easily arise, throttling your project implementation and impacting your schedule.

- Negotiate access to timelines, sprint backlogs, burn-down charts, and other project management artifacts. Frequently review and keep an eye on issues you might be able to unblock (such as an open question or stalled ticket). Do not, however, follow up on details incessantly.

- Ask to be tagged on tickets relevant to your project, so status updates and comments are pushed into your inbox. Ensure rapid response if tagged to encourage continuation.

- Working through engineering leads and project managers, ask them to bubble up issues and information from the rest of the team.

- If finding blocks of time to problem-solve together is challenging, suggest scheduling "open hours"—a time when you will mutually be available if needed.

- Offer to take ownership for updating stakeholders with progress and blockers. If this is explicitly agreed upon to be part of your role, you have an excellent reason for gathering information from the team on a regular (but not too frequent) basis. Keep yourself informed and keep stakeholders in the loop, giving the team air cover. (See more in **Chapter 2.**)

- **Hold lightweight check-ins**—Engineering is a highly complex activity requiring deep concentration. Context-switches, interruptions, frequent breaks, and urgent emails are highly disruptive. Nonetheless, issue identification, resolution, and status updates are important.

  To balance these competing needs, establish a regular "stand-up." Borrowed from Scrum, the stand-up is a place to share recent accomplishments, affirm upcoming goals and activities, and surface emerging issues. Depending on your team's velocity and the rate at which problems arise, you might require check-ins daily, every other day, or weekly. The longer the cycle, the higher the risk you leave issues unresolved.

Don't delay holding the first stand-up too long after kick-off, since this is your chance to ensure the team has started strong and is aligned.

Ideally, hold stand-ups in the same place, so everyone gets in a routine. Literally standing up is customary. Keep it short—15 minutes should be sufficient. Avoid gathering in a meeting room where you're inclined to get comfortable and take time to small-talk, set up, and wait for others to arrive. Don't prepare documents—stick to artifacts you already have. Ideally, an engineering lead or project manager (or Scrum master)—not the product manager—runs the meeting.

All team members must be on time and attend in person (unless they are remotely located, and then they should join via video conference, not phone to ensure full engagement and "facetime"). If many members of your team are remote, then hold the entire stand-up over a group video conference, with everyone joining from their desk.

The format is simple—each member of the team has a turn at answering three questions:

1. What did I **work on/accomplish** since the last stand-up?
2. What will I **work on/accomplish** next?
3. What **impediments** are in my way?

Team members are expected to be transparent and share good and bad news. If, for some reason, a member of the team has not been able to complete something they committed to or is stuck in any way, they should volunteer the information. If a team member isn't forthcoming for some reason, others are expected to ensure the three questions are asked and answered by everyone.

The stand-up is not a place to resolve issues or to ask or answer questions outside these three. If there are impediments, team members agree on who will be responsible for follow-up. Usually, this is a smaller subset of the team and, if it is a severe blocker, they meet immediately afterward.

Apart from providing their own updates, the product manager's primary responsibility in stand-ups is to observe and identify common issues. These can then be taken "offline" for further exploration with the project manager or engineering team. Here are some good questions to ask yourself:

- Is the project moving at a pace where I can see it coming together?

- Are team members marking work as "done" or "code complete," but issues such as bugs or unfinished testing remain open?

- Has the team worked on what they promised to in the last stand-up?

- Is what the team is working on next aligned with my project's priorities? Or are they working on something for someone else?

- Do I hear the same tasks come up again and again? Does that suggest something is stuck?

- Are any impediments related to the clarity of requirements? How can I assist? How can I do better next time?

- Are impediments addressed within a day or so? (If the problem is still being talked about at the next stand-up, there may be a more significant issue.)

- Are potential issues not being raised? (Be on the lookout for body language or a quiet team member.)

- Do I see a sense of urgency and engagement? What can I do to encourage and motivate?

- **Be prepared to make trade-offs**—You need to have a practical mindset. As details surface the full complexity of implementation will become apparent to the development team, and they may request to compromise on designs or features to make engineering easier. Listen to the technical explanation behind the request and brainstorm options for workarounds. You don't have to agree on the spot—take responsibility for gathering data to ensure the alternative will work for the user and business, and return with an answer as quickly as you can.

As covered in **Chapter 9**, scope, timeline, and quality are often at odds. Engineering owns quality, and quality should not be easily sacrificed, or you'll quickly earn an undesirable reputation.

If you dig in your heels every time a trade-off is needed, you'll add risk to your project and earn a reputation for being unreasonable. But

Engineering Doesn't Work for You

Product managers often seem in an unfair position. Resource availability, the development process, and the pace at which delivery happens are beyond your direct control. Nonetheless, you are often called to task when product implementation isn't moving fast enough.

In such a situation, here are the worst things you can do:

- Throw your team members under the bus (blaming them or engineering managers for slow delivery).

- Attempt to micromanage engineers directly (driving them toward specific deliverables, checking on progress many times a day).

- Set aggressive deadlines in the hope that this will create a sense of urgency.

Instead, take some alternative strategies:

- Break down scope until incremental but regular delivery is possible (even if small). As confidence builds, you can add more complexity.

- Encourage investigation into underlying issues such as lack of development tools, immature testing processes, or low resource levels, then suggest and support improvements.

- Track and draw attention to sources of disruption and time spent on non-development tasks (which reduce team throughput).

neither should you agree to every tradeoff. Shortcuts are okay but not when they grossly impact user experience or value.

- **Block and tackle**—Yes, it is your job to provide air cover for your team, even if that means more pain and work for you. You want them focused on solving difficult technology challenges to drive success for your customers and your business. Stakeholders who go "directly" to engineering with requests, feedback, or distractions not only disrupt your project but can result in your team suddenly working on projects other than yours. And you may be seen as someone who doesn't do enough to avoid distractions.

    Especially if you're a more junior member of the company, it can be nerve-racking to try to redirect a senior stakeholder. As always, an objective and flexible approach works best:

- First, seek to understand. Ask open-ended questions. What is the underlying cause or context for the disruption? (Try the five-whys from **Chapter 4**.)

- Reiterate how your initiative benefits the business and why it was a priority in the first place. Share context and data. Explain how the disruption added risk or extended the timeline.

- Sometimes the disruption is more important, enough to force a reprioritization—in that case, make implicit trade-offs explicit. Inform the stakeholder of the impact, accept the change, and communicate it to the team.

- If you think you can identify one, offer to help find an alternative path to address the need that is prompting the disruption. You don't need to generate solutions on the spot—promise to return with options by a specific timeline.

- Ask that the stakeholder work through you if anything comes up in the future, rather than go direct to the development team. Tell them you'll either identify a workaround or offer trade-off options with estimated impact while keeping the team focused on agreed-upon goals.

If needed, ask your manager for help or approach the stakeholder jointly with the engineering lead and project manager.

If the issue appears to be endemic, track the cumulative impact so you can escalate it and negotiate time and resources for your team to complete their work. Your team will be frustrated if held to its commitments despite disruptions. Help them avoid this.

- **Motivate the team**—Little things matter in keeping your team excited, engaged, and productive. Reinforce goals and context to keep the "why" top-of-mind. Share any good news from customer validation or stakeholder updates. Bring in cupcakes or spring a round of beers at a happy hour. Ask the company to support the purchase of T-shirts with a fun design. Celebrate team achievements. Thank them sincerely. It is easy to lose sight of the little things that matter when everyone is heads-down.

3. Product Review

Regularly review the cumulative results of the team's work with stakeholders, to keep them informed and aligned. Showing a partially working product early, to get addressable feedback or to surface misunderstandings, is preferable to waiting until you have a fully working product that may not meet expectations. A scheduled review (or demo)—say, every two weeks—ensures that a long period of time will not lapse between gathering stakeholder feedback. It also provides an excellent opportunity to reinforce the project's business importance and validate progress toward specifications.

It is good form for the product manager to allow the team to shine and let individual engineers demo their work. It helps the team be more visible, motivated, and accountable. Even though not all team members are polished presenters, it is more valuable to work through that awkwardness than have one person dominating the limelight.

Reviews can be frequent (such as at the end of each sprint if you are using Scrum) or on an ad-hoc—but not infrequent—basis when implementation reaches key milestones. Make this one of a few more substantial meetings, which all engineering, design, and product contributors attend, along with internal stakeholders who are interested in the product. Prepare well, so you are set up for success.

· ·

Dropping the Ball Instead of Blocking and Tackling

For the third day running, I noticed the head of customer service in a water-cooler discussion with one of our most experienced engineers. Not thinking much of it at the time, I later found out the engineer was busy addressing some bugs reported in customer service emails, which affected "only" a few customers.

Unfortunately, the engineer was supposed to be working on a time-sensitive, mission-critical project expected to drive 30 percent of new revenue in the next year.

Taken aback, I asked the developer how the work had been prioritized. Red-faced, he told me customer service had shown him the emails and that he felt bad for the customers and for the customer service department for having to deal with it.

I met with the head of customer service. Far from being angry or upset, I just asked him for his perspective. He told me that he hadn't meant to disrupt other priorities but that the last time an issue such as this had come up, he'd forwarded the ticket to the product team and hadn't heard anything back. So this time, he approached engineering directly to get attention.

Had I responded to the previous issue with clarity about where it should be placed relative to other priorities, and then provided a workaround to customer service to keep the customers happy, I'd have avoided the situation. As a result, I'd failed to intercept a potential disruption.

One other lesson I learned was that there is power in creating trusted relationships and influence. I remain impressed at how the customer service lead had built such an informal yet powerful relationship with engineering that the developer was happy to drop his other work!

· ·

- **Secure buy-in**—Certain attendees may be prone to derail progress or bring up unrelated issues (such as revisiting prioritization decisions or business goals). Or you may know that the product demo won't be as polished or as complete as a specific stakeholder might expect. In either event, seek buy-in ahead of time. Remind them of the purpose of the review, give them a preview of what is to come, and ask them to bring up concerns with you directly now (rather than during the review when it may deflate a hardworking team).

  If helpful, recruit a stakeholder to send a message or reiterate a point during the review that you have been making. This is particularly useful if your team needs to hear from someone other than you (for example, if the team appears to lack a sense of urgency).

  Prep stakeholders to emphasize the importance of the work the team is doing and the impact on customers and the business. Have them call out names and specific achievements. It is a huge morale boost for the team to know that senior stakeholders value their work.

- **Schedule and validate demos**—In collaboration with engineering leads, assign a presenter to each part of the demo and ask them to prepare (or script) it. Ensure the demo is fully working—demos tend to be on development servers, which might not work according to plan in the review. Time everything to run for no more than an hour, including an allowance for open discussion. Suggest they do a dry-run for any team member new to this. To avoid unnecessary busywork, make sure there is no slideware—but only a working product.

  What can be demoed is sometimes not obvious—it doesn't all have to be compelling user-ready features. Engineering can show small increments of work such as a command-line script or function, API input/output, or a rudimentary UI or manipulation of data. Even infrastructure work can be demonstrated (for example, ask, How can you show me that the storage upgrade has been successful?).

- **Structure and guide the demo**—Remind all present of the purpose of a demo and (if necessary) what they can expect and the groundrules for how you would like stakeholders to engage with you and the team. Reinforce the project goal and remind everyone that the project is in progress (since what they will see is likely to be incomplete). Ensure the review, though, does not turn into a status discussion.

  Step back and let team members take you through their sections in turn. It is okay if the demo isn't polished, particularly early in development. Have them talk through what a rough design, a proto-type, or the code does, so stakeholders can follow along.

If a team member skips over important context during their demo and stakeholders appear lost, ask the presenter for clarification in the form of a question (resist the urge to state it for them). For example, "When you clicked on Submit, where did the data go and what happened next?" If something goes wrong in showing the demo, acknowledge it, make a note, and keep moving.

Invite feedback from stakeholders by asking them questions. Avoid getting defensive or explaining away limitations. Stakeholders can sometimes be overly critical. Probe for understanding—having them share the underlying business context is more valuable than just reacting to a feature. It helps everyone make better decisions in the future. If something comes up that isn't immediately relevant, listen for a bit to confirm your suspicions and then respond with "Great question—can you and I take that offline?" (and follow up afterward).

Don't forget that internal stakeholders are not customers, so don't take to heart every piece of stakeholder feedback. Consider what they say through the perspective of your customer and adopt only what makes sense in that context.

Open up the floor to discuss how things are going. Specifically, pose these questions:

- What are the overall impressions of the stakeholders? What are they positive about? What concerns do they have?

- Are we on the right track with the scope of the product and prog-ress to date?

- What additional business context and priorities come to mind relevant to the initiative?

- Does the team have any "asks" of stakeholders? (This may include support, resources, or information.)

- What are your next steps? (Make commitments to follow-ups.)

Follow up by sending a short note to everyone who attended the demo. Summarize what you heard and surface any significant issues that were not shared. It is common in a large meeting, particularly when all levels of seniority are present, that not all concerns are raised.

- **Conduct your own QA**—Even if you have quality assurance team members supporting you, do not completely rely on them. Typically, QA is looking for technical issues and confirming that the product is working according to the specifications written. Two common issues tend to go unresolved unless you do your own QA:

  1. *Interaction and visual design polish*—If your product has a user-facing interface, it is possible that the intricate UI/UX and visual tweaks that make it intuitive and delightful were overlooked. This is not to say engineers don't care about these tweaks, but polish is often very hard to specify and communicate in designs. It is also challenging to know what will work for the user until you try it out.

  2. *Hidden requirements*—Even the best product managers won't catch everything the first time. You may realize you're missing edge cases. It is common to find, after using your product, that features don't make as much sense as you'd thought or work quite the way you imagined in your head.

  Recruit your designer and some engineers to help you conduct this review. And your demo is a strong candidate for some more robust usability testing with prospective customers.

  Now, though, is not the time to change user stories already completed—these are new requirements for future iterations and new estimates.

4. Retrospective or Post–Mortem

An often overlooked tool is the retrospective. It enables the opportunity to inspect, learn, and adapt your processes and ways of working. There is always room for improvement. The retrospective provides a safe space for the team to share recent experience while it is still fresh in their minds.

The goal is to identify actionable and constructive improvements. Generally, you wish to uncover:

- what went right and what went wrong,

- the issues' underlying causes, and

- ways to avoid similar situations in the future.

Structure your retrospective carefully. Participants should avoid getting personal and stick to the facts. Sometimes teams get out of the office and go somewhere fun, to warm up and break down communication barriers.

You can start a retrospective by revisiting outcomes from the previous retrospective. What changes did you make, what worked, and what didn't? If the team did much better and the improvement became a new good habit, then celebrate. If it didn't, discuss why and resolve to tackle it again. (Chances are, if it was the highest-priority opportunity for process improvement last time, it probably still is.)

Then discuss what went well and what didn't go well in the cycle just completed. Remarks should be captured on a whiteboard or in a shared document. Themes tend to come up again later.

Here are two popular approaches:

Methodology 1—Did/didn't work:

a. *Green post-it*: What worked [continue doing]
b. *Orange post-it*: What didn't [stop doing]

(If you prefer, you can add a third category, "start," to create a "start-stop-continue" list.)

Methodology 2—The 4Ls:

a. *Liked*: What did the team enjoy? What processes, decisions, collaborations, or activities went right? Emphasize the positive.
b. *Learned*: What new things did the team learn? Perhaps it was something surprising and unexpectedly effective that you want to do again.
c. *Lacked*: What were the things that were tried but could have gone better? Perhaps a decision was made but turned out to be the wrong one or was made too late.
d. *Longed for*: What things were missing that the team desired? Perhaps some activity, process, tool, or data was absent.

A simple four-step structure will ensure maximum and equal participation from all involved. Use post-its and a whiteboard, or an online document you can all share and simultaneously edit.

1. **Individual brainstorm**—Write down as many thoughts as you can. Try to make equal quantities in the different categories (don't make them all bad thoughts, for example).

Areas for Retrospective Brainstorming

In the event your team is stuck or needs encouragement to be frank and forthright on where they observed issues, use this simple checklist to spark ideas.

- ☐ Clarity of vision
- ☐ Roles and responsibilities
- ☐ Context and supporting data
- ☐ Scope and specifications
- ☐ Designs and user validation
- ☐ Assumptions and risks
- ☐ Planning
- ☐ Timeline, throughput, and velocity
- ☐ Quality and testing
- ☐ Tools and documentation
- ☐ Collaboration and communication
- ☐ Focus (distractions) and priorities
- ☐ Decision-making
- ☐ Meetings
- ☐ Resourcing

2. **Roundtable**—Take turns to elaborate briefly on one to three ideas (doing three at once speeds up the process).

3. **Group similar ideas**—Find any themes or related issues that emerged.

4. **Vote and commit**—Decide on a few areas (no more than three) to improve, and commit to change.

Unless the team is very high-functioning, addressing just a few actionable and high-impact issues each time is all that is required. Communication and awareness improve merely by sharing feedback on other issues. One or two committed next steps provide the team focus and something they can all agree on fixing. Elect an owner to drive improvements, adding them into subsequent initiatives until the new habits are adopted or no longer relevant.

CHAPTER 9

Navigate Challenging Trade-Offs

Generate value quickly and sustainably by managing the tension between scope, time, quality, and resources.

What you'll learn in this chapter

1 The ability to comprehend the inherent trade-offs necessary between scope, speed-to-market, quality, and resources when building technology products.

2 Techniques to manage stakeholder expectations for project scope and delivery dates, and effectively communicate trade-off decisions with stakeholders.

3 Tips on how to avoid the hidden impact on your product and your engineering team's morale that can come if you fail to address technical debt over time.

Managing Trade-Offs Is a Balancing Act

Given a finite amount of resources (in cost and personnel), a product manager must balance three parameters: scope, time, and quality. Relaxing or tightening any one of these parameters necessitates tightening or relaxing, respectively, the constraints on either or both of the other parameters.

Scope includes the features and functionality you will provide your users, and the tools, reporting, and systems required for the business to operate the product. You can capture scope as an organized backlog of the validated features and technology needed for successful product delivery.

Richer functionality is usually considered desirable, so that you delight customers and generate greater business value. Too little scope, and your product might not meet your customers' expectations, or you may fail to anticipate and handle edge cases, which lead to user confusion. However, including too much scope can delay your delivering *anything*, increase technical and usability complexity, and de-focus and frustrate your team (especially if scope is added later in the development cycle).

Time is the time-to-market, or the speed at which you deliver a functioning product that will serve the stated goals of the business and your customers. It is measured in *elapsed time* and not resource allocation (such as person-days).

A faster time-to-market is usually considered desirable because you deliver solutions to customers' problems more quickly (unlocking direct business value). In turn, this also frees up resources to start working on other projects (avoiding opportunity cost). However, at a certain point, accelerating time-to-market begins to take its toll on the usefulness of the product—compromising functionality, usability, and quality—and team morale.

Quality concerns the health of underlying technology and systems supporting the product (their interoperability, robustness, stability, scalability, recoverability, maintainability, reusability, and learnability). Think of meeting design standards for user experience (usability) as another quality consideration.

Not surprisingly, greater quality is generally considered desirable. You don't want to give end users new features if they are only going to be frustrated by instability or performance issues. You also do not want your development team wasting inordinate time addressing bugs or refactoring existing code when they could be efficiently creating additional business value. You should not expect perfect quality right from the start either; this

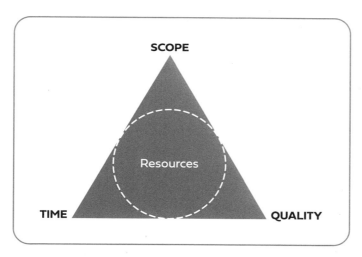

FIGURE 9.1 *A scope-time-quality-resources trade-off framework*

leads to overinvestment or "gold-plating." It may be better to get the product into the hands of your users so that you can learn where the real issues
are and improve your product's quality incrementally over time.

Figure 9.1 is a simple framework to visualize the balance between these
three concepts as a triangle, the area of which is equal to the total amount
of work you can do given a set of resources. Increase the resources, and
(theoretically, at least) the area of the triangle can grow to increase
throughput. When the area of the triangle must remain constant given a set
amount of resources, however, then any change in scope, quality, or
time-to-market will necessitate a resulting constraint on one or both of the
other parameters.

Many versions of the framework are used in industry—some using
resources/cost as one of the points in the triangle (with quality holding
constant) and others using a four-point framework (resources, scope, speed,
and quality). These frameworks all have much of the same premise—you
cannot optimize for all, or even most, parameters. Trade-offs are inevitable,
and it is your responsibility as product manager to preempt possible issues,
highlight choices, and respond with solutions when compromises are
required.

Although simple in concept, managing trade-offs is one of the most
complex responsibilities you will face, as every situation tends to present a
unique and nuanced set of constraints and challenges. In this chapter,
I will introduce principles and techniques to increase your likelihood of

making good decisions while maintaining visibility into possible future issues.

What Is Over-Scoping and How Do You Manage It?

Increasing scope to incorporate more features can reduce your ability to ensure a high-quality deliverable. It can also extend the time until launch. As illustrated in **Figure 9.2**, while delivering "more" might seem customer-centric, it can backfire—you may frustrate customers if the product becomes harder to use or if you make them wait longer to receive any functionality at all. Focusing on fewer features allows you to execute faster and with higher technical quality and usability.

Specifically, *scope creep* is a process where scope is added after a project has been defined and kicked off. Not all scope creep is bad. Sometimes you genuinely uncover needs that you did not or could not determine at the start of a project. The key is to minimize the sources for unnecessary or later-stage scope creep while managing an objective and collaborative process for necessary scope inclusion.

Let's look at how over-scoping happens, and how you can address it:

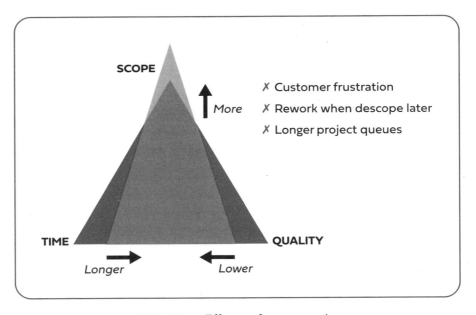

FIGURE 9.2 *Effects of over-scoping*

1. Initially Over-Scoping a Product Initiative, Cutting Later

Many product managers generate a long list of requirements and negotiate for as much as possible to be slotted into the time available. Trying to deliver more features and functionality may seem desirable, but it can be a trap. You'll end up with a tightly-packed schedule, putting pressure on your team and overpromising on what you can realistically deliver. Invariably, well into development, it becomes apparent that scope must be dramatically reduced to make a deadline.

Is more scope inherently better? No—less is more:

- **User experience complexity**—What you leave out, as much as what you put in, is what makes a product elegant and easy to use. Too many secondary features make it harder for users to achieve their primary goals. Extra features become distractions: users take longer to learn to use a product and to discover where the features are, and they may have to take more steps to complete their tasks and make more decisions than necessary. Added to this, when there are too many variables, user validation becomes harder: you wonder, "Is poor usability due to confusion between too many feature options, or is the feature itself the problem?"

- **Greater technical complexity**—More scope creates code complexity and a higher likelihood of errors. Bug counts rise, performance lags, cross-functional dependencies occur, and you find it harder to isolate where a problem has occurred. Every piece of functionality you add has to be maintained. That means you will later spend resources supporting features that may not deliver much value—taking you away from other more valuable activities.

- **Longer customer wait times**—Delivering *something* earlier is usually better than delivering *everything* later. Over-scoped projects tend to delay giving customers some satisfaction, in the hope of making a bigger splash. Most customers prefer that you address their top priorities quickly, even if that means delaying other requests. If you wait too long to deliver something to the customer, pressure mounts for you to move faster. Partially complete or broken features are often dropped at the last minute, disappointing stakeholders and customers regardless.

- **Wasted effort and rework**—As well as time spent in scope elaboration and negotiation meetings, it is likely the team has created

Avoiding Over-Scoping, Later Cutting

- Use prototypes and user testing to challenge your scope assumptions. Look to eliminate or reduce features as much as validate them. (**Chapter 5**)

- Use the "top-down" specification approach to constrain scope tightly from the outset. No should-haves or nice-to-haves, only must-haves. Maintain a list of items that has been agreed as out-of-scope for later reference, should an idea come up again. (**Chapter 6**)

- Create your product backlog early and groom it often to create visibility to known scope. Brainstorm to surface and preempt possible requirements that would otherwise later arise as scope creep. Then carefully critique and prioritize against your goals. (**Chapter 7**)

- Split releases—deliver new scope in smaller increments to provide reoccurring value. Said another way, deliver smaller, regular updates at a frequency suitable to your customers. (**Chapter 10**)

- Promote simplicity as a product principle in your organization. Work to optimize your product interfaces for a lack of clutter. Revisit existing features to ensure they're being used by a large enough number of your customers to justify continuation.

designs, completed validation, and built technical infrastructure to support features that aren't really needed or (due to time constraints) won't be built. Cutting scope later doesn't mean just dropping features; it often means that the user experience team needs to redesign the user interface and that engineering needs to re-architect, to account for the eliminated features.

- **Opportunity cost**—For each piece of scope prioritized in the current project, there is a future project in the queue waiting for resources to be available. You can't address your future project's important needs while you add features and functionality of lesser value to your current project. The longer they go unaddressed, the more the urgency increases. In addition, new bugs, issues, and ideas will be added to the queue, and delays will grow longer. And your business will suffer from what is called opportunity cost—the cost of not addressing issues might be lost customers and delayed revenue.

2. New Stakeholder and Customer Requests that Aren't Aligned with the Goals

As the product takes shape, customers and stakeholders will provide feedback. Much of this feedback should be incorporated if it improves the agreed-upon outcomes. Sometimes feedback is not aligned with the original project goals but includes new ideas and feature requests. Or perhaps the request is aligned, but it requires more effort and delivers less impact than features the team has already decided to work on. The later this occurs in a project's delivery schedule, the more disruptive it can be.

Unfortunately, new requests are often easy to justify and to tack onto a project in progress. Senior stakeholders or influential customers may see your project as an opportunity to include something they have long desired. They can be hard to say no to. As such, requests circumvent the same objective, rigorous scrutiny that would have been applied at the beginning of a project.

Instead, new requests should be held to the same standard as anything considered at the start. Know and articulate your goals—where you need to be to win the customer or fulfill the vision. That will make it is easier to say no to incoming requests and your own ideas. Failure to do so may result in the following:

- **A launch delay**—Each new item of scope added into the product backlog necessitates that you renegotiate delivery dates. While any new scope item might have minimal impact (adding a few days here

· ·

De-scoping Can Be Removing Features that Aren't Being Used

A client was rebuilding its core mobile product from the ground up, moving the same feature set to an entirely new technology platform. The plan was to rebuild every feature currently in the service: the rebuild would take eight months.

Unfortunately, the old technology platform was challenging to support. A fast-growing subscriber base, moreover, was placing it under more and more stress.

We conducted a discovery process to "de-scope," looking at actual usage data for individual features and conducting user surveys. Instead of having to rebuild everything they already had, the data showed they could safely shed 30 percent of the existing features because users weren't using them at sufficient quantity or frequency.

The client saved several months in development. More than this, the user experience was simplified (reducing technical and testing complexity, and making the product more intuitive for the end user). And what was next on the roadmap (a new revenue opportunity) would start much sooner.

· ·

Handling Stakeholder and Customer Requests

- Say no nicely—capture ideas in a backlog for later consideration (to show you listened), then reiterate your goals and current focus. (**Chapter 2**)

- Default is out, not in—assume a piece of scope *isn't* required and set a high bar for justifying why it needs inclusion. Use the same ruthless prioritization approaches to requests as you did when prioritizing your original plan. (**Chapter 4**)

- Make the impact of each new inclusion clear on the launch timeline or on previously agreed-on requirements within your backlog. Often, once stakeholders see the fallout, they change their minds.

- Left-field requests are common during customer and internal demos. Always start with reaffirming and validating project goals and use them as a mechanism to filter and contextualize new asks. ("How does that align with what we set out to do?") (**Chapter 8**).

- Don't become a source of change requests yourself. Despite your influential position, product managers must be disciplined and focused. Add your ideas to your idea backlog for later consideration rather than adding them to a project in mid-flight.

and there), many additions can substantially extend a launch date. Sometimes, the impact and the implied trade-off is unclear. When it later becomes clear, stakeholders push to avoid delay and ask the team to figure out how to fit it all in without affecting the schedule.

- **Analysis paralysis**—Even if faced with pushback when requesting new scope, stakeholders may continue to negotiate for its inclusion by asking the product manager to complete a "small" amount of analysis (such as high-level requirements and potential schedule and resourcing impacts) before finalizing a decision. Sounds perfectly reasonable, right? Well, unfortunately, no. Defining, planning, validating, and estimating are not free services—done correctly, they require resources and take the team away from completing the current priorities. The very act of context-switching means your team loses focus and gets confused as to what the goals are.

- **Lower return-on-investment** (ROI)—When giving a project the go-ahead, decision-makers usually consider it a good investment, where the business benefits greatly outweigh the costs to build it. Adding scope after the "green-light" decision circumvents your company's governance mechanisms, increases project costs, and delays realization of benefits. It weighs down ROI, making the project much less attractive—so much so that it might not have been approved in the first place.

3. New Necessary Scope, Not Evident at the Start, Needs to Be Added during a Project

It is usual, early on in a project, to understand some scope well but to underestimate the extent of the work yet to be identified. Unfortunately, most teams are overly optimistic in assessing how much scope is known and forecasting how quickly they can implement what is known.

Examples of scope commonly discovered later include the following:

- Refined and new requirements that you can identify only as the product takes shape through customer and stakeholder testing and demos.

- Significant but less-apparent use-cases, exceptions, error-handling, and edge-cases that manifest themselves as the product is tested internally or through user feedback.

- New technologies with high uncertainty that require "invention," with proofs-of-concept, before you can establish scope and effort.

- Seemingly straightforward requirements where no one fully appreciates the complexity until details are understood.

- Internal requirements from business and technology support teams, which manifest when demoing the emerging product.

- Requisite integration with tools and back-end systems (particularly legacy technologies), the complexity of which wasn't obvious earlier.

- Unanticipated dependencies on other teams or technologies, which are not readily in the team's control.

- Time addressing bugs.

The following problems can result if you don't carefully manage this type of necessary scope inclusion:

- **Constant schedule slippage**—If you're in a situation where you've created and communicated a schedule based on the best-case

Managing the Inclusion of Necessary New Scope

- Get buy-in from stakeholders early to ensure you've thought about your project from their perspective. Otherwise non-functional, internal requirements may become evident only later. (**Chapter 2**)

- Use the early stage of a project to focus on product discovery and customer validation rather than jumping into implementation. (**Chapter 5**)

- The top-down specification framework establishes and communicates goals and high-level scope from the beginning of the project. Consider additional needs based only on new market, customer, or business information that wasn't clear at the start as well as needs aligned with your stated goals. (**Chapter 6**)

- To preempt your team from becoming frustrated by apparent scope creep, explicitly set the expectation early on that new necessary scope *will* be identified through validation and *will* be refined through collaboration during execution. Regularly reinforce this as a team norm. Agree that scope changes might mean you need to renegotiate existing delivery commitments.

- Create a well-documented "scope intake" approach to consider new requirements against goals, current priorities, and timeline. Make this the only way new scope gets added to a project (and ask your team not to work on anything not filtered this way).

- Hold retrospectives regularly to identify approaches to improving the level of early scope detection for the future. (**Chapter 8**)

scenario of knowing all scope up front, then each discovery becomes another slippage announcement.

- **Negative perception of project clarity**—It is unreasonable to expect product managers, designers, or engineers to know 100 percent of all scope at the start of a project. It is also unfair to refer to the discovery of new *necessary* scope as "scope creep," yet that may be how it is perceived. The implication is that the product manager should have done a better job defining requirements at the outset. This might impact the product manager's reputation and create dissatisfaction among engineers sensitive to changes midstream.

    Note though, failure to follow due process—such as prioritizing ideas rigorously, completing specifications, conducting regular user

Early Stakeholder Buy-In Is Critical to Avoid Scope Creep

A product manager on my team was launching functionality to help users build their own customized video playlists. The idea was to help them discover and schedule educational content in the sequence and times that made sense to their learning goals. The business objective was to increase stickiness and engagement and, in turn, improve subscriber retention.

We were two weeks away from launch when the product manager held a pre-launch review. A broad group of stakeholders across the company attended—but many were hearing about and seeing the functionality demoed for the very first time.

Far from excited, the marketing and customer service teams both reacted with surprise and concern. The meeting turned into a discussion about delaying the release until they had enough time to consider all the implications. They started identifying new features they wanted to make customer support easier.

The product manager had not spent enough time building broad support and ensuring voices were heard—and now the project looked like it was going to be blown out by last-minute requirements.

Several senior people had to intervene and work through the issues—as it turned out, very few of the new requirements were necessary, but it took a lot to convince the other teams to implement workarounds instead. All this last-minute scrambling could have been avoided with a more thorough buy-in process to garner support and discover hidden requirements.

validation, or building a deep and thorough backlog—is laziness. If you are changing priorities or discovering requirements that could easily have been anticipated earlier, do not blame your team for losing respect for you and becoming frustrated at the addition of new scope.

How to Handle Making Delivery-Timeline Commitments

Companies may set deadlines for good reasons. For example, you may have the following:

- Customer dependencies that require your project be delivered by a certain date, to manage a complex implementation or roll-out.

- A cyclical nature in your business, such as for e-commerce services or enterprise businesses where sales tend to peak or ebb in certain months.

- A marketing event or major conference at which you have a set opportunity to unveil the product for the world to see.

Deadlines can also be helpful and necessary:

- They allow the organization to plan on other long-lead activities such as launching your product into the market, an advertising program, and communicating with and rolling it out to customers.

- They increase the predictability of when the engineering and design team can start working on the next priorities.

- They ensure that new improvements are regularly released.

- They allow your company to manage dependencies between teams and technologies.

- They create accountability and a sense of urgency among team members.

However, some product managers and stakeholders set fixed dates that are aggressive and arbitrary, often in the hope of motivating the team to work harder. This behavior is unfortunately endemic in the technology industry. Yet, as illustrated in **Figure 9.3**, if you set tight and immovable deliverable dates that are incompatible with the expected scope, available resources, or quality requirements, you might inadvertently cause the team to

- cut too many features, even those critical to users, disappointing customers;

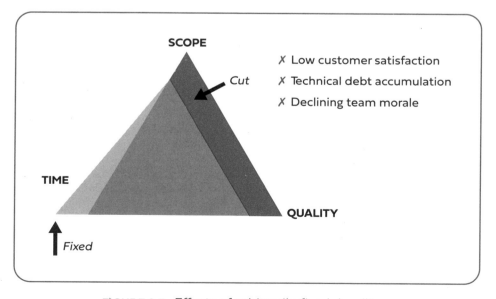

FIGURE 9.3 *Effects of arbitrarily fixed deadlines*

"Under-Promise, Over-Deliver" Doesn't Work

"Under-promise, over-deliver" is a catch phrase that sounds like you're performing. You pad scope estimates and communicate timelines that are too conservative because you want yourself and your team to look good when you beat them.

Unfortunately, in taking this approach, you are actually doing the following:

- Playing politics: this approach is manipulative, as it is in your interest and not in the interest of customers or the business.

- Delaying other priorities: even if you finish early, that might mean other teams aren't ready.

- Making other teams scramble: they have built their own plans around your communicated timeline.

Over time, your timelines won't be taken seriously. They'll start discounting them with the thought "Oh, that really means four weeks instead of six!"

Estimates must be transparent—including contingency and confidence levels—and based on analysis and facts that you can share.

- skip time in validating the product with customers and increase the likelihood of usability issues and incomplete features;

- under-invest in quality to ensure a bug-free product and lower technical debt; and

- lose pride in their work, lose motivation, and feel unappreciated—knowing they will have to come back to address issues later.

There needs to be some comfort with ambiguity in your organization and a willingness to focus on value-driven outcomes rather than delivery milestones. While it is reasonable to be expected to make time-based commitments, you must manage why, how, and when you make them.

1. Negotiate to Complete Enough Product Discovery to Increase Confidence When Later Establishing Dates

Early in a project's life, you will typically uncover things you didn't think of, and scope (and outstanding questions) will grow in size. There will usually be tension between the business, which desires to set a firm delivery date as early as possible, and a product development team wanting to avoid making commitments until they can be fully confident in their schedule.

The trick is to find a balance. Negotiate for the ability to delay date commitments long enough for sufficient discovery and validation, so you can understand the scope and effort required to deliver a quality product to the market. Sufficient discovery and validation includes

- doing customer validation (prototypes and testing),

- creating and elaborating on specifications and requirements,

- pursuing technical exploration (eliminating key technical risks, planning architecture, and proof-of-concept on new technologies),

- completing high-level effort estimates for known scope, and

- developing a resourcing plan to deliver your solution successfully.

Here are some good ways of knowing you have moved from a "discovery" mode into a more predictable "delivery" mode:

1. The rate at which you identify substantial new scope slows, falling well below the rate at which you are completing work. That is, you are delivering more requirements than you are finding new ones to add.

2. Your team's throughput (velocity, if you are using Scrum) has stabilized. You are in a much better position to confidently set dates because you can base your estimates on experience and on remaining scope.

2. Build Conservatism into Your Project Plan to Address Unexpected Issues

Do not expect a development team to be willing to make an aggressive date commitment without "all" the scope clearly articulated. However, you don't want to be required to create an inflexible, detailed requirements document upfront, negating opportunities to adapt to what you learn from team collaboration and customer validation efforts.

Even after you complete your initial product discovery, you have probably only uncovered roughly 60 to 70 percent of probable scope. Moreover, it is natural to be optimistic about how quickly you will deliver against that.

There are two things to consider when establishing a delivery date for your project: (1) the date (or more correctly, a date range), and (2) your confidence level in hitting that date. When you must discuss timelines with stakeholders, do so in the following way:

Negotiating Time to Complete Discovery

- In stakeholder discussions, define and emphasize measurable value-driven outcomes rather than delivery dates as your primary metric of success. Explain your unproven scope assumptions and your need to validate them before establishing deadlines.

- Set a "date for a date"—agree with stakeholders that, for a period, you'll be in discovery mode, at the end of which you will feel confident that you can come back to them with likely delivery dates.

- At the start of the project, put all possible scope into your backlog, whether clear and understood or just "placeholders" for areas to explore. Give each a high-level estimate so that you are aware of how much total potential work there is to do. (See *"Getting a Product Backlog Started"* in **Chapter 7**.)

- During the kick-off, explicitly declare you are in "product discovery mode." Identify tasks that will maximize learning, risk mitigation, and customer validation over all else, such as building prototypes and technical investigation.

- Set interim milestones, rather than a single date, to deliver progressively against a broader goal. Each provides a check-in point in which you can revisit commitments with stakeholders.

- **Include a contingency**—Explicitly budget for effort toward unexpected scope and issues that will invariably occur. The best way to get stakeholders to agree to this is to gather data on previous projects—past performance is an excellent predictor of the future. (Keep in mind this might be a sensitive subject if it reflects poorly on previous owners.) By looking at initial planned versus actual delivery dates, you can get an estimation for a percentage-based contingency. If you do not have the data, then allowing for 20 percent extra time over the planned schedule is a good place to start. Be transparent about your contingency budget; don't just pad your estimates.

- **Provide a date range**—Rather than a specific date, provide dates for average, best, and low-end cases. Alternatively, rather than setting a hard date in the middle of the month, you can communicate that delivery will occur anytime over that whole month.

Communicating Date Slippage

While no one is happy about a delay, stakeholders usually understand that building products is a complex process. They want to help in any way they can—by removing organizational barriers or managing customer expectations, for instance.

The three most important things to remember:

1. Deliver news early—don't delay in the hope the issue will resolve itself. Waiting will only make it harder for the company to adapt.

2. Deliver the message straight and don't make excuses or blame others. Stick to the facts and don't make it personal.

3. If at all possible, provide a path forward (or several options). Even if some impact is unavoidable, provide a workaround or action plan. Usually, the stakeholder will jump quickly on board and will trust you to address the issues the best you can.

- **Include a confidence level**—Anytime you share your timelines or delivery dates, include a confidence level (or set of caveats), which your development team has agreed to. A good rule of thumb is to communicate several dates at a 50 percent-plus and an 80 percent-plus confidence level (but this will depend on your culture and audience). Occasionally, you might hear a stakeholder—in a moment of optimism—mention only your earlier date, omitting the upper range and confidence level entirely. If you do, gently remind them.

At the start of your project, your date ranges are broad and your confidence low, but this will improve as you learn and execute more. As the project progresses, closely monitor how quickly your team is working through the backlog to increase the level of fidelity for date estimates. At some point, you'll be in the position to be highly confident about a specific date and the business can start coordinating other activities toward it. Make a commitment too early, and the chances of disappointment are high; too late, and the business has no time to plan supporting activities (marketing, customer roll-out, and management of other dependencies).

3. Build a Sense of Urgency through Context Setting, Rather Than Aggressive Deadlines—and Actively Manage Stakeholder Expectations

As a product manager, you are in an unenviable position. You have stakeholder pressure to speed up delivery of your projects while also playing a critical role in protecting the team from distraction and anxiety. In this situation, product managers tend to exhibit one of three behaviors:

- Product Managers who *amplify* stakeholder concerns genuinely have considerable ownership and passion for their products and desperately want to please stakeholders and customers. Unfortunately, they also tend to turn even the smallest concern into a crisis for their team. They may set aggressive dates or interim deliverables, perhaps checking in on their team's task-completion status frequently. No one enjoys working with a taskmaster.

Tale of Two CEOs

The CEO for a community product (UGC, or user-generated content) was incredibly frustrated at his team for a lengthy delay in the delivery of tools and automation to materially eliminate spammers (removing fake accounts or robot-generated marketing messages) from the platform. The team was understandably feeling under pressure—it was a complicated system that had many moving parts (complex data analysis, high-velocity database transactions, lots of edge cases). They had gotten bogged down in the sheer enormity of the task. Meanwhile, the problem was getting worse, and the CEO was pushing for an aggressive timeline commitment.

The key? Pick one specific, high-urgency use case to define, build a solution for, and ship. Not only did it take just six weeks to complete—but the proof-of-concept also provided valuable insight into scope and technology needs, gave the team much-needed confidence in their approach, and got the CEO off their back.

Contrast that with a CEO at an enterprise software company. His team was months into building a system to manage online customization and sales for automobiles. The team tended to be overconfident with estimates, only to run into complexities, blow the latest deadline, and make excuses. This tested the CEO, who was not known for being patient.

With the team unable to set a deadline they could commit to, he demanded the team ship on a date of his choosing. They shipped on time, but it was a poor-quality product, with the team then working overtime to fix the self-inflicted problems. Had the team sought to demonstrate progress and a sense of urgency, make thoughtful but conservative estimates, and manage the CEO's expectations, they might have avoided these problems.

Balancing Stakeholder Expectations and Team Motivation

- Employ strategies for setting context to encourage your team's sense of urgency. Help them to understand the "why" and see the value in their work and its impact on customers. (Chapter 2)

- Ask questions if progress seems behind. But be sure you don't become a micromanager who is always checking up on task completion, especially mid-sprint.

- Avoid getting caught off-guard making ill-considered date commitments in meetings, stakeholder conversations, and especially in front of customers. The only thing worse than being put on the spot is responding with an aggressive "crowd-pleasing" date that you'll later regret. Rehearse your answer.

- When referring to dates, call them target or planning dates instead of launch, delivery, or release dates.

- Be particularly wary of what dates are communicated externally. Keep scope and dates vague (at the monthly or quarterly level).

- Some product managers simply act as a conduit to *pass-on* unfiltered communication to and from their team. While being highly communicative, they do little to shield the team. They add little value to their communication as they do not themselves take on the stakeholder management challenge, leaving their team exposed to too much interference.

- Some product managers are good at *absorbing* and positively channeling stakeholder communication. They stoically represent their team's work to stakeholders and protect their teams from too much direct stakeholder interference. They trust that their teams can rise to the occasion to address challenges provided they get the time and resources they need. They choose carefully what stakeholder concerns to communicate back to their team and how they do so.

Absorbers are the most effective product managers, providing air cover and not being overly date-driven. Most of the time, the team is left to do its best to solve problems and works toward a final deliverable with a sense of urgency (and without burning out).

But should you always be an absorber? In rare situations, you might want to act differently. When all else fails, a small (but not uncontrolled) crisis can jolt people into action. Do not overprotect the team—when a message must be loud and clear, it is okay to pass it along unfiltered.

Usually, however, instead of pushing the team to commit to an aggressive scope or dates, provide frequent business updates that maintain a sense of urgency. Remind them that what they are doing is important and why and reiterate that you're counting on them.

On the flip side, you must set and reset stakeholder expectations. Provide them with frequent status updates and reaffirm commitments previously made. If anything looks like it might slip, be honest as early as possible, so they can adjust their plans or help you. Come to them with recommendations. Never hide bad news.

The Challenges of Managing Quality and Technical Debt

Quality issues tend to arise in four key areas:

1. The customer cannot easily use the solution. This may be because you cut too many corners in creating and validating user interactions, trying to make the product quicker to engineer.

2. The engineers were not given enough time to design and architect their code and thus did not make the software easy to write and maintain or flexible enough to change. This makes future development costlier and more time-consuming than expected.

3. There was insufficient testing to ensure the software did what it was expected to, leading to excessive unanticipated issues once live.

4. You did not give due consideration to possible post-launch issues that can happen at scale. These issues might include poor performance or failure to build adequate tracking into the solution (making issue diagnosis difficult).

It's easy to overlook quality issues because they are tricky to anticipate and tend to manifest later in the product lifecycle, often well after launch. It's also easy to sacrifice quality as the impact isn't easy to quantify and far from immediate.

The most significant challenge in balancing scope and time-to-market with the inherent quality of the underlying technology and systems supporting the product is that poor technical quality only really becomes apparent at these times:

- In the final stages of the development process, during performance and systems-wide testing, which surfaces excessive bugs and extends your planned time for testing (*interoperability*).

- Early in a product's life, when customers discover edge cases and bugs you didn't anticipate (*robustness*).

- In production, either as the product slows or fails unexpectedly or uses excessive system resources after launch (*stability*) and, notably, at "peak" loads (*scalability*).

- After a failure, which tests how quickly you can restore a service (*recoverability*).

- When you attempt to build upon the product, such as fixing bugs, you require significant effort (*maintainability*). Alternatively, building new features upon existing features takes much longer than expected due to refactoring (*reusability*).

- When engineers cross-train other engineers unfamiliar with the system, and it takes an excessive amount of time to come up to speed (*learnability*). Poor quality and lack of documentation are likely culprits when you notice the same senior-level engineers must be involved in almost all projects touching technology areas in which they have deep expertise.

Technical debt is the total accumulation of all the small and large trade-offs and technology choices you have made in the past, all of which impact quality. As the name suggests, when technology matures and you continue to build on the shortcuts, left unaddressed, they accumulate as "debt."

As illustrated in **Figure 9.4**, many technology companies pay too little attention to quality, overvaluing new feature development and undervaluing the hidden effects of poor quality. Poor quality, however, doesn't just impact product performance; it also saps the morale of the team, which is forced to work in a challenging, hard-to-maintain, easy-to-break legacy technology environment. The team feels overworked, and they lack pride in their outcomes. Eventually, team members will start to leave.

To improve your ability to preempt quality issues:

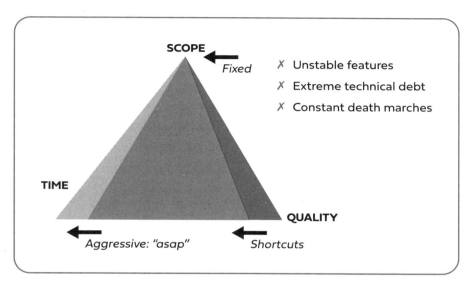

FIGURE 9.4 *Effects of consistently ignoring quality*

1. Include Time in the Project Plan for Architecture, Design, Code Review, and Thorough Testing

As a rule, engineering owns quality. Product management provides support by informing and respecting necessary quality activities and enabling adequate time and attention so engineering can achieve the following:

- Architect how the systems will work—considering past, current, and possible future needs.

- Learn new technologies and understand how legacy systems work—perhaps completing proofs-of-concept to decide the best approach.

- Design the technology, algorithms, and services (such as APIs).

- Conduct design and code reviews with one another.

- Cross-train and collaborate with other teams to share knowledge.

- Rewrite or extend older core components on which your new features will rely.

- Extend developer tools and scripts for repeatable code integration, testing, and deployment.

- Build in logging and automated tests and validate that code passes these tests.

- Complete performance, dependencies, and security testing.

- Fix bugs.

Budget for it. As a rough estimate, testing and debugging generally take about 30 to 50 percent of the time it takes to produce product or code in the first place (but your team can help guide you). Encourage the team to add technology tasks to the backlog to provide visibility and an opportunity to explicitly prioritize these needs.

Negotiate an appropriate investment in quality and scale given the lifecycle of your product and customer expectations. In general, engineering teams hate having to come back to re-engineer components, preferring instead to "get it right the first time." An initial product release ought to meet or exceed quality expectations, particularly if you grow faster than anticipated. In the rush to get to market, you don't want to make so many technology trade-offs that performance is unstable.

Be careful, however, not to overinvest in a fully-scaled solution too early when launching new or beta products that may not need the level of sophistication of more mature products. You still don't know if you are building a product of great value or not. As illustrated in **Figure 9.5**, ensuring the highest possible quality at all times can work against you. Over-emphasizing quality and scale at this point might prove very wasteful (delaying time-to-market and the opportunity to gather necessary customer feedback to guide your product's future, and consuming valuable resources) especially if the product later fails or evolves in a significantly different direction after the initial launch.

2. Involve Support Teams Early to Define Internal "Non–Functional" Requirements

In addition to involving your development team, involve technical operations, QA, business operations, and customer service teams early on. This will help you to achieve the following:

- Identify non-customer-facing and performance requirements that might not be immediately obvious.

- Head off last-minute delays when these teams uncover unanticipated needs in their ability to support your product.

- Help to "right-size" quality—get everyone on the same page regarding what is the sufficient, but not excessive, scale and support required.

Examples:

- What level of scale will you need? (Your expected growth in customers, database transactions, complex and hardware-intense functionality, availability.)

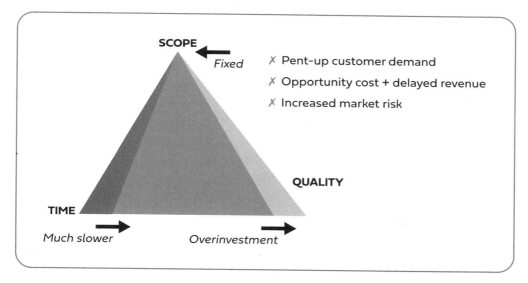

FIGURE 9.5 *Effects of overinvesting in high quality before it is warranted*

- How will the software be monitored once in production?

- What tools, metrics tracking and reporting systems are used by internal teams that must either be extended to support your product or tested for dependencies that might render them inoperable?

Too often, these teams are brought in too late without enough visibility to an upcoming product release, support tools, documentation, monitoring, hardware, or test automation.

3. Gradually Eliminate Technical Debt

Too much technical debt will eventually slow the pace of development and make even simple functionality far costlier to build. Unfortunately, debugging, refactoring (making existing code better), documenting, and rewriting (replacing existing code) are essentially engineering tasks that have no immediate, apparent business benefit. As a result, it is easily undervalued, overlooked, and deferred.

Examples of technical debt:

- Reported bugs left unaddressed.

- Gaps in automated-test code coverage.

- Duplicated code (for example, having APIs that do, more or less, similar things, or choosing to write new code rather than reuse existing code).

Managing Technical Debt over the Lifecycle

When you're working on a feature for the first time, your emphasis should be on getting it to market quickly. This may require quality trade-offs, as your imperative should be to deliver something to customers from which you can start learning. Should the feature fail, you won't have wasted work trying to scale it or build in flexibility.

During development, engineers should take thoughtful shortcuts in areas where this is better for the business but with the promise that they can come back to fix them later. Many product managers destroy this goodwill, however, by not respecting technical debt and budgeting for cleanup work afterward.

Instead, use these techniques to show you're a good partner:

- Follow up each release with a period of clean-up, especially immediately after launch, when issues are more likely to occur. (**Chapter 10**)

- Dedicate occasional projects purely to technical priorities or "feature hardening." Some companies create themed sprints to ensure some balance, such as dedicated "feature sprints," "customer request sprints," or "technology sprints."

- Don't just fix issues with new features. Periodically address some bugs and usability irritants for features that are already live in production. Avoid addressing low-priority bugs, however—no one likes bugs, but, honestly, many of them don't matter. Fix those that do.

- Ask engineering to provide quality metrics that you can show stakeholders alongside product metrics. This will allow you to highlight quality concerns, justifying further investment in fixing the underlying technology. Example quality metrics include automated test code coverage, performance, uptime, and bug counts.

- Old, unused code that once served a purpose.

- Shortcuts to get a product out quicker (if you ask for something to be delivered earlier, you might hear an engineer quip, "Do you want it done fast or right?").

- Older code languages and practices from the past that do not reflect modern-day approaches.

- The natural variance that occurs when many coders are involved, whether junior or advanced (each will have a slightly different approach to solving the problem at hand, and some, perhaps many, may no longer be at your company to provide insight or training).

- Inefficient database transactions, memory leaks, and CPU usage, all of which hog resources.

- Inadequate or missing documentation, such as comments in the code, release notes, and deployment/support instructions.

- Unexpected dependencies between systems or challenges (a lack of modularity and flexibility).

- Legacy systems, perhaps even those considered best-of-breed in their time, that have now been superseded (possibly among the hardest technical debt issue to address, as replacing deeply integrated legacy systems is akin to performing a heart transplant).

Some level of technical debt is manageable and indeed desirable. Accumulating some debt means you are making decisions to go faster—to get something out to your customers or to try an idea out before deciding to commit to serious investment in it. The problem arises when you don't give engineering opportunities to "pay off" the debt at a later stage.

Recognize that technical debt is a ticking time bomb. Collaborate with your engineering team to invest sufficiently in its removal. How much time should you budget for this? A good rule of thumb is to expect to invest 20 percent of developer time in the activity—but the time you need will vary with how much debt you have already accumulated and how mature the underlying system is.

Adding Resources May Not Be the Easy Answer

In theory, you can relax a project's scope, timeline, or quality constraints by increasing the budget for resources, usually by introducing additional developers. As shown in **Figure 9.6**, imagine extra resources making the scope-time-quality triangle larger and more flexible to meet the needs of each parameter. If a team is in a situation where it is unable to relax any of the first three constraints to deliver a quality product within a set timeframe, then adding resources may achieve this goal.

However, three critical considerations suggest that adding resources is rarely a viable trade-off:

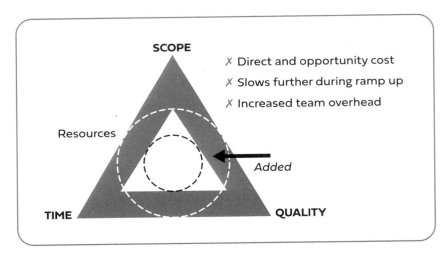

FIGURE 9.6 *Effects of adding resources to a project that is already late*

- **Increased direct cost**—Adding resources can significantly increase a project's budget. Adding them late in a project typically comes with even higher direct costs since you need to bring on your most experienced talent or expensive vendors.

- **Opportunity cost**—When viewed across an entire organization, increasing resources for one project may starve something of equal importance elsewhere. Resource allocation is a zero-sum game—some project or business unit elsewhere loses the resources redirected to your project. Calculating the impact is complicated: you are either forgoing future growth or delaying resolution of an issue that will need addressing eventually (such as deferred maintenance). Redirecting resources may require re-prioritization of projects all over the company, and very senior people might need to make those decisions.

- **Brook's law**—Also known as the "mythical man-month" (from Fred Brooks's 1975 book of the same name),[10] Brook's law encapsulates the idea that bringing resources to a team already busy and behind in implementing a project can cause it to slow even further, well before you receive any benefit. Training, onboarding, context-switching, and increased communication overhead divert the team from working on the project as you bring new people up to speed.

If you must add resources to a project, then, be highly selective and thoughtful in doing so:

- **Focus new resources on targeted and isolated components**—For example, get them to work on features not already started, to review and test code completed by others, or to catch up on automated testing that might have fallen behind.

- **Make the changes as early as possible**—Adding resources earlier in the project will get a longer payback for your ramp-up cost.

- **Bring on team members of proven caliber**—Add people with deep experience in the code base, so that ramp-up is minimal.

- **Consider pair-programming**—Get new people to work closely with an existing team member so they can learn as they go and be less likely to slow down their colleagues.

Feeling the Effect of Resource Reallocation

A consumer mobile client wanted to accelerate its timeline improve user-engagement features, which, in turn, would increase revenue for the business. As a public company, it had made revenue projections to the market, assuming these features would have been available earlier. So further delays in delivery might prove detrimental to the share price.

Sacrificing quality wasn't an option either—millions of users depended on the service. Putting customer satisfaction at risk would only lead to even more revenue pressure later.

Time, quality, and scope were all fixed. The only option was an aggressive increase in resourcing to accelerate delivery. Senior management was very open to this and would support whatever was needed. That is, until they understood the knock-on effects:

1. Additional engineers would increase total company R&D costs by 15 percent when R&D costs were already considered too high for a public company in its space.

2. They would have to pull experienced talent from across the organization away from other projects (backfilling those projects with new and more-junior engineers). These projects were also of paramount importance, both for increasing revenues and longer-term strategy.

In the end, the project got a few more people, but the impact would have been too significant to implement the full plan. The features launched well behind schedule but, despite the negative impact, the alternative would have been worse.

Common Organizational Challenges that Make Managing Trade-Offs Harder

Here are some specific situations you might find yourself in that make driving trade-off discussions even more challenging—with some high-level strategies that may help you to address them. Recognize that, if faced, these situations may be over-constrained and imbedded in the company culture—and you can only do your best.

REACTING TO ONE-OFF CLIENT REQUESTS

When deal- or sales-driven, scope and dates are commonly defined up front (particularly if there is a legal commitment), and they are subject to a client's demands or schedule. You may face very specific requests and customizations by a top client or prospect, communicated through the sales or business development team, and these may be required to win a deal.

Counter strategy In these instances, always endeavor to get involved early in any discussions that will dictate fixed commitments for your team—if possible, ask to be involved in setting deal terms or contracts. Recommend leaving scope high-level (and not prescriptive) and keeping timelines broad. Ensure stakeholders understand the required resources to support the requirements and the implications for other priorities, before client commitments are finalized.

To ensure long-term maintainability, whenever building any solution for a single client, abstract scope and build it as a core feature of your product, which can serve multiple clients, and not as a "one-off" feature. Customizations are often quickly implemented with low quality, and future development of the platform either breaks what isn't a core part of your overall market solution or requires constant maintenance.

OPTIMIZING FOR SHORT-TERM GOALS

Businesses that emphasize hitting aggressive quarterly business targets and responding solely to incoming customer requests often do so at the detriment of quality and "bigger bets"—projects that, if successful, can generate break-out, outsized gains. Since longer-term investments do not deliver economic returns immediately, they give priority to projects likely to quickly increase sales and customers, even when these results are not sustainable.

Counter strategy Elevate longer-term, value-driven metrics and ask your engineering team to identify and report on quality parameters as a way to highlight their importance and level the playing field.

SEEKING A BIG-WIN

In startup companies, often before a major financing round, there will be a strong desire to demonstrate a "big win." This might be landing a new customer or delivering an impressive product capability. Larger companies may face similar challenges when expected to announce significant new products or functionality at conferences or marketing events.

Counter strategy Treat these for what they are—executives need to show potential investors or external stakeholders enough, but they may not need a fully-functioning, immediately saleable product. Discuss with stakeholders the minimum requirements to meet their needs. Perhaps a high-fidelity prototype will do.

WORKING WITH AN INEXPERIENCED OR RISK-ADVERSE TEAM

Less mature teams struggle with the ambiguity inherent in embracing ongoing trade-offs. They may interpret a lack of fully detailed, up-front requirements and timelines as stemming from laziness, a lack of commitment to goals, or excessive ambiguity. They dislike taking quality shortcuts because they see this as wasteful, even when exploring products that are not guaranteed to succeed.

In particular, organizations that fear failure struggle, particularly early during the discovery phase, when experimentation is required to formalize scope and timelines are hazy. Perhaps team members worry about their reputations and the possibility of missing deadlines they cannot guarantee.

Counter-strategy Establish and communicate a set of product principles, emphasizing how you want to work. Include learning and discovery of the "right scope" through hypothesis-generation and experimentation, operating without all scope up front, being flexible on dates, and being willing to take calculated risks in quality (with the commitment to clean up technical debt progressively for successful products).

OPERATING IN A COMMAND-CONTROL ENVIRONMENT

A strong CEO, founder, or other leaders concentrate decision-making at the top, confidently directing the product based on his or her vision and belief. While this person's instincts may be excellent and help focus the team, communication can break down as organizations grow and become more complex. A single individual cannot possibly understand all the nuances and impacts to make insightful trade-off decisions.

Counter strategy: When faced with this situation, while you should not ignore their guidance, treat their requests like others. Evaluate where they fit in the scope priorities and explain the impact on timeline and quality. If they are prescribing highly specific scope requirements and timelines, employ the five-whys technique (introduced in **Chapter 4**) to understand the underlying need. Then you can suggest alternative approaches and workarounds that may not be as constraining. Rarely take even a senior leader's request at face value.

If In Doubt—Ship Early, Ship Often

If you are ever in any of these situations where you feel overly constrained on scope, quality, timelines, or resource trade-offs, then focus on "the number one rule" for product managers: Ship! Deliver working product into the hands of customers and stakeholders—code, features, or functioning "early versions"—even if they are imperfect (but not disastrously so).

Shipping builds momentum and confidence in the team. It keeps stakeholders happier. It provides something to test with customers. It highlights any urgent quality issues you need to address. By shipping small increments of code frequently, you start to figure out what scope is essential and thereby improve your ability to estimate the timeline for the remainder of the project.

CHAPTER 10

Launch for Impact

Bring your product into the market smoothly, exciting customers and stakeholders with your solutions.

1 How to ensure smooth deployment of new functionality to users, in close collaboration with your technology teams.

2 How to work effectively with your organization to successfully manage an impactful and exciting market launch.

3 Disciplined techniques to reduce risk prior to launch, and to address high-visibility issues after launch, so as to maximize customer satisfaction and meet business expectations.

Launch to Delight Customers and Keep Stakeholders Happy

Launching new products and functionality is one of the more complex processes in an organization.

- It involves the coordination of many technology and non-technology stakeholders across an organization, each doing their piece in sequence.

- It is a period of high visibility, when all eyes are on a much sought-after product or improvement, and seamless stakeholder management and communication are critical.

- It is when customer-visible quality issues are most likely to arise—and your response must be with urgency now that the product is being used at scale.

Generally, technology organizations coordinate product releases and launches using their own processes, with varying levels of maturity and risk adversity. A product manager at one organization and a product manager at another may have very different roles—from being a fairly uninvolved stakeholder to directly overseeing launch.

Regardless, your long-term success depends on how well your product performs once in the market. Although you may not directly control all aspects of bringing the product into the hands of your customers, you must both understand all the moving parts associated with launch and play your role to reduce risk, evangelize the coming improvements, and quickly address issues as they arise.

It can be helpful to tease apart three distinct components of launch, as outlined in **Figure 10.1**. Not all (and not even most) launches include all three components. For example, it is common to skip a beta for low-risk changes or if your company doesn't (or can't) run betas. And small enhancements or purely back-end changes to an existing product are customarily deployed without market announcements.

1. Technical Deployment

A production environment is an externally available system that allows customers and end users to interact with a product. Before reaching production, most software will go through several environments accessible only to internal users, including staging for end-to-end testing.

Technical deployment	Pushing new products, features, or fixes to a production environment, which may or may not be visible to end-users
Beta release	A trial of a new product or new version of an existing product released to a limited audience
Market launch	The public declaration of the general availability of a new product or functionality

FIGURE 10.1 *Three components of product launches*

The final step—deploying to production—must be done with great care and adherence to a strict process. Your engineering and technical operations teams will manage this process. But you must be on hand to provide support, make critical decisions should issues arise, and communicate outcomes to stakeholders.

A *technical deployment* may be one of three variants or a hybrid of the three:

- The introduction of new or improved user-facing functionality.

- A fix (such as addressing bugs) to a current product.

- Releases with no apparent end-user changes, such as refactored code, new APIs, or upgrades to tracking and data systems.

Major releases might have a code name or number sequence (such as 1.0, 2.0, 3.0). Small releases may be referred to as "dot" or "point" releases (such as 1.1 or 2.5). Patches are usually even smaller, used to address a particular issue, and quickly rolled out.

You can reduce risk by limiting the complexity (the level of features and functionality) and the number of end users initially exposed to a new deployment. You can even deploy new code, while entirely hiding new functionality from users, through a "feature flag": a configuration component used to toggle a feature on or off (known as a "flag flip"). This allows you to safely deploy and validate new technologies before making the new features or products generally available to a wider audience.

But beware. Even if you are making back-end deployments only or are initially hiding new functionality, you can still inadvertently introduce regressions (bugs) elsewhere that adversely affect user experience or product availability.

2. Beta Release

A *beta release* allows for an externally accessible but controlled production environment where select users are permitted access to interact with the new product. You can control access to a beta product for long enough to ensure stability, improve quality (sometimes called hardening), and validate that there are no adverse effects on business metrics. Users may also provide feedback, and you can make adjustments before committing to general availability.

Many organizations do not use betas at all, or they use them only for certain products, while others consistently keep products in betas for an extended time. Occasionally, when consumer interest is lacking, a product never makes it out of beta, allowing the company to cut their losses and avoid a costly roll-out and marketing program.

3. Market Launch

Market launch is making the product widely available—often involving a product marketing campaign. Since you'll be serving customers at scale, unanticipated problems or complaints can quickly have serious, high-visibility consequences. Unfortunately, early in a new product's life is when issues not addressed in pre-launch testing are most likely to surface.

Customer scrutiny aside, management, partners, and investors will be watching your product closely. And they'll be monitoring any negative impact on the company's reputation or business metrics. Many people across your organization will need to be involved in the lead-up to launch, not just engineering. It's at this point that your internal communication and coordination becomes particularly critical—you need to keep all activities aligned and ensure everyone knows what to do.

Product marketing can be as simple as an announcement email to customers but might also include press events, customer roadshows, sales training, and online marketing to drive awareness and adoption. You must participate in this post-launch phase to ensure the product is successful. Unfortunately, it is often right at this point that many product managers take their eyes off the ball. But that's a mistake—success comes *after* market launch, not *upon* launch.

Smaller, Iterative Deployments vs. Big-Bang Launches

Product releases that include extensive changes and introduce multiple new features quickly are chaotic, unpredictable, and complex. *Big-bang* launches tend to have many dependencies, require more time for integration and testing, and need greater roll-out and post-launch support.

They are commonly seen as a way to maximize a marketing push or to delight customers with an impressive suite of enhancements. Or they happen when organizational pressure to get a product to market (to hit a predefined delivery date) outweighs appreciation of the risks.

Given all the changes, customers might need to relearn to use your product. They are more likely to be disappointed when the many promised features fail to materialize (due to last-minute scope cuts) or are buggy and difficult to use.

If your product release is tied in with a substantial marketing campaign, you must not only hit a high-stakes deadline but also get everything right on first-go—putting unhealthy pressure on your team.

In general, small iterative deployments are preferable. Simplify matters by introducing fewer new things at once—and do so more frequently. Not only will you dramatically reduce risk, but you will also make the launch process repeatable, and thus smoother, as you do it more often and learn how to do it a little better each time.

Smaller deployments also help break a vicious cycle. The more scope you add to a release, the more time it takes to deliver it. In turn, this extends the time between releases, making users wait longer for vital enhancements. Smaller releases mean you deliver some benefits earlier and more often. Of course, you will want to balance this to avoid customer fatigue from too-frequent updates.

Techniques for Successful Technical Deployments

Technical deployments are inherently internally focused. You will usually act in a support role, assisting engineering, quality assurance, technical operations, and project management. You must understand specific policies and issue-resolution processes—and make sure that all involved parties are working in close coordination and following procedures as follows:

1. Support and Budget Time for Adequate Test Coverage

QA and engineering will conduct thorough testing through the implementation phase. As components of the product start coming together and interacting, bugs will inevitably come to light. Bugs can be perplexing, and it can be hard to track down their underlying causes.

Later in implementation, engineering will conduct systemwide testing. They will want to ensure efficiency and stability, checking such things as CPU usage, database integrity, response time, and memory leaks. Comprehensive testing and monitoring—including load testing, data, and logging, and observing the impact on other components (including external vendors)—is required before deploying to production.

While QA and engineering own quality, as a product manager, you have primary responsibility for supporting them in the following three ways:

- **Budget sufficient testing time in the project timeline**—Account for testing in any plan or delivery date. Even if engineering has thoroughly unit-tested through the development cycle, you might need to budget 30 percent of your timeline on systems-level QA and debugging (leaving 70 percent for core development).

- **Triage incoming bugs**—In consultation with engineering and business stakeholders, you are responsible for deciding which feature bugs you must fix before launch and which can wait till later. You can use a simple priority level—starting at P0—to categorize severity; P0/P1 issues are the most severe, and if they persist as the desired launch date approaches, it may be preferable to delay.

  You will find an example categorization framework to use for bug prioritization at http://www.influentialpm.com—you can customize it to help inform what constitutes P0 through P4 bugs for you.

- **Test your own product**—Do not leave testing solely to QA. Test every part of your product and report bugs. As you are closest to your customer, you are best able to detect usability or customer-facing issues. Remember though, now is not the time to ask for changes or new requirements.

You should be extremely responsive to requests from your engineering and QA counterparts. If you do not already sit together, you might consider declaring a conference room as a "war room" for large, complex releases. Collocating the team there reduces communication overhead, encourages collaboration on bug detection and fixing, and builds morale.

The Origin of the Word "Bug"

Folklore has it that Rear Admiral Grace Hopper coined the phrase in 1947 after finding a moth stuck between points in a relay. The actual origins may be more mundane—nonetheless, it is a fun trivia question to pose to your engineering team.

Thomas Edison, in 1878, wrote about bugs as little faults in his inventions, requiring months of intense study before success could be reached. The term appeared again in 1931 in an advertisement for Baffle Ball, as a mechanical pinball game marketing itself as lacking bugs (glitches). And in 1944, Isaac Asimov wrote of removing bugs from his robot imaginations in his books.

Bug may have been derived from the Middle English *bugge*—the same root for bugaboo or bugbear (fear, irritation, and loathing)—or from the Low German *bögge*, which brought us hobgoblin and gremlin.

2. Understand and Follow Deployment Policies and the Plan

A *deployment plan* includes each step, in sequence, that is required to successfully roll out the product. It should be well documented, identify who will do which tasks, and highlight any particular technical steps or scripts required. Doing so will avoid missteps (and missed steps).

Bug-Outs

I worked as a product lead at an enterprise company, and we were close to completing a major site redesign. We decided to identify outstanding bugs and to build internal excitement for the coming product by running a "bug-out."

We recruited as many people in the organization as possible, across all departments. We made the product available to them on a staging server for 24 hours and provided them with accounts for the bug-reporting system, with instructions on how to report bugs. We asked them to include steps to reproduce bugs and screenshots. As an incentive, we announced a prize for the participant reporting the most bugs rated P0 through P3.

Everyone hit the product hard, trying to find and report bugs. Rather than treating it as a long and laborious task, we turned finding bugs into a fun game. The resulting list of bugs was long, but overall we were encouraged to see few major issues that we hadn't already found. It increased our confidence that the product was ready.

A (slight) downside of the bug-out is that some stakeholders requested last-minute new features and design changes instead. But we marked these requests for consideration at a later date.

Many companies have developed processes and technology to ensure deployments occur smoothly. They may use *continuous deployment,* which allows small increments of code to be released continuously into production. Systems will automatically roll back should a key business metric be affected or users impacted. As confidence grows in the product's stability, more users will be progressively redirected to the new release.

Avoid deployments at times when you have insufficient engineering and technical operations resources to respond should a major issue arise. Organizations with smaller engineering teams or with less-mature testing and monitoring might choose to avoid deploying late in the evening or on Friday or just before a public holiday. It may be tempting to break this rule, since hitting the launch button feels like you've achieved a milestone by the end of the week. But you don't want a system failure over the weekend as the team's response time might be slower, you risk disrupting engineers' social plans, and key team members may be unavailable.

Larger organizations tend to manage deployments to minimize customer impact, choosing times when they know their customers won't be actively using their product. In such a case, they might *prefer* late nights and weekends as deployment windows.

Seasonal businesses might have blackout periods that last many days, even months. As an example, one U.S. e-commerce company avoids any major product release from the week before Black Friday until after the New Year to protect their Q4 holiday sales (which account for 40 percent of the year's total).

While major product launches are in a blackout, it is usually still permissible to make minor changes and fixes. But expect stakeholders to treat exceptions very conservatively, often requiring executive sign-off. They will want assurance that the release will be of great business benefit and very low risk.

3. Determine Your Role in Post-Launch Monitoring and Issues Escalation—and Include a Roll-Back Plan

Once in production, because the product is now serving customers, your quick and thoughtful response to issues is of paramount importance.

Your technology team should have a *service* or *support-level agreement* (SLA) that describes how to handle issues. An SLA defines what constitutes an urgent, major, important, or cosmetic issue and determines the appropriate response time, communication plan, and escalation procedures. It serves as an internal "contract" between your technical operations, engineering, product, and customer service teams, as well as other groups.

An example SLA is provided online at http://www.influentialpm.com.

Your technical operations team will have systems monitoring for downtime, latency, and other problems. They will report uptime, response times, and other performance and operating metrics. They will also find and address performance bottlenecks, such as issues with database-intensive applications and edge cases that emerge under high load.

It's also necessary, however, to make sure that individual product features are functioning as expected. While the overall system may appear to be okay, perhaps a key feature has stopped working as expected. The need to monitor important and specific features is often initially overlooked. And when something breaks, it isn't detected until after users complain.

Say you have a simple website that allows registered users to post comments on articles. You may need to implement automated testing and monitoring not just on the overall web server and back-end systems but also on the login, password recovery, registration, post-a-comment, and edit-a-comment features. Without this, should anything break, your site might appear to be operating fine, but the product will not be working as expected.

To reduce your risks, work with your team to add sufficient (but not excessive) and product monitoring at the feature level:

1. Discuss available internal and third-party tools for feature-level monitoring.

2. Walk through the main components and flows of the product and identify what can break.

3. Agree on which features have higher levels of severity, and how quickly issues affecting them need a response.

4. Ask customer service to monitor user complaints and alert you as needed.

▶ **Chapter 4** introduces the five-whys technique while you can learn more about post-mortems in **Chapter 8**.

5. Hold a post-mortem or five-whys analysis every time an issue affecting customers goes undetected. This will help you to address gaps continually, as you uncover them.

Finally, wherever possible, establish a *roll-back plan* that allows you to back out of deployments that have proven to be problematic. They give you time to stabilize and solve issues, reducing urgency and any ongoing customer and business impact. Essentially, a roll-back event occurs when the problem is severe enough and when the solution is unknown or will take too long to address. It restores your production environment to the state it was in immediately before deployment, letting the business operate as usual while you address the problems.

Generally, you want to avoid roll-backs. They can be complicated, perhaps leaving users confused and disrupted by the sudden change back to an older experience. They may also result in a small amount of data loss.

But a roll-back is preferable to an extended period in which the problem is compounding, customers and stakeholders are getting increasingly frustrated, and your team is verging on panic, not knowing the cause or solution. When you need to address a severe problem quickly, your team might take risks, such as patching untested code to production, potentially making the problem worse.

The Impact Of Ignoring Feature-Flags and Roll-Back Procedures

A consumer company introduced a free trial for its popular subscription-based product as a way to increase conversion from website visitors. The intent was to generate trial users who, after a positive experience with the product over the trial period, would be more likely to become fully paid customers at the end of the trial.

The team had spent several months enthusiastically preparing the one-month trial. They worked on new homepage designs, back-end changes granting access to the new trial-user tier, updates to the payment and cancelation processes, and new marketing emails and advertising. When the service launched, it was immediately rolled out to all users.

At first, it seemed a big success, with thousands of users opting for a free trial. However, after the first month, it was clear something was wrong—the conversion rate from free to paid users was well below expectation, and the business was losing revenue quickly. The issue: many users who had previously paid for just a single month of the service were now just opting for the free month. While the free trial drove incremental paid users, it was not enough to offset the loss in first-month revenue.

Executives decided to roll back and remove the trial offer. But, in their enthusiasm for the project, no one had anticipated that a roll-back might be necessary. There was no roll-back plan and no way to switch off the feature for any of the visitors. Instead, a new project had to be started to unwind all the changes.

It took several months until a new release was available. And, all the while, revenues continued to fall, stress levels rose, and delays impacted other projects.

Technical Deployments Checklist
☐ Sufficient systems/integration testing in project timeline
☐ Bug prioritization categorization framework
☐ Testing your own product
☐ War room for large, complex releases
☐ Deployment plan documented
☐ Deployment blackout policies agreed
☐ Service-level agreement (including product manager responsibilities)
☐ Product feature-level monitoring (post-mortem every time something material breaks)
☐ Roll-back plan

A roll-back allows you to take stock, find the root cause, correctly code and test the fix, and deploy it with greater confidence. While you, the product manager, are not likely to be responsible for creating the roll-back plan, ask for it to be outlined to you and then ask for a test run to ensure it will work.

Beta Releases—Benefits and Approaches

Betas allow for a full or partial release of your product to a limited audience, even with incomplete features and known bugs. Such an audience is likely to be tolerant of issues and of changes to, or even removal of, features. They're also willing to provide feedback and agree to have extra data collected about them. However, running betas usually requires a more sophisticated and complicated production environment so the new and existing products can be run side by side. Betas also require an organization to be patient while they are run—and tolerant of possible changes and even consequent failure. To run a successful beta, employ the following strategies:

1. Limit Risk by Giving Your Release to a Subset of Users First

The point of a beta is to reduce risk. You limit business exposure while gathering quantitative and qualitative user data and business metrics that allow you to adapt your product in preparation for a confident market launch.

How you select which customers will become beta users depends on your business and capabilities, but how you make your choices might also bias the quality of the data you get back. Here are four strategies to help you find and choose beta users:

1. **Opt-in beta**—Users can select a switch to receive the new version while being able to switch back to the old if they change their minds. Usually, data collected in this phase is only applicable to early adopters or loyal users who are more curious to try out new offerings. However, this strategy can be advantageous in enlisting your most tolerant and supportive users. They are more forgiving and more willing to give feedback.

2. **Random allocation**—With this option, you direct a percentage of users to a new version for evaluation. Users are selected randomly and assigned to a test cell so that behavior, loyalty, or interest do not bias results. Through the random allocation of users, data collected in this phase will accurately portray how the product will perform once rolled out to all users.

3. **Limited beta**—This restricts the absolute number of users for a new product, often by invite only. You can limit exposure, scale slowly, more fully test your product, and buy time to respond to unexpected issues. And you can gradually increase access over time. New startups also deploy this technique, hoping to create buzz for their product by limiting its availability.

4. **Internal beta**—Also called "dogfooding," this is a particular kind of limited beta, available only to a select group of stakeholders. Access is often password-protected or approved after an authentication process, with the goal that internal stakeholders provide feedback before customers become involved.

2. Deploy the New Version to Run in Parallel with the Existing Product

If your product is an upgrade to an existing version, a beta release requires that you deploy the new version in parallel with the current product. Running two versions in parallel is simple in concept but can add substantial complexity to your production environment:

-   You may require separate physical or virtual servers, one for the old code, and the other for the new. The two versions must not interfere with each other's performance and stability.

- Once you have assigned beta and non-beta users, you must ensure they are directed consistently to the correct version, so they do not have a confusing or disjointed experience. This is particularly challenging when users aren't authenticated right at the start of a session. If they come back later, you may not recognize they have visited before and give them the incorrect version.

- You must ensure data integrity across both versions (they must share infrastructure in common or use data replication). You must ensure backward compatibility with your previous version or synchronicity across multiple databases.

It is the responsibility of engineering, not product management, to design, build, and test development, staging, and deployment environments, including the beta platform. However, you must be aware of these complexities, contribute requirements, and make sure sufficient time and resources are invested in them. Fortunately, in recent years, third-party platforms have come onto the market to help manage betas and A|B testing that, once integrated into your platform, can greatly simplify the process.

When running a beta release in parallel with the release version, moving the beta into general availability is easy. You simply switch to the new version (previously in beta), making it the default experience for everyone. This can be done progressively, in stages (10 percent, 20 percent, 40 percent, 100 percent). If possible, keep the old version available to users who prefer to use it for a set period, before deprecating it.

3. Gather and Apply User Feedback, and Validate Critical Business and User Behavioral Metrics before General Availability

Most users, knowing they are in a beta, will be more tolerant of issues, unannounced updates, and less-polished features. If you are putting a user into beta, then consider communicating those possibilities explicitly. Make sure that the website, emails to them, and other customer messaging states that they are in beta and that the product is subject to change. As an added precaution, give them the ability to roll back to the previous version if they so desire.

Give users a method to report issues, bugs, and ideas. Send them surveys or interview them. Because a beta has a limited number of users, you can manage feedback volume and focus on what you most need to learn, without significant customer risk.

Betas are highly useful for validating core business and user-behavior metrics on a smaller audience while still doing so at a statistically relevant level. You can detect and potentially eliminate problems before they have a strong negative impact, or build confidence in expected positive outcomes (against your stated KPIs). In particular, if you have randomly assigned users into beta, you can compare their behavior against those using your current product (your control group) to understand the relative impact of your beta.

Use the primary, secondary, and counter-metrics laid out in your specifications (**Chapter 6**) to develop a short list of metrics and specifically look for leading indicators that might have dipped unexpectedly. These could be signs that your product has caused an undesirable change in user behavior or that there is a technical issue that has gone unnoticed.

These are some typical unintended consequences and leading that may suggest you have a problem:

- Revenue dips (fewer transactions, lower conversion or renewal rates)

- Reduced user activation (downloads, visitor "bounce rate," registration)

- Lower user engagement (time spent, page views, repeat usage)

- Abandonment (dropout—the percentage of users who leave before completing a goal)

- Decreased feature usage (when you change a user interface, you may inadvertently reduce discoverability for some features and their usage)

- Impacts on one platform that are not obvious on others (a metric or issue is more pronounced on one device type, browser, or channel)

Techniques for a Successful Market Launch

Market launches are inherently externally focused. The product manager participates in (and often leads) a set of activities to complete the non-technical steps required to get a product successfully into the hands of customers. Depending on the size and profile of your product launch, these steps may be relatively straightforward or, for complex launches, might require months of planning. Follow these strategies for a successful market launch:

1. Build a Launch Team with a Point Person from Each Department

A launch requires coordination and planning involving many cross-functional players. It can be a challenge to keep everyone aligned and productively working toward launch goals. However, you don't want to miss out on input from a critical player just because you want to keep the team small and efficient.

One possible solution is to create a go-to-market team, or *launch team*. This team will include *one* accountable point person in each key internal function, who will support (or be impacted by) the launch. Ensure that each member understands and commits to

- participate in launch-planning meetings (held weekly, say),

- proactively represent the needs of their department,

- oversee and complete (or delegate and ensure completion of) their department's tasks in preparation for market launch,

- communicate product-release status and progress back to others in their department, and

- evangelize and support the success of the product to others in their department.

To build your launch team, start early—possibly weeks or even months in advance of a substantial release.

First, recruit your launch team and discuss any concerns or needs they might have. If you have several people in a department who could be representatives, try to ascertain who is most likely to be a positive influence and make the necessary commitment.

External team members don't have to be the most senior in their departments (although for high-profile launches, they may well be). They just need to be able to represent their department's needs, take responsibility for coordinating with you, and communicate back to their teams.

Figure 10.2 identifies typically good candidates for your launch team. Depending on your situation, the generic framework here may or may not apply, but you can adapt it to suit your organizational structure and decision-making processes.

- The *executive sponsor* has a unique role. He or she
  - is senior enough to remove bottlenecks across the organization;

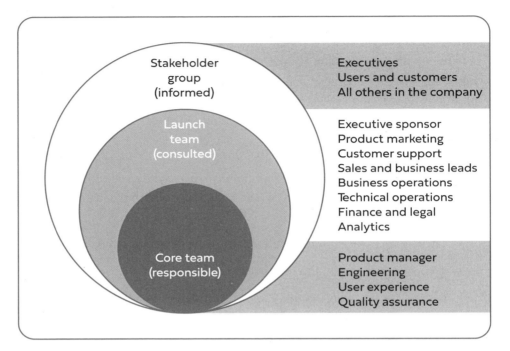

FIGURE 10.2 *Members and Responsible-Accountable-Consulted-Informed (RACI) model for a launch team*

> ▪ provides other executives visibility on the project, reiterating why the product is vital to the business; and
>
> ▪ keeps up team morale by, for example, publicly recognizing contributors and communicating the product launch's importance to the business.

- *Product marketing* drives the marketing program (including PR, user communications, and outreach). This representative often also owns responsibility for copy and creative assets that appear within the product.

- *Customer support, customer success,* or *client services staff* are the front line for making sure customers can successfully implement and use your product. Depending on your organization, this group may have responsibility for anything from answering customer inquiries to customer roll-out and onboarding. It may be necessary to develop training materials, and you'll need to give them time and help to become expert in using the new product.

- *Sales* and *business leads* need to understand what the product will do, how to sell the product, and preempt likely customer objections. They will need to be confident that the solution is of high quality and value to the customer—otherwise, they won't be comfortable selling it.

- Other *business operations* teams might also need to support or operate your product. For example, they may need to produce content, advertise the product, train other teams, or manage vendors. They may need to adjust their business processes and will need time to implement processes and train their staff.

- *Finance and legal* might need to be aware of revenue impact, pending budget requests, or sign-off on any regulatory or legal requirements (such as updated terms of service) for launch.

- *Analytics* needs to ensure product data is captured and reflected in updated reporting. They also need to be aware of and prepared for any impact the product release could have on their data systems. For example, they need to know if a new service might influence some critical business metric (so they don't misattribute the change to some other action), or if tracking changes are required.

Meet regularly to keep up momentum. A launch team ensures that more concerns are aired earlier rather than later and that everyone has a chance to prepare for the product release.

When the launch date is getting close, call your launch team together for a formal *readiness review* to work through any remaining concerns and reaffirm that everyone is a "go" for launch—perhaps physically signing a go/no-go document. And inform them as soon as you know if a launch commitment might be delayed—they can help minimize the impact.

2. Establish Key Performance Indicators, So You Know What Success Looks Like

It's essential to define and set measurable business targets *before launch*. What happens if you don't have up-front agreement on your KPIs?

- **Goal misalignment**—Some will think the product was successful and others will not. For example, you may have launched an improved version of your product to increase customer satisfaction, but some of your colleagues thought the product's intended focus was to generate direct revenue. You declare the launch a success when customer satisfaction rises—but if they do not also see an immediate revenue improvement, they deem it a failure.

- **Retroactive goal-setting**—Also known as "hindsight bias," you review various metrics after launch and highlight those that look promising, declaring the launch a success. You lose objectivity. The "gains" may not have been of sufficient benefit to warrant the investment in the first place.

- **Mistaking launch as the marker of success**—After launch, everybody goes off to work on something else. A few months later, someone notices the product isn't performing very well. The team abandons what they were working on to fix it.

Agreeing on metrics and targets will help you decide what matters and when you can genuinely declare your product launch successful.

> ▶ **Chapter 11** covers product metrics that can be candidate KPIs of your launch. **Chapter 6** covers product specifications, which must include defining primary, secondary, and counter-metrics.

As highlighted in this chapter, in the section on betas—it may also help to declare counter-metrics. These are not necessarily expected to be improved by the launch of the product but, should they decline, there would be a problem. For example, a product launch might be designed to improve conversion of site visitors into paid users. However, if user satisfaction (such as NPS) or customer retention sharply declines, then the product is not a success. Benchmark metrics before launch and consider agreeing in advance on what variances are acceptable, If, for example, a decline in a counter-metric is under 5 percent, you might have agreed that the problem wouldn't be considered severe enough to warrant a roll-back (or even worth addressing).

Few launches are perfect the first time. Having KPIs in place will help you communicate expectations and be receptive to post-launch measurement. Then, if the product is missing the mark, you can go back and figure out why, and make the necessary changes.

3. Communicate with Customers and Partners

Before a major launch, contact key vendors, partners, and customers if they might be affected. Do not surprise them with sudden change. Expect a passionate response if changes are substantial—even if you're introducing improvements that will be good for them.

Once you have many customers using your product, any change can be a big deal. If possible, give your users time to switch gradually and engage them in the process.

Here are some practical ways to get customers and partners onboard:

- **Announce changes in advance or very soon after**—Send out an email, newsletter announcement, or other notification of the release. For SaaS offerings, notifying clients well in advance is strongly recommended (especially if you expect downtime as you complete the upgrade or if your end-users will need retraining to continue to use your solution). Unless you are making dramatic changes, advance notification is not as necessary for consumer applications, but users appreciate hearing about new valuable features, and a launch is an opportunity to get your dormant users reengaged with your offering.

- **Engage your customer or user community advocates**—Work with customer service and marketing to develop a simple outreach program. Notify them of the work you've been doing and ask if they'd like to provide input. Even if you are unable to integrate much of their feedback, the very process of asking for input helps smooth ruffled feathers. This strategy is particularly useful when you reach out to key influencers, such as recognized brands, marquee clients, or frequent participants in community forums. Turn them into advocates, and they will help others embrace the change.

- **Have a roll-out program**—If you are working on an enterprise product, partner with sales and marketing to create a phased roll-out of the upgrade for existing customers. You might choose to upgrade specific verticals or geographies one at a time. Alternatively, the update cycle might mirror the natural sales cycle—in that the upgrade doesn't occur until after a customer renews, sometimes a year or more in the future. Often the new version of the product becomes a key selling point for renewal. As a result, it is not unusual to be required to support the last two (or three) versions of your product. **Figure 10.3** gives an example of a generic four-phase roll-out.

- **Listen closely for post-launch feedback**—Identify channels through which customers may express their feelings, positive or negative:

  - Customer service phone calls, emails, chat transcripts, and feedback forms

  - Sales leads

  - Implementation personnel (onboarding, integration, sales operations)

ROLL-OUT PHASE	TIMING (assuming year-long renewal cycle)	TARGET CLIENTS
1. Early adopters	0–2 months	• Reference clients (possibly already using your beta) • Clients most vocal in demanding the new features
2. Low-risk accounts	2+ months	• Newly signed clients • Small clients (forced upgrade)
3. Follow renewal cycle	At renewal due	• Clients as they reach renewal date • Clients with unique integration or specific feature needs
4. Late adopters	12+ months	• Highly conservative, change-adverse clients • Clients with regulatory needs that you're not fully compliant with yet • Clients using deprecated platforms (such as browsers, operating systems, and third-party systems) that you will no longer support in your new version

FIGURE 10.3 *Example roll-out plan for an enterprise product update*

In-Product Education

Onsite tutorials, walk-throughs, and introductory pop-overs to educate users about your product enhancements don't appear to work as effectively as you might think. Most users immediately dismiss them. That's because they don't want to re-learn your product, or because they are trying to get something done and you are just getting in their way. Focus instead on making your product intuitive to use.

- Social media, third-party blogs, mobile app stores, and user communities

Proactively monitor feedback and respond accordingly. If a key client has something to say, alert sales and offer to jump on a call with them. If there's a problem that is likely to cause concern, communicate what you have found to stakeholders, along with your action plan. Don't wait for them to come to you. Respond honestly and don't make promises you can't keep.

Partnering with Product Marketing

Product marketing (PMM) can be one of a product manager's greatest allies in making a product launch successful. Of course, not all product releases include a marketing budget and resources. However, should you be lucky enough to be part of a big marketing push, make sure you make the most of it.

In general, product management owns the definition and prioritization of the feature set and is responsible for delivering a solution that addresses the stated value proposition and differentiation. Product marketing owns the messaging: how to communicate the product's benefits to the customer. Product marketing can also help you with a range of activities, including customer acquisition, copywriting and messaging, PR, and sales training.

Use the following techniques to increase your chance of success in working with product marketing:

- **Engage early**—Engage the PMM as soon as your project kicks off, perhaps after you've completed discovery but have not yet progressed too far into product execution. Putting a product-marketing campaign together is complicated. Marketing usually keeps a calendar of all its campaigns and activities. See whether there are conferences, events, or other marketing initiatives you might leverage—or perhaps impose a blackout date for your launch. Companies usually want to focus the public's attention on a few key things at once, and you will want to avoid having your product drowned out by something more important. Likewise, understand if there is a budget for driving customer acquisition or advertising. Manage date commitments very carefully and make sure you aren't stuck with a release date that can't be changed at all because of a marketing campaign.

- **Launch brief**—To "talk the same language," provide product marketing with a brief overview of your product from the customer and market viewpoints. Your differentiation factors will be critical in making the product newsworthy—marketing requires a hook that will get influencers, press, and customers interested. Focus on benefits, not features—discuss features or technology only in terms of how they support delivery of the benefits. Also share known risks and gaps—if you know of "gotchas" (bugs, missing features, advantages competitors have that you do not), make sure marketing knows so they can work around them.

  In **Figure 10.4**, you can find a product-marketing brief template. And an example is provided online at http://www.influentialpm.com.

- **Reference customers and testimonials**—Have beta customers or current users provide testimonials before the official market launch. Include quotes from their management team, as well, and write up case studies. Ideally, get permission to publicly refer to them before they start using the product (particularly if they are getting a preview at a discount). Seek market backing from industry supporters, vendors, or product-development partners, and from standards or official industry bodies.

Be careful not to overly rely on a press release or a splashy launch event. Public relations is an essential tool for building brand and reputation over the long term. But while it might give your team a boost and lead to a short bump in interest in your product, it won't replace serving customers well over the long term.

Likewise, be very careful not to generate too much hype or set expectations too high, externally or internally. Your early adopters can be your greatest champions or your most aggressive detractors. Fail to meet expectations, and you can easily lose credibility with industry, potential investors, and management. Make sure your plan promises only what you know you can deliver.

1. **Internal positioning statement**	• Product vision
	• Target customers **(Chapter 3)**
	• Problem statement/pain points **(Chapter 3)**
	• Pricing (if known)
	• KPIs and spec **(Chapter 6)**
2. **Top three customer benefits**	• Value proposition and differentiation/unique selling points **(Chapter 3)**
	• List of prioritized features to support each
	• Include mocks, designs, screen captures or photographs where possible
3. **Benefit/top feature comparison table**	• You versus top 2–3 competitors, and/or
	• Your product's previous model/version, and/or
	• Your existing product on another platform (for example, if you are launching a new mobile application, compare it to your existing web version)
4. **Gaps & Risks (for internal use only)**	• Missing features or functionality that customers may have wanted
	• Known issues and bugs
	• Competitor strengths over your product
	• Any other areas PMM should avoid
5. **Availability**	• System requirements and platforms
	• Compatibility with previous versions
	• Regions, segments, or markets in which it will be available
	• Partners or distribution channels
	• Date range or roll-out plan

FIGURE 10.4 *Product marketing brief template*

Market Launch Checklist
☐ Launch team formed
☐ Regular launch team meeting scheduled
☐ Launch KPIs defined, benchmarked, and agreed upon
☐ Advanced customer notifications and announcements distributed
☐ Customer and community advocates outreach completed
☐ Roll-out plan defined and socialized
☐ Post-launch feedback channels monitored and responded to
☐ Product marketing brief written and distributed
☐ Reference customers recruited and testimonials gathered

Managing the Post-Launch Period

Don't think of your product launch as *the* marker of success. Launch is just the beginning. Success should not be declared until the product is running stably and meeting stated KPIs.

As **Figure 10.5** (the bathtub curve) illustrates, products have a higher tendency to fail early, during burn-in (when issues become apparent for the first time), or they fail late in life during wear-out (when accumulated technical debt and older technologies become harder to support).

Immediately after launch, issues invariably arise that can be detected only once you have users stress-testing your product at scale. Have part of your team—those who built the product—form a *ready-response* team, and charge them with measuring performance and addressing issues in a disciplined, proactive manner. Much like "first responders," they can be quickly dispatched to an incident and then can carefully assess the situation before taking decisive but considered actions.

1. Advocate to Not Reassign the Development Team Immediately after Launch

Particularly when a project is delayed, managers may be inclined to immediately re-deploy scarce engineering resources after it is launched. They may assign your team members to new projects that were scheduled to start right after your launch—especially when the next new project already has a deadline and has been "waiting" for resources to come free.

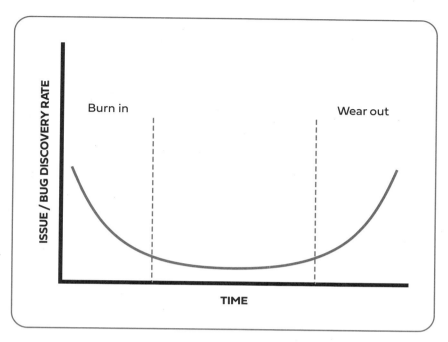

FIGURE 10.5 *The "bathtub" curve predicts a higher rate for discovery of issues early in and at the end of a product's life*

In the meantime, issues with the just-launched product can remain undetected—until they become severe enough, surprising everyone. But with no one left to address the issues, developers who worked on the project must be pulled back to fix what they can while simultaneously working on their new priorities.

So if possible, negotiate to keep some or all of the development team engaged in the project for at least a few weeks after launch—and then slowly ramp down as confidence rises. Aim for each part of the system to be supportable by at least one expert engineer (without having to go outside the team). During this time, when not working on emergencies, the team can be cleaning up, removing technical debt, and addressing bugs.

2. Proactively Review Business Metrics and Performance

Although you may be deep in execution and post-launch cleanup, monitor customer feedback and KPIs to ensure the product is successfully meeting the stated goals. Go looking for problems! Don't wait for a reporting dashboard that highlights an issue to be published or a stakeholder to question why there's been a sudden drop in a business measure. To avoid such a situation:

- **Measure and communicate performance**—Monitor the success criteria you established before launch. It may take several days, weeks, or even months for trends to stabilize. If you notice negative, inconclusive, or inconsistent trends, communicate your observations and include an action plan. Determine, also, if the product has had any unexpected effect, given the counter-metrics you defined. Even if you have conducted a beta, you must continue monitoring for a long period post-launch.

- **Close the loop with customers**—After allowing a short period for customers to learn and get used to the product, conduct a series of interviews to ensure they are adopting the product and that it is helping them achieve their goals. Gather feedback for planning future enhancements.

Post-Launch Isn't Just Maintenance

In more traditional processes, launch might be followed by a "maintenance" phase. But this assumes that the product delivered was right the first time and now needs only to be maintained. In reality, up to 30 percent of development resources are spent addressing issues and optimizing for already-launched products.

At one company I worked at, immediately after launch, we'd plan on reallocating the team to work on a new initiative. However, too often, this meant that engineers had to respond to unexpected issues arising in newly deployed services while also trying to get the (already delayed) next project underway.

To solve the problem, we spread support across the organization and allocated bug-fixing to any engineer who was free. Often, however, only the original coders knew enough about the system to solve unexpected issues quickly enough. This created SPOFs—single points of failure—as some engineers had such specialized knowledge that it was always more efficient to have them solve new issues quickly than have other engineers learn.

Ultimately, we found better alternatives:

- Budget time for post-launch cleanup and support, with a more gradual ramp-up for the next project.

- Keep teams together rather than disbanding them. Give them similar projects so that groups of developers get to own their systems for longer (and their bugs too).

- Use pair-programming, rotations, and cross-team code-review to force knowledge sharing.

- Empower product managers to optimize for business objectives rather than for schedules. Allowing them to delay new projects when optimizing or enhancing an existing product will contribute more to business goals.

- **Follow up on technical performance with technical operations**—If a problem emerges, technical operations will usually come to you. But it doesn't hurt to ask them to share the data with you. Question them about their observations. Ask them what they believe constitutes a stable product and whether yours meets their criteria. Likewise, monitor the rate at which new bugs are being reported. After a while, these should be declining to the point where they are well below the rate at which they are addressed (nearing stability).

3. Follow a Disciplined Process to Determine Root Causes for Issues before Acting

It is understandable that you feel pressure to address issues as quickly as possible. However, now more than ever, it's critical that you be disciplined in following an established process to deal with post-launch issues and ensure their effective resolution.

Before addressing a problem, ask yourself two questions:

1. How important is this?

2. Do we really know what the root cause is?

Without taking some time to conduct analysis, you might fix what appears to be the problem, deploy an untested "patch," and discover the situation is no better, or maybe even worse. While a sense of urgency is a highly commendable trait, a lack of discipline in a crisis is not. So practice a no-heroes policy.

You must delineate when the team is in *exploration mode* (assessing the issue and investigating causes) and *action mode* (fixing and deploying a patch). Take action only after the priority, risks, and path forward is clear.

Root-cause analysis is used to form hypotheses and validate possible causes. This analysis looks beyond simple explanations—perhaps the issue is the tip of a larger iceberg. Ensure your team is meeting to validate assumptions and getting second opinions on the resolution plan. Keep the launch team informed of the status of issues, progress, and resolutions. This can be a challenge, since it might take time away from addressing the issue or feel like you have to deliver too much bad news. However, when updates are not forthcoming, stakeholders start getting nervous—they think, perhaps, the team isn't aware of the problem or needs help.

Communication during Production Issues

When an issue occurs, limit how much information engineering team responders must communicate to you and offer to own the job of providing updates, as available, to well-meaning, concerned stakeholders. Protect the team. If you or your stakeholders require lengthy explanations and frequent status reports, you will distract them from what should be their primary focus—solving the problem.

4. Hold a Launch Retrospective to Discuss Process Improvements

After the dust has settled, but also while the issues are all fresh in your mind, take time out to openly discuss what went well and what didn't. Encourage honest input from everyone so that you can learn how to make launches more successful in the future. Hold a meeting and invite all core and launch team members who played a key role.

The retrospective must be blame-free. It helps to set the scene by communicating that everyone *believes they did the best job they could given the situation, what they understood at the time, and what resources were available.*

Your agenda can be simple. The intent is to focus the conversation and make it a comfortable experience, rather than a free-for-all, and to avoid self-criticism. Consider including these kinds of topics on your agenda:

- Remind everyone of the retrospective "rules of engagement." The retrospective must be blame-free. It helps to set the scene by communicating that everyone *believes they did the best job they could given the situation, what they understood at the time, and what resources were available.*

- Ask what went well (or, at least, better than last time).

- Ask what can be improved.

- Of those things that can be improved, ask what few things the team will commit to for next time.

While these three questions may be sufficient, some additional questions will help prompt an open and fact-driven discussion:

- Review, step by step, the launch process, starting at two or three weeks before. What went smoothly? What didn't?

- What is the ratio of bugs detected before launch as opposed to after launch? What did we miss?

- Were the development/deployment processes and environments set up to help us be efficient and effective?

- Did we meet the launch goals?

- How did we work as a team?

- What is the quality of internal communication like? External communication?

▶ In **Chapter 8** I cover some approaches and a simple four-step structure for running effective retrospectives.

Ask participants to write down their thoughts ahead of time. Post-it notes work well to get most issues out on the table, as does sending the facilitator a list before the meeting to compile (and anonymize) the feedback. Bring a list of known problems, their causes, and other observations to the meeting so that you cover everything.

The product manager should *not* run the retrospective. Ideally, find a third party who has no personal investment or ask a widely respected development lead on your team.

Depending on how frequently you launch new products, a good target is to get about three to five key recommendations from each retrospective.

Post-Launch Checklist

☐ Form a rapid-response team—gradually reassign team members to other activities as the product stabilizes

☐ Review business, secondary, and counter-metrics

☐ Close the loop with customers

☐ Follow up on technical performance indicators to ensure stability

☐ Define and follow a disciplined issues-diagnosis-and-resolution procedure

☐ Conduct a post-launch retrospective

☐ Celebrate individual and team achievements

5. Celebrate

It's too often overlooked, but you should celebrate all the hard work that has gone into getting your product realized and into the hands of your customers. Sure, the product may not be perfect, there is almost certainly more work to do, and perhaps you're already thinking about the next project. But take some time out to let everybody reflect, relax, and savor their achievement.

Celebrations can be simple, like grabbing a beer or ringing a gong. Or you might take a boat trip, go to a restaurant, or take a couple of days off to make up for the extra hours that everyone put in.

A few pointers:

- Invite a senior stakeholder to say a few sincere words and rub shoulders with all who contributed. Ask him or her to emphasize the business and customer impact the team is making.

- Publicly acknowledge individuals, but be liberal in calling out as many of the core team members as possible and be specific about their contribution (no, "great job" is not sufficient). Be aware, however, that some team members may not like to be in the spotlight, and sometimes forgetting someone is worse than acknowledging nobody.

- Get together a collection of positive emails from customer service or directly from clients. Share these testimonials.

And once the celebration is over, be sure to put the launch in context.

Launch is just a brief moment in time. Enjoy the high of shipping quality product to your customers, but then get back to business. Don't wait to perfect a product before launching, but establish a rhythm to ship value frequently. It is better to start iterating and learning.

A Disciplined Process to Manage Post-Launch Issues

When responding to post-launch issues, follow these steps to systematically conduct root-cause analysis prior to taking action.

1. Report and document issue

   - Date, time, person who reported it and description of what occurred
   - Step-by-step instructions on how to reproduce it
   - If issue is user experience related, include screenshots

2. Assess severity to business and customers

   - What critical business parameters are adversely impacted?
   - What percentage of users/customers are affected? How are they impacted?
   - Are there any workarounds and what are they?

3. Assign a priority

   - Based on priority decide whether to address and with what urgency
   - Communicate priority and status to stakeholders
   - Stop here unless priority is high—otherwise proceed to next step

4. Determine root causes

   - Reproduce issue (if it cannot be reproduced, follow up with the reporter—don't just close it)
   - Develop hypotheses
   - Validate hypotheses (with data)
   - Identify risks and assumptions (How might we be wrong? What might we be missing?)

5. Implement a fix

   - Agree on an approach to fix or patch the issue
   - Code the fix
   - Test the fix—try to break it
   - Deploy fix—using standard deployment procedures
   - Retest in production to confirm the issue has been resolved
   - Communicate resolution to stakeholders

6. Hold a retrospective

   - Conduct a five-why's post-mortem
   - Agree on action items to reduce chance of something similar happening again

Measure Success

Utilize meaningful metrics to track and increase the value you deliver to customers.

What you'll learn in this chapter

1 Five categories of customer-centric metrics for measuring a product's performance and to show where to focus for improvements.

2 How to design useful customer- and business-centric metrics and the common pitfalls to avoid.

3 Frameworks and example metrics you can use for your product.

Five Customer–Centric, Product–Performance Metrics

Most useful product-performance metrics fit into one of five categories that, in combination, provide a complete picture of your product's health and financial viability:

1. **Product flows**—Can customers achieve their goal with your product? And how do they achieve their goals?

2. **Actionable value-based indicators**—What are the leading indicators of customer behavior that show they get value from using your product?

3. **Customer satisfaction**—Is your product meeting, failing, or surpassing customer expectations? What specific areas need more attention?

4. **Customer relationship funnel**—How well do you optimize each stage of the journey to guide customers toward a more meaningful relationship with your company and your product?

5. **Customer lifetime value** (LTV)—How valuable is your product to your customers over the long term, to support a financially viable, sustainable business?

As illustrated in **Figure 11.1** as you go down the list, each, in turn, represents a stronger indicator of long-term product success—with optimized product flows being the weakest and a healthy LTV being the strongest. However, each also requires increasing amounts of time to gather sufficient data and observe trends, sophistication in tracking and analysis, and complexity in developing effective strategies to address issues.

Collectively, the five categories provide a holistic picture of your product's performance: you can track the usability of your service, you can appreciate its value as perceived by customers and as revealed by underlying customer lifecycle behavior, and you can understand the economics of supporting and scaling your product. **Table 11.1** provides a summary of each category, their purposes, and the kinds of actions you might take based on the insights surfaced—which I will cover in more detail in this chapter.

You must define and monitor specific metrics across each category—tailoring their methodologies to suit your unique service offerings, the life stage of your product, and the data-analysis capabilities of your organization.

While you should define a range of metrics to track, highlight a few (or perhaps only one) that are critical based on the maturity of your

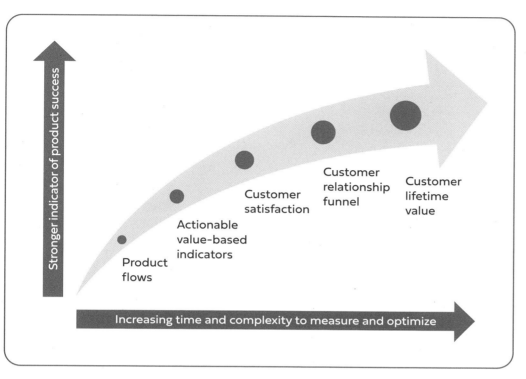

FIGURE 11.1 *Five categories of customer-centric, product-performance metrics*

product and your next greatest challenge. Doing so will give you and your team focus, helping prioritize those efforts that will have the most impact on performance. Having too many metrics can create confusion and, when some are in contention with each other, prioritization becomes harder.

In this chapter, I discuss the key attributes of all good metrics and then introduce each of the five categories of product-performance metrics and associated frameworks. Each company adapts its definitions, methodologies, and approaches for gathering, analyzing, and reporting data. This chapter aims to provide a starting point to orient you to the metrics that matter, understand how to define metrics for your product, and know how to avoid common pitfalls.

At http://www.influentialpm.com, I include examples of frequently used metrics definitions, sample charts and reports, and analyses and exercises to apply, to go more in-depth on what is covered here. You'll also find a list of commonly used analysis tools; this list is periodically refreshed given the fast-changing nature of this ever-evolving industry.

TABLE 11.1 The five customer-centric product-performance metrics summarized

WHAT IS IT?	WHY MEASURE IT?
1. Product flows	
The portion of users who successfully (and without friction) move from one part of your product to the next—all the way to goal completion.	Most products have complex interfaces with multiple choices available at each step—each decision point is an opportunity for user confusion or abandonment.
2. Actionable value-based indicators	
Specific customer behaviors or interactions with core functionality in your product. They indicate that customers are getting value from your product.	Repeat, frequent, and lasting usage is a proxy for successful customer-value creation (and a leading indicator of customer retention). Leading indicators enable quicker detection and resolution of issues.
3. Customer satisfaction	
How delighted customers report they are with your overall service (and the underlying factors for satisfaction or dissatisfaction).	Not all your current customers feel loyalty to or get everything they want out of your product, even if they frequently use it. Customer satisfaction is a leading indicator of long-term retention and advocacy.
4. Customer relationship funnel	
Your ability to successfully transition customers through each stage of their lifecycle journey with your product.	Potential and current customers vary in their level of engagement and their understanding of why and how to use your product. Your product must transition them gently from one stage to the next to avoid abandonment.
5. Customer Lifetime Value (LTV)	
Your ability to attract new customers cost-effectively and retain them long enough (and at a high-enough gross margin) to make your product profitable over the long term.	Acquiring loyal and satisfied users is not enough to scale a sustainable business. You must be able to extract business value over the lifetime of each customer. LTV avoids short-term thinking (such as solely focusing on quarterly revenue targets).

HOW DO YOU MEASURE IT?	WHAT ACTIONS DO YOU TAKE?
• Analyze user progression from each entry point through each interaction (for example, from one screen to the next). • Track on a session-by-session basis (each visit).	• Identify areas of friction leading to dropout. Focus your ideation and testing on eliminating them. • Declutter interfaces to help users complete their most critical tasks. • Reduce steps to goal completion.
• Target the most critical user-centric goals of your product and pinpoint behaviors that illustrate progression toward them. • Track by user cohort and over multiple user sessions. • Use comparative metrics (expressed as a percentage or ratio).	• Understand why users do not use your product as often as you might like. • Focus product development on those changes you identify as most likely to encourage repeat and deeper usage. • Regularly remeasure using new-user cohorts to track improvements over time.
• Conduct regular surveys of both occasional and habitual users of your product. • Measure the product's benefits and functionality—both overall and in specific areas—to pinpoint root-cause issues. • Quantify results and complement them with qualitative research to add more detail.	• Use poor results to advocate for delighter product improvements, even if they don't immediately appear to have short-term revenue or direct business benefits. • Prioritize adding or improving features that have low satisfaction but high importance.
• Split all users into lifecycle sub-segments, such as leads, trial users, paid users, and loyal long-term users. • Track the percentage of customers who move successfully from one lifecycle phase to the next, to pinpoint where dropouts occur and where improvements are needed.	• Determine which steps in the funnel suffer the most dropouts (lowest rates) for product-development focus. • A|B test initiatives that will help edge more users incrementally to the next stage in the funnel.
• Calculate the average revenue per user, less variable costs, taking into account churn over the lifetime of paying customers. • Monitor each channel or customer segment separately so you can optimize customer acquisition costs (CAC).	• Understand which customer segments are most valuable (useful when deciding which features to prioritize). • Provide information about which channels to invest in and scale, and when to do so (when CAC < LTV). • Assist in product-pricing analysis (sometimes charging less is better if it lowers churn so that LTV improves).

Attributes of Useful Product–Performance Metrics

Useful metrics focus a team on achieving a shared, actionable goal, and they are easily and frequently measured, so the outcomes and lessons are clear. Not all—not even most—commonly tracked metrics are helpful in this way. Useful metrics have common traits that make them inherently "good":

1. Useful Metrics Are Actionable

Actionable metrics sufficiently pinpoint where you may have a problem so you can identify potential solutions—or, at a minimum, they enable you to form a firm hypothesis, so you can do further research or run an experiment. Actionable metrics can also tell you where you *don't* need to do something and should focus on something else instead, which is incredibly valuable when prioritizing work for your under-resourced team. When selecting a metric, ask yourself what you would do if these numbers went up or down, or stayed the same. If you can't identify specific actions, choose a different metric.

Inherently, comparative metrics, such as ratios (with a numerator and denominator) and rates (fractions and percentages), tend to be actionable in that you can generally isolate the effects of product improvements over time and spot variations and trends. Unlike absolute numbers, they are less subject to non-product influences. If uncontrolled externalities easily influence a metric, you won't learn anything.

Similarly, an actionable metric must be frequently measurable. If you are to iterate quickly, the metric must give you fast feedback. The loop between taking action and seeing a result should be as short as possible—ideally measured in days or weeks. Quarterly or yearly is too slow.

That said, be aware of potential downstream, lagging effects. For example, for a change in the product designed to increase customer conversion, you will quickly see if users purchase at a higher rate, but it will be some time before you can see if those customers engage with and later repurchase your product at levels similar to those of your previous customers.

2. Useful Metrics Are Meaningful to Product Goals

Many metrics (such as those measuring short-term financial objectives) have little to do with actual product performance. Product metrics, when relevant, get right to customer-centric goals. They help you identify where the product could be improved. They measure the value you are delivering to your customers, which, in turn, generates positive business results.

Product managers should be aligned with (and induced to pursue) what's good for the customer. Simply pursuing short-term business goals might lower long-term value, and the team might do "what it takes" to hit them (which may not be strategic or right for the customer).

Every company likes to see increased revenue. But if increasing revenue is the only goal, then the team might allocate all resources to maximize short-term sales—at the expense of long-term sustainability. Or the team might prioritize one-off development efforts to secure client deals, incurring an opportunity cost in *not* building functionality for their broader target market.

Meaningful product metrics measure sustainable, scalable business value for beneficial, long-term customer outcomes. They should not be deal-driven or prematurely promote scale or growth before the product is ready.

3. Useful Metrics Avoid Averages and Correlation Bias

Averages mask the underlying user behavior and trends. For instance, if you have 100 people using your product, and 90 percent of them use it for 10 seconds and 10 percent use it for 2 hours, is that better than 100 percent of users using it for 10 minutes each? An average total of time spent (12 minutes versus 10 minutes) would suggest it is but arguably the product is failing to adequately serve the vast majority of its customers.

Always complement averages with medians and distributions. The median tells you how a *typical* user behaves, whereas averages can be unduly

The Dangers of Overusing Averages

When tracking advertising performance for a media company, we initially used a metric called "average engagement time," which focused on understanding how long users spent interacting with the brand once they clicked on an advertisement. We reported a healthy time-spent metric of about 30 seconds (better than a TV ad!).

A different picture was revealed, however, when you looked at the overall distribution curve. There was a very sharp spike, where many users spent as little as five seconds, and a long tail, where fewer users would spend 30 seconds or more. Imagine a standard distribution curve but with the peak pushed sharply to the left.

We knew that, while we still had high-performing solutions, we had too many disengaged users. We needed to find ways to capture their attention longer. So we set about improving the quality of the initial experience.

We also knew that *average time spent* was artificially inflating our impression of what the *average user* was doing. By switching to a median (the point at which 50 percent of users were to the left of the line on the curve and 50 percent were to the right), the reported time spent fell (to about 20 seconds). The results were still better than those of most online advertisers and gave a more accurate picture of how much time the typical user was interacting with the brand through our solution.

influenced by outliers. Distributions will surface interesting and unusual "blips" where an issue might be hiding. Segment all your data by different audience types, channels, and platforms—then search for those secondary drivers that may lead to valuable insights and breakthrough ideas.

Similarly, do not confuse causality with correlation. Correlation is an apparent relationship between two variables that change together. That doesn't mean one causes the other. To determine if causality exists, you can only use techniques like split-testing, so that discrete groups of customers experience different versions—one a control and the other the feature you want validated. Since you eliminate all other influences, the feature must produce the outcomes.

4. Useful Metrics Are Clear, Shared, and Robustly Measured

Choose simple metrics with clear, precise definitions for shared understanding. Have a transparent methodology for consistently calculating them. Create a data dictionary and, for each metric, include the following:

- A clear, descriptive naming convention (with no ambiguity).

- The rationale for why the metric is important to the business.

- The precise period over which it is always measured.

- A documented technical methodology for tracking and calculating it.

- Ways to handle edge cases and outliers (what gets excluded or capped in the analysis).

Correlation vs. Causation

A team member was evaluating the effectiveness of a new feature on the site. He dutifully gathered data, dividing users into two groups: those that had used the feature and those that had not. He then ran an analysis to see if either group spent more time with the product, came back more often, or stayed on longer as paid customers.

The results were positive—those who had used the feature outperformed the others.

Unfortunately, he had incorrectly assumed that the new feature was the cause of improved engagement. All he had proven was that users who were already more engaged with the product were more likely to try out new features than less-engaged users.

The results were inadvertently biased: there was a correlation (highly engaged users tend to use new features), but there was no causation (the new feature was driving increased engagement). The correct way to have established actual cause and effect was to run a randomized A|B test (where some users got to see the new feature, while others did not).

- Sorting, filtering, and sub-segmentation options (by customer type or channel, for example).

- The expected ranges: "out of range" means there is likely either an anomaly or a calculation error.

- A history of actions or events (product launches, optimization tests, externalities, metric methodology changes, lost or corrupted data) that may have impacted the metric over time.

Help stakeholders internalize the definition, familiarize themselves with reports, and agree that your chosen primary metrics are those that matter most. You will help avoid situations where a stakeholder reacts to a negative impact on a secondary metric when the key metrics are improving.

Data hygiene is of paramount importance. Your data warehousing and tracking systems must be thoroughly tested, reliable, efficient, and automated. If data can be lost or incorrectly reported, then your metrics won't

A Shared Understanding of Metric Definitions across Stakeholders Is Essential

We launched major improvements to the website's search-engine optimization and thought the results a momentous success. While most traffic continued to come through the homepage, search engines now also indexed thousands of "deep-links": pages with content that hadn't previously been picked up by search-engine crawlers. By making them search-engine-friendly, we suddenly increased visitors to our website by about 30 percent.

However, these deep links were also less effective at converting visitors to paying customers. So the site's *average* conversion rate fell (the homepage continued to do well, but now we had more than doubled the traffic to lower-converting pages). The net effect was very positive—we were driving more overall sales—but stakeholders were confused by the results.

We had carefully defined neither our conversion-rate metric nor the need to segment performance for homepage traffic from that for deep-link entry pages. A lower average conversion rate even had some managers thinking that total sales were down and that we should consider a roll-back to *reduce* traffic to the poorer-performing pages.

After many meetings to educate everyone on the actual outcomes—showing the data behind segmented conversion rates that led to increased sales—we finally achieved agreement. But not without some deep disappointment and frustration for the team that had put in such hard work to achieve our goals. Had we first clarified the opportunity and our project goals, and gotten agreement on the metric by which we would measure success, we might have avoided the post-launch crisis.

be accurate. *Your* credibility is damaged when data is proven inaccurate. Ideally, any member of your company should be able to take the same source data, reproduce your analysis, and draw the same conclusions.

1. Improving Product Flows

Each user session with your product is a discrete journey. They have come to your product to achieve a goal—but do they? Or did they drop out without completing what they intended? Did they take too long or follow an inefficient path? Did they become confused at some point?

Start with the customer entry points into your product and then trace the user journey, step by step. Review every decision a user must take, every page or component, every action and result. Look for friction points getting in the way of your users completing their tasks.

Thanks to the advent of many easily integrated out-of-the-box tools, product-flow analysis is one of the simplest ways for a product manager to get the insights necessary to guide usability and flow improvements. However, you must invest time in defining trackable events, adding them to product requirements and understanding and carefully interpreting what the data are telling you.

Imagine the hypothetical website *Centsible* introduced in **Chapter 7**. As you will recall, users are invited to take a quiz to learn more about personal finance and to set up a credit card for tracking their spending (and receiving offers and advice). This flow is illustrated in **Figure 11.2**. Users visiting *Centsible* are offered two choices. The first is for a user who is not ready to signup yet, to learn more about personal finances and what *Centsible* can offer ("take a quiz"). The second choice allows a user ready to start receiving personalized advice, to register, and "link a credit card." Each path has a number of steps that can be analyzed for maximum goal completion and optimal user satisfaction.

Say the product manager has noticed that only 30 percent of potential applicants make it to their goal and wishes to increase that to 50 percent or more. The product manager decides to understand under lying issues within the flow—developing hypotheses around possible causes and looking for telltale signs in the data. Once found, the product manager can do further customer research or A|B testing to improve each step—and ultimately increase goal completion.

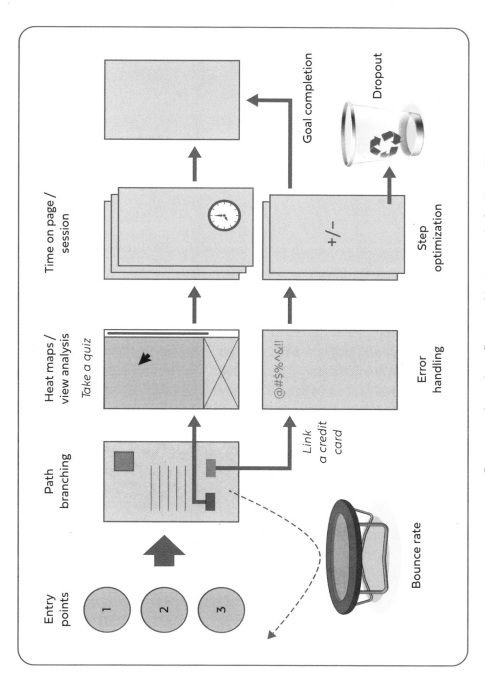

FIGURE 11.2 *Conceptual product-flow tracking example for Centsible*

Consider the Entire Customer Journey

Many products rely on users interacting with touch-points outside of a website or application. Advertising, app store listings, social media channels, email, push notifications, and customer service interactions are all part of your customer's experience with you. So, too, are any physical touch points, such as reliable shipment and delivery of physical goods.

These external elements can create a disjointed experience or be the greatest obstacles to improving your service. Always map out the entire customer journey and look for improvements, especially ones that don't require much engineering time.

Specifically, the product manager may investigate the following:

- **Bounce rate**—The bounce rate is a single-page session. Often it indicates the user did not find what they came looking for and left after scanning only one page or screen. A high bounce rate for *Centsible* might suggest the product manager needs to work on improving the first-time experience and messaging. Perhaps they should experiment with landing pages and personalization technologies to make different traffic sources more relevant and to "speak" to the unique needs of that user. Bounce rate can be misleading, however, and particularly if your service delivers value in a single pageview.

- **Path branching**—Product flows are rarely linear. Choices on a page logically represent different directions a user can take, which branch out to achieve different goals and link back to previous pages. Too many choices increases cognitive load and potentially confuses the user (getting them lost). In *Centsible*'s case, it might be better to focus the user on completing one primary objective ("take a quiz") and encourage finishing the other ("link a credit card") later.

- **View analysis**—You can use tools (such as *heat maps*) and user studies to analyze clicks, mobile gestures, and scrolling behavior. More advanced tools can even evaluate what users are scanning, reading, or hovering over. You might think core features and content are in plain sight, with crystal-clear messaging, but then find that users are searching all over the page for what they want or clicking on other items by mistake. A close look at the heat map for the quiz feature in *Centsible* may suggest users are paying more attention to one area of the page much more than others.

- **Error handling**—Track and determine frequently occurring error conditions that are irritating users. These errors are likely the result of incomplete or unclear messaging or page design. Never assume it's the user's fault. Instead, make it your responsibility to guide them, helping them to avoid errors and to recover as quickly as possible when a user-driven error occurs. The *Centsible* product manager might look at how to avoid incorrectly entered credit card information blocking a user from going further, perhaps through more real-time verification and more explicit error messaging.

- **Engagement time**—Some services prefer to optimize for longer *time-on-page* or *session time*, while others shorter. For *Centsible*, a user interacting with the quiz and learning more about personal finances for a longer time on the site is likely desirable. However, conversely the product manager probably wants to reduce the time the user spends linking a credit card.

Reducing Drop-Off

Working on a user community product, we were measuring dropout during registration and profile setup. While many users completed initial registration, we had a 30 percent drop-off during the steps required to complete an account profile. This was hampering our ability to grow active users.

We brainstormed some alternative approaches. Some were simple (such as enhanced messaging). Others were quite radical (such as eliminating the entire profile setup and letting users join the community immediately).

The simpler options did not make enough progress—we were still asking too much of our first-time users. The more radical ideas were dismissed outright because they created other problems—notably, the risk that bad actors might create invalid and duplicate accounts and behave in unacceptable ways, putting the integrity of the community at risk.

We tested several different combinations, asking less of users, to find what would reduce dropout, while providing enough real-world validation to protect the community. The answer: asking for the user to upload a single profile photo and enter an email address was sufficient. All other attributes we could ask for later, once the user had experienced enough value from the product.

In addition, we added a photo-validation tool that helped our customer service team quickly find profile photos that were not of real people or were duplicate accounts, and to block these.

More Strategies for Flow Optimization

- Speed matters. So make sure your product loads quickly by reducing the overall page and image size. Test response times across target environments (not all users have the high-bandwidth broadband that you enjoy).

- Your user experience team can help organize navigation and overall information architecture so that users quickly find what they need. Remember that your internal jargon and terminology may not make sense to your users.

- Identify the top user goal for each step. Increase its prominence and optimize messaging. Eliminate the less-travelled paths (or link to them in minor menus or side panels).

- Steps that have high levels of user commitment, such as making a purchase in a checkout flow, usually have very high dropouts. Require as little user-entered data as possible, reduce clutter, and minimize competing calls to action to focus the user.

- Consider both in-page progressive revealing of secondary information upon a user's hover or click (which can be done using JavaScript) and infinite scrolling techniques. These will keep the user from having to load a new page or click Next or More or overwhelm the user with too much initially (while still making additional information easily accessible).

- Ensure your time tracking correctly measures actual user interaction with the service. Background windows or applications can overinflate calculations, adding to session time when the user isn't actively engaged.

- Review logs for frequently occurring errors and experiment with instructions, form validation, and instant feedback to help users avoid them.

- Evaluate whether users successfully recover from an error in one try. If not, then your error messages might be vague or written for an internal audience. Don't leave writing error messages to the development team unless you want them to say something like "Error #U4395: Input Invalid."

- **Step optimization**—The product manager might also look to increase or decrease the number of discrete steps necessary to complete a task. Each step is an opportunity for the user to *drop out*—to abandon your product before goal completion, whether through confusion, impatience, or disappointment that they are not getting the value they came seeking. Focus on eliminating or improving the steps with high dropout. For the remaining steps, provide feedback along the way, so the user feels closer to their goal.

   Consider the "cognitive" load for each step. Having fewer steps is not always better as it means you must increase the complexity for any one step. For example, upon reviewing of the link-a-credit-card flow, the product manager may discover that asking for all the user's information on one page was overwhelming and that breaking this into two or more pages reduced abandonment. Sometimes you improve goal completion by adding steps to reinforce your value proposition and guiding the user slowly toward the end goal.

   > ▶ Use KJ brainstorming techniques, RICE prioritization, and split-testing—overviewed in **Chapter 4**—to determine and execute against your product-flow optimization strategy.

   Armed with a better understanding of where the greatest pain points in the existing flows are, a product manager can focus on the highest leverage steps. (Don't try to optimize too much of your product experience at once, as this can become wasteful and it will be harder to discern which of the changes drove benefits.)

   Brainstorming with your team, you can test promising ideas to improve your product flows over time. Don't overlook the simple layout and messaging changes that can make a massive difference and are easiest to test and deploy.

2. Vanity Metrics versus Actionable Value-Based Indicators

Vanity metrics often make their way into company collateral or management updates. They show a nice hockey stick from left to right, illustrating how big and impressive your product has (or will) become. They may look good, but vanity metrics can mask severe fundamental business and product issues—they are distractions from understanding what value users get from your product offering:

- They are included only for bragging rights; they give an illusion of success, such as impressive growth, but perhaps without sustainable customer or business-value generation.

- They over-optimize for short-term decision-making (such as temporary boosts in revenue or delivering product features just to win a deal).

- They are incomplete, painting only a partial picture (the real problems lurk under the surface, masked by apparently positive results).

- They tend to be highly correlated with other metrics, failing to isolate product decisions from other factors (such as sales and marketing activities or external market trends).

- They do not lead naturally to more in-depth analysis and actionable changes.

For example, which metrics are better indications of product success?

- Mobile app *downloads* that sit on the mobile desktop unused? Or fewer app downloads, but ones that are *actively used daily*?

- An e-commerce service's *total customer base*, each submitting an order exactly once? Or a smaller community of *loyal re-purchasers?*

- Your social media *followers* who passively view and "like" your content? Or a sub-group of passionate community users who frequently *engage* with and *share* your posts?

- A media site that attracts millions of *monthly active visitors* who stay there for an average of 10 minutes a month? Or 100,000 passionate readers regularly engaging for an extended *time-on-site* of 30 minutes a day?

In each of the above examples, it is more important to optimize for the second metric than for the vanity metric that precedes it.

Actionable metrics are those that pinpoint and measure specific *behaviors* that customers exhibit within your product, which demonstrate they find sustained, substantial value from using your service. Actionable value-based metrics conform to the *"Attributes of Useful Product-Performance Metrics"* covered at the beginning of this chapter. Specifically, they have some or all of the following characteristics:

- They are comparative over time and against different cohorts. You can measure them frequently and consistently. In particular, you'll usually find them stated as rates—not as absolute numbers.

- They are leading indicators of retention—in that they predict (correlate with or perhaps cause) users continuing to use your service.

- They align the goals and best interests of the user with the activities of the product development team.

- As their name implies, they're actionable (with further analysis) and bring focus—in that they guide the product team to identify initiatives that result in improving that specific metric.

- They isolate the effect of product improvements from externalities or other activities. An increase in a rate after a product improvement signifies that the product change caused the benefit, and not something else.

That is not to say that your company shouldn't track registered users, revenue, client growth, and so on—and also occasionally make decisions to optimize for short-term improvements. But such metrics are not appropriate for product manager accountability. They may create unintended incentives to focus on activities that don't generate long-term value for either your customers or company. By also tracking actionable metrics, you can balance competing goals and empower your product team with the primary charter of driving value for the user.

Actionable metrics can exist at a very high level, measuring the overall performance of the product. High-level metrics are usually owned by a senior product leader in charge of the whole product. More specific metrics might drill into the performance of particular features, perhaps measuring the percentage of users who discover the feature and complete some task—these are best owned by the product manager in charge of that area of functionality.

In general, actionable metrics will be some variant of one or more of the following:

1. **Activation rate**—The ratio of users who both can and do start an activity, whether that be users (at a high level) meaningfully adopting the overall product, or (at a granular level) discovering and trying a specific feature. For example, if 1,000 visitors come to the *Centsible* website and 300 of them start taking a quiz, the quiz activation rate is 30 percent.

2. **Conversion rate**—The ratio of users who started and completed an activity or transaction. Conversion can refer to users opting to pay for your service, or simply a user's success in achieving a goal with your

product. For example, *Centsible* may define a conversion event to be when an unregistered user signs up and links a credit card (since they can now potentially earn revenues from that user).

3. **Retention rate**—The ratio of users still actively using a service at the end of a given period, who were using the product at the start of the period. Retention can be a measure of repeat purchases, paid renewals, or simply continued usage of a product over time. In *Centsible*'s case, they may discover that each month about 5 percent of active users over one month do not come back to engage with their product the next month. Their monthly retention rate is 95 percent.

4. **Frequency of use** (also known as "stickiness ratio")—The portion of users, out of all active users over a long period (say, monthly active users [MAU]), who return to engage with the service over a shorter period (say, daily active users [DAU]). The stickiness ratio is DAU divided by MAU. Increasing frequency means users become more active, generally a positive thing for most services.

5. **Engagement time**—The total time the average active user engages with the service over a defined period (over multiple visits and not just one session). Engagement is critical for content, social, and gaming applications and less so for transactional services (such as e-commerce and enterprise). For example, if the average *Centsible* user returns three times in a month and spends 10 minutes reviewing their personal finances, total engagement time is 30 minutes per month per user.

6. **Match rate**—A measure of how accurate the recommended content is to the end user. This metric is specifically useful for services with heavy personalization, a marketplace, or targeted advertising features. One of the goals for *Centsible*'s "take a quiz" feature is to tailor content recommendations to the user's answers. By measuring how many of those content recommendations are then consumed by the quiz taker, *Centsible* can improve the quality of its quiz and its ability to match useful content to the user's needs.

7. **Referral rate**—A measure of virality that addresses the following question: Assuming your product is delivering value to customers, to what extent do they promote and advocate your product to others? Imagine *Centsible* asks users to share their completed quiz scores with friends and family. The percentage of users who do so is the referral rate.

In the online resources at http://www.influentialpm.com, you can find a detailed overview of these seven common actionable metrics and examples, which can be adapted to your needs.

Actionable metrics can be a particularly important addition for regular monitoring and reporting of an enterprise company's products. In business-to-business companies, the focus tends to be on a deep understanding of sales metrics (such as lead-to-conversion rates, client deal sizes, transaction volumes, and win-loss ratios). But, after a successful sale, it may be a year or more before the customer is up for renewal—how do you know whether the client is getting value out of the service in the intervening time without subsequently measuring end-user behavior?

Sales metrics are appropriate for a sales team but should never be the sole metrics for the supporting product team. If you are also tracking

The Dangers of Vanity Metrics

We were presenting the monthly dashboard, and among the metrics were some vanity metrics such as 20 million total registered users and 4 million monthly active users.

During the end-of-month review, the CEO asked whether the fact that only about one-fifth of registered users was active was a problem or not. Was this to be expected after six years of operation? Admittedly, we should have expected many inactive accounts by then. But how many?

Attention turned to the monthly active-user metric: 4 million. This represented about a 6 percent drop over January. This led to a discussion about possible causes for the lower performance in February and what to do about it until a product manager at the meeting pointed out that February has three fewer days than January.

Following the meeting, I convinced the CEO to introduce a few additional actionable value-based metrics to focus attention instead on how successfully the product delivered on users' needs. As a result, the following metrics became part of the dashboard:

- "Stickiness ratio" (Did users frequently use the service?)—Calculated as the number of daily active users divided by the number of monthly active users

- "Goal-completion" (Did users achieve the task they came for?)—Measured by the number of user sessions that ended with a transaction divided by the total number of user sessions started

The product team had responsibility for improving performance on these metrics and reporting progress.

(Incidentally, for our specific service, we chose not to track "total time engaged per month"—cumulatively, how much time users spend on the product—even though it qualifies as a value-based indicator. Since our goal was to get the user to transact as quickly as possible, it would have been in conflict with our user's needs.)

successful customer onboarding and integration, and employee account activation and engagement, you can understand the health of each client account. These are leading indicators—low adoption likely correlates with (but won't be the sole source of) cancelations. By monitoring these metrics too, you have plenty of time to address any issues in the product before the renewal period.

3. Quantifying Customer Satisfaction

Behavioral metrics are good proxies for (or leading indicators of) customer value creation. But measuring satisfaction—by asking your customer for feedback—is a more direct way to track loyalty and the likeliness of retention.

Customer satisfaction can help you evaluate your product at two levels:

1. Overall, how well is your product performing relative to competitor benchmarks or customer expectations?

2. Specifically, in what benefits (features and functionality) are you failing, meeting, or exceeding customer expectations?

Accurate measurement can involve substantial work—preparing high-quality questionnaires, identifying and qualifying customers to survey, and following up to increase participation. You then need to analyze, interpret, and link results back to in-service customer behavior (to correlate satisfaction with the customer's real-world experience with the product). Doing this well requires leveraging experienced data analytics professionals, many hours of preparation, and infinite patience. As a result, it is often done too infrequently. However, measuring customer satisfaction need not be so complicated.

It's possible that your company has customer research personnel who frequently survey users. If so, approach them to see what they already monitor. If necessary, ask if you can add some questions specifically about your product and get access to their raw data (as opposed to secondary reports). If you aren't currently surveying customer satisfaction, I'll introduce a couple of simple approaches to get you started.

1. Overall Customer Satisfaction

A popular methodology to measure overall customer satisfaction is the *Net Promoter Score* (NPS). NPS reduces customer satisfaction down to a single, highly visible metric (and sets a very high bar). To determine your NPS score, ask users the question,

> "On a scale of zero to ten, how likely are you to refer/recommend [your product] to a friend or colleague?"

As shown in **Figure 11.3**, once you have results, group together detractors (people who rate your product from 0 to 6) and promoters (who rate it 9 to 10), then subtract the percentage of the detractors from the promoters. Ignore passives (those who give a 7 to 8 rating).

Always follow up the NPS question with one or a couple of qualitative questions to understand why the respondent answered the way they did—otherwise NPS is not actionable.

Merely making customers happy or satisfied is not sufficient to reach an NPS in the 50-plus range. You must delight most of your customers, such that they become advocates.

NPS has received some valid criticism. Some common issues:

- Without a large enough sample set, it lacks statistical significance and, as such, can vary wildly from one measurement period to the next.

- It is subject to bias in the customer selection process and overemphasizes recent customer experiences.

- It is not comparable across industries—some industries consistently rate very low in NPS across the board. NPS is useful for comparing your product to competitors but not to outside-industry players.

Detractors	0–6	%D	
Passives	7–8	%S	**NPS = %P – %D**
Promoters	9–10	%P	–100 ⟷ 100
Total		**100%**	

FIGURE 11.3 *Scoring an NPS survey*

- Many products are not inherently referral-based, such as intimate, sensitive, everyday, or "boring" products. For example, you are unlikely to go out of your way to recommend taxation-preparation software, self-help tools, or personal hygiene items to your colleagues and friends. A low NPS does not mean the customer isn't satisfied—they might just not be comfortable being a vocal advocate.

- Without secondary root-cause analysis, NPS isn't very actionable.

Nonetheless, if backed up by more sophisticated customer surveys, research programs, product tracking, and reports from customer service, NPS can provide a quick and easy (if imperfect) way to elevate customer satisfaction to a top-of-mind quantifiable business metric.

NPS Is Sensitive to User Perception and Other Biases

I was working on an online skills-development product. We'd built a vibrant subscriber base of self-trained consultants and professionals, enjoying weekly content releases. Anecdotally, we heard stories of changing peoples' lives—professionals previously stuck working in poor jobs able to break into new careers, older employees using the product to keep their skills current to compete alongside crops of young graduates trained in the latest techniques, and mothers able to reenter the workforce after a long hiatus.

But NPS was very low. We sought to understand the disconnect and discovered users' reasoning. Far from being dissatisfied with the product offering, their unwillingness to refer the product to others was a deeply personal fear: "I'm embarrassed. I don't want any of my friends or colleagues to know I don't know how to do that skill already!"

A similar case occurred for an on-demand workforce marketplace. The NPS was negative until they realized that no one user would refer another user since the referred user might be competition in the on-demand labor pool. Simply adding to the NPS question "if it didn't impact your business opportunities," NPS rose by 60 points.

And at a niche video-content company, NPS survey completion rates were very low. In the research, users responded that their "friends and colleagues wouldn't be interested in this content." After changing the question to "recommend this product to someone like you," survey completion rates soared.

Finally, be careful of selection bias. One company consistently rated NPS in the 60s, but a closer look revealed they were only surveying users who had been active for at least 20 minutes. Half their users had moved on by then (an example of survivor bias). After launching a revised survey strategy that reached all users, NPS fell by 10 points—which is still an excellent score.

2. Ranking Customer Satisfaction of Specific Benefits and Functionality

A simple approach to evaluating satisfaction with specific benefits, functionality, or features is to ask customers a two-part question with the option of four multiple-choice answers (or rankings on a scale from 1 to 4) for each component of your service, as outlined in **Figure 11.4**. Four options are better than five, because this eliminates fence-sitting (neutral) responses (such as "Neither satisfied nor dissatisfied"), forcing customers to express an opinion one way or the other.

Components you can survey for can include specific features and flows, or benefits and user outcomes. Test basic needs or table-stakes and your key differentiation features. For example, for the *Centsible* application, you might may ask users to rate their satisfaction on:

- Ease of use
- Application speed and stability
- Account set-up
- Link credit card
- Review spending activity
- Usefulness of quizzes
- Breadth of personal finance content
- Effectiveness of personal finance content
- Quality of personal finance management recommendations

Remove biased language (for example, word as "application speed" rather than "fast application") and ensure each description is meaningful to your audience at a glance. Provide an optional free-form comment box for users to write thoughts or justifications for their choices. You may find clues to problems or misunderstandings in your questions.

Asking for ratings for both satisfaction *and* importance provides invaluable data. You can use the responses to force-rank features and functionality into the following four quadrants to inform product-optimization priorities:

- **Cut**—If you have a dissatisfying element in your service that is of limited use to customers, consider cutting it altogether to simplify the user experience and reduce maintenance complexity. If cutting is not possible, consider making the element less prominent and put minimal effort into further development.

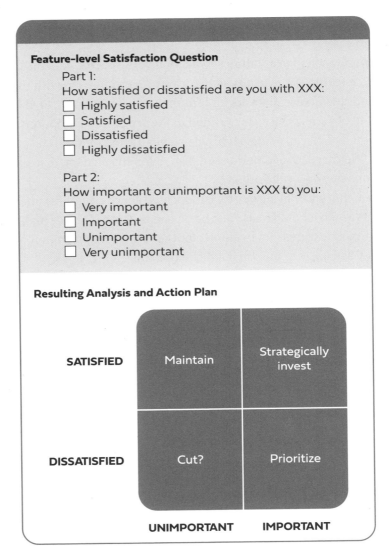

FIGURE 11.4 *A simple customer satisfaction survey question and matrix*

- **Maintain**—Don't invest further in features that are meeting customer expectations but do little to differentiate your service. Keep monitoring usage trends, however, in case a feature turns out to be more critical than once thought.

- **Strategically invest**—Perhaps counter-intuitively, consider additional investment in high-satisfaction, high-importance areas, so you make customers even more delighted and put even more distance between yourself and alternatives.

- **Prioritize**—Invest in high importance but low-medium satisfaction components. Some features may need considerable work to close the gap between what you have today and what customers expect.

Follow up your surveys with more in-depth, qualitative analyses—user interviews, other surveys, and firsthand customer feedback from your customer service department.

Complete surveys regularly (perhaps quarterly) so you can identify if investments are achieving the results you hoped for or if new gaps have emerged. Note, though, that you should try not to change your methodology or questions too dramatically from survey to survey—if you do, comparative analysis becomes challenging.

▶ Combining customer satisfaction surveys with the Kano analysis (**Chapter 4**) enables you to measure current satisfaction and prioritize future features in one exercise.

Unless you must use anonymous surveys, link your NPS and satisfaction data with actual user behavior data from product tracking. Connecting these data sets can give you insight into which particular experiences are affecting satisfaction, either in positive or negative ways, and help you understand how a positive NPS is correlated with frequent use of your overall product. You'll be able to analyze perceptions versus usage, helping you to uncover more trends or disconnects between stated and demonstrated preferences. Different user types might value varying features: for instance, highly loyal customers will be more likely to emphasize satisfaction with different components than first-time users (or irregular users).

4. Breaking Down Your Customer Relationship Funnel

Customer relationship funnels can be mistaken for, but differ substantially from, the product flows already introduced. Unlike product flows, a funnel

- is from the customer's perspective (not that of the product);

- represents the lifecycle stage (current mindset or depth of relationship) that the user is in with your business or service;

- maps the entire relationship and, as such, is likely to include many interactions with your product (not just a single visit) across all customer touch-points over a long period of time.

Figure 11.5 represents one of many funnels you can use to conceptualize the user's journey with your product. There is no hard and fast rule to the nomenclature or the steps in the customer funnel. Companies vary in their language—especially that used with consumers versus enterprise businesses—perhaps combining or adding some stages.

Imagine a funnel that represents a customer's relationship with your product or service: it starts from the very first time they become aware of your product, perhaps through advertising or a recommendation. At this stage, they don't know much about it—only that maybe it could solve a problem they have. They are unclear about your value proposition; perhaps, even suspicious.

After they learn more about your product—say, by visiting your marketing website—they might become more interested. They see that you might solve their problem and explore your product's website to learn more. They are now in the *consideration* stage. Here, you must do an excellent job of educating them about your value proposition and overcoming their objections.

Next, some of them research, download your application, register for your product (if you provide it for free), agree to a trial, or purchase your product (if you offer a paid product). They are in the *acquisition* stage.

Many product managers fall into the trap in believing the hard work is done after they acquire a user. However, now you must get them to start

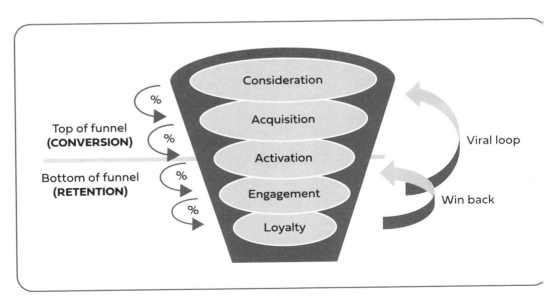

FIGURE 11.5 *An example consumer business customer funnel*

using your product (the *activation* stage), or they might give up quickly and maybe ask for a refund. You'd better get them hooked—as a one-time user is not very valuable. Customer dropout at this stage can be substantial, which is why careful attention should be paid to making "first-time use" (also called onboarding or adoption) a compelling and enjoyable experience. First impressions matter!

The *engagement* stage, when the customer or user interacts more fully and frequently with your service, follows. Now they are beginning to get value from your service but have not yet become habitual users. They are still evaluating, and you still have much to prove.

The next stage is *loyalty* (or advocacy). Your customer is habitually using your product, and you're likely earning ongoing revenue streams from them. Keeping them coming back is paramount. If you retain and delight these users, they will be more likely to refer others into the "top of the funnel" (into the awareness stage, thus completing a *viral loop*). Or perhaps you have additional services you can upsell them.

Any elapsed or dormant user is one that stops using your service for any reason. They present an opportunity for a *win-back* (also called a reactivation)—the process of remarketing your service and convincing them to try it again. These can be some of the lowest-cost customers to acquire, especially if you have improved the service or launched exciting new functionality since they last engaged with you.

Conversion (the top of the funnel) commonly defines the moment the user or potential customer first becomes a revenue-generating user (direct or indirect) of the service, which may happen at the same time as, or some time after, acquisition. *Retention* (the bottom of the funnel) is the process of keeping existing revenue-generating users engaged and continuing to use your product.

Since users can drop out at any stage, the path from awareness to loyalty looks like a funnel: wide at the top and narrower toward the bottom. Funnels allow you to sub-segment customers into levels that reflect their depth of relationship with you, helping you to pinpoint

1. where the greatest opportunities for improvement are (which is usually where the largest percentage of dropouts occurs), and

2. the friction points, actions, and behaviors that encourage (or discourage) users to take the next step.

Track the percentage of users who graduate from one stage to the next (along with those who drop out) to identify where your greatest opportunities lie.

Strategies for Funnel Optimization

- Conduct A|B tests on messaging, landing pages, and trial offers to increase conversion rates. Outsized gains can come from seemingly small changes. (**Chapter 4**)

- Deliver first-time customers a superior onboarding experience to increase the likelihood they will become loyal customers. Low customer retention is often really a result of a poor activation experience. First impressions are made within hours or days.

- If your company is focused only on sales, conversion and growth, advocate for customer delighting features to improve engagement and retention. These initiatives often have longer-term payback periods and are therefore easily deprioritized.

- Your most loyal users are your greatest advocates and can be leveraged to drive word-of-mouth and viral growth. Consider giving them tools and an incentive to drive referrals.

- Lifecycle marketing (CRM, email, push notification, community, and other "off-line" programs) is an essential tool for bringing users back to your product—keeping them engaged and progressing through later stages of the funnel. Partner closely with your marketing department to invest in post-purchase retention programs, not just to drive new sales.

For example, if you have a step with a 60 percent dropout, and you successfully decrease this to 50 percent, you have moved 25 percent more customers down to the next stage. This is better than focusing on a step that already performs at 90 percent and driving it up to 99 percent (getting 10 percent more customers to the next step).

By cohorting users (that is, aggregating users into a group based on receiving the same product experience over a similar time period) you can see where your product improvements are successfully moving users further down into the funnel.

5. Understanding Customer Lifetime Value

Customer lifetime value, or simply lifetime value (LTV), is the superior metric for measuring the financial performance of a product—better even than revenue or return-on-investment. That's because it captures the customer's total gross margin contribution across their entire lifecycle with you, from their conversion to the day they leave your service.

Figure 11.6 illustrates a simple LTV formula. It is calculated by taking the average revenue per customer (ARPC) and subtracting the cost to deliver the service to the customer (COGS). By dividing this by the churn rate, you can calculate your product's LTV. (This formula assumes a consistent average monthly churn rate. For the purposes of discussion, we'll assume measurement is on a monthly basis and the same month-to-month—but that doesn't have to be the case. For example, many enterprise B2B services renew annually.)

- **Average revenue per customer** (ARPC)—ARPC is the expected monthly revenue earned from each customer. It includes revenue derived from direct sales or subscriptions, from indirect advertising or third-party revenue streams, or from upsells of additional products and services to existing customers. It is sometimes referred to as ARPU ("user" instead of "customer")—which is commonly used when users don't directly pay for your service but you might still derive revenue from their interaction with your service.

- **Cost of goods sold** (COGS)—COGS factors in all *variable* costs associated with servicing and delivering the product to customers, such as supplier time and materials costs, customer support, retention incentives, and product returns or refunds. (Visit http://www.influentialpm .com for a more thorough breakdown of COGS and why you do not factor in *fixed* costs.) Subtract COGS from ARPC, and you have your monthly *gross margin* per customer.

$$LTV = \frac{(ARPC-COGS)}{churn\ rate}\ ; or$$

$$LTV = \frac{(ARPC-COGS)}{(1-retention\ rate)}$$

FIGURE 11.6 *LTV formula for a constant churn rate*

- **Churn rate**—As mentioned previously in this chapter, churn rate is the percentage of customers lost each month. Even the best-run consumer and SaaS services report losing 2 to 5 percent of their customer base every month.

- **Customer lifetime value** (LTV)—This is simply the summation of the monthly gross margin divided by the churn rate, and it represents the profitable value of an average customer over the entire relationship with that customer.

In reality, calculating your LTV is rarely as straightforward as the formula shown in **Figure 11.6**. To be sufficiently sophisticated, you will need to model out how cohorts of segmented customers pay on an ongoing basis for your service and determine how many of them stop paying for your service, for example, on a month 1, 2, 3, and so-on basis. It is common for users to churn in higher proportions earlier in their relationship with you, while deeply loyal users are slower to churn. For a detailed example, see the online resources at http://www.influentialpm.com.

LTV analysis is incomplete until you compare it to the *customer acquisition cost* (CAC) or *cost per acquisition* (CPA)—the initial cost of acquiring the customer. Some teams assume that acquiring users is the most critical early goal for a new product—they want to build the user base as rapidly as possible. However, to be profitable, ensure that

$$LTV > CAC.$$

Generally, LTV analysis should be broken down by channel, whether paid distribution channels (expensive), advertising and marketing channels (better), referrals (cheap), or organic and viral methods (free!). Often one channel will have a lower CAC or a lower churn rate and is, therefore, more attractive than another. LTV analysis allows you to make better decisions on when best to scale up and to partner with your marketing acquisition team on which channels to focus on.

If your LTV for a particular channel is less than the CAC for that channel, then you are losing money on each new customer. That might be okay under certain circumstances if you

- understand how to make LTV profitable over time, *and*

- know how your economies of scale will lower CAC and COGS, *and*

- are in "land-grab" mode to build a large, defensible footprint, *and*

More Strategies for Improving LTV and CAC

Product managers are responsible for total market success of their product and therefore must engage throughout an organization to influence long-term superior economics.

- Price-test and vary your business model (perhaps offering premium tiers or upselling opportunities) to increase ARPU. Price-testing is never easy, so be sure to research extensively proven methodologies and understand the risks.

- Offer longer terms (particularly for enterprise and subscription businesses) in exchange for substantial discounts (for instance, 30–40 percent off for users who opt for a one-year commitment over month-to-month payments). Such changes lower monthly ARPU—however, they often increase LTV because they also lower churn.

- Seek superior COGS (renegotiate with suppliers, invest in development resources to lower the cost of service delivery and customer support, and automate internal business systems).

- Collaborate with marketing to optimize CAC, starting with segmenting LTV by channel and increasing the mix of lower-cost channels.

- Leverage unique differentiators such as network effects (the value derived from a community of interconnected users), personalization (customization driven from your unique understanding of user data), and other features that raise the barrier for exit—making it less likely that users will move to alternatives. (**Chapter 3**)

- have patient executives or investors willing to lose money while you figure out your unit economics.

Otherwise, it might be best to concentrate on creating and limiting yourself to a smaller but more loyal user base until you have control over the profitability of your business (which should be, at least, break-even).

Such is the power of LTV analysis: it can highlight where your best opportunities are, not just within your product, but within your entire business model—it's a very powerful, actionable metric.

CHAPTER 12

Advance Your Career

Evaluate your skills and identify professional growth opportunities.

1 Perspectives on how to view your strategic role and responsibilities in a modern technology organization.

2 Five superpowers that outstanding product managers possess and that you can acquire.

3 How to view your product management career trajectory, with advice for aspiring but nontechnical product managers.

No, You're Not the CEO of the Product

Often thrown about as a catchphrase, "the product manager is the CEO of the product" is not entirely true. You don't have the power of a CEO to assign people to specific roles or tasks—quite the opposite. You have no direct authority (although that doesn't mean you can't get things done through influence). And you are unlikely, particularly early on in your career or at larger companies, to own a real profit and loss statement (P&L), set the overall vision for the product, decide budgets, allocate resources, negotiate strategic partnerships, or establish product pricing. In many ways, product managers are not at all like CEOs.

But it *can* be helpful to think of yourself as the single, directly responsible individual (DRI) ultimately accountable for product success.

Doing so forces you to think broadly and strategically. You are charged with being the voice of the customer. You understand the product vision and align other team members around it. You take responsibility for establishing, communicating, and measuring business goals. (If your product isn't as successful as you'd hoped, what have you learned about your customer and how can you evolve your product to address those new insights?)

Thinking of yourself as the DRI for the product also forces you to focus and execute. You must communicate effectively and collaborate with a cross-functional team, coordinating across business functions and with design and engineering. If your product isn't being delivered on time or to scope, what can *you do* to get it back on track? If stakeholders aren't appearing to be supportive, what can *you do* to generate buy-in or gather feedback?

Martin Eriksson, cofounder and curator of the excellent product management blog *Mind The Product* (http://www.mindtheproduct.com) proposes a simple but powerful Venn diagram (**Figure 12.1**), made up of the following elements, to illustrate how you can think about your central role in driving product success:

- **Business**—Focus on creating value for customers, and ultimately for your company, by connecting business objectives to product outcomes. Appreciate and align yourself with the organization's purpose and goals, and know how what you are doing relates to those. Eliminate business risks and seek to generate sustainable revenue streams. Understand the basics of essential business functions such as marketing, sales, business operations, and finance. Work closely with

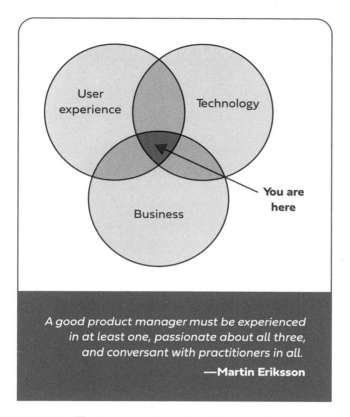

*A good product manager must be experienced
in at least one, passionate about all three,
and conversant with practitioners in all.*
—Martin Eriksson

FIGURE 12.1 *The intersecting role of the product manager*

customers and external partners, and partner with internal business teams at your company. Be ready to work within real-world business constraints, resource limitations, and deadlines.

- **User experience**—Develop empathy by getting out of your office and meeting regularly with customers. Dig deep into user research and behavioral data. Ensure the product experience meets high standards. Regularly validate your product with end users and collect improvement feedback. Collaborate with design, user testing, consumer insights, and creative and brand teams to deliver superior and delighting experiences.

- **Technology**—Develop an understanding of your technology platform and vital engineering tasks. Make yourself available to your development team to clarify questions, discuss priorities, collaborate on solution options, and make trade-offs. Product managers require the closest of relationships with their engineering teams: developers, quality assurance, and the technical operations personnel who will support your product once it is released.

Usually, a product manager will be an expert in one or two of these areas, perhaps having previously worked in a business function, in product design, or as a developer. You don't need to be an expert in all fields—you can rely on the expertise of others. You *do* have to enjoy learning the fundamentals, however, and be comfortable working seamlessly across all three specialties. You're responsible for bringing all three together to make progress toward a common product goal. That's why you are at the center of Eriksson's Venn diagram.

If you apply the practices outlined throughout the book, you will eventually master the mindsets, techniques, and relationships necessary to become an outstanding product manager. However, each product manager's journey can be quite different—given unique company environments, adaptations of different tools and processes, formal and informal training programs, and the kinds of managers and mentors with whom you surround yourself.

In this chapter, I will help you contextualize your journey and spot potential gaps you can address proactively. In the resources online at http://www.influentialpm.com, you will find skill-assessment templates and examples to help you identify your current strengths, so that you can develop your skill-development plan.

The 3Ps of Product Management: Product, Process, People

To ensure you are effectively working across all aspects of product management, use a simple 3Ps framework (see **Figure 12.2**). Refer to this framework regularly so that you don't overlook anything substantial, and reference relevant chapters when you need reminders about the tactics you should employ.

Product	Why we build and what we build (and what we don't) in our products
Process	How we discover, prioritize, validate, develop, launch, and evolve our products
People	Who we serve or partner with and how we engage to be successful with our products

FIGURE 12.2 *The 3Ps of product management*

1. The Product *P* Stands for All Aspects of Delivering Solutions of Value

It may seem obvious that product managers manage a product. However, simply defining *what* the product is, is insufficient. As we have seen, specifications can be initially quite vague and fluid, nailed down only through collaboration with customers, stakeholders, and team members.

Deciding what *not* to build is often as critical as deciding what to build. Often delivering smaller product increments can accelerate time-to-market, minimize investment, reduce risk, and enable you to start learning before you determine what to build next. You must address the many goals of your organization optimally, while also addressing the needs of your customers through goal-driven methodical prioritization techniques. These are the decisions and trade-offs you must own, assess, and balance.

Arguably more important, it is the product manager's responsibility to define, communicate, and reinforce *why* the product should exist. What is the customer problem you are solving, for whom are you solving it, and why is it worth investing in?

Finally, product managers must "close the loop" and identify and track the core metrics that show the value you are delivering to your customers and your business—and iterate and evolve their product to optimize for this value.

2. The Process *P* Stands for Following the Organization's Approaches to Managing the Product Lifecycle

Product managers must understand how work gets done in their organization to be successful. This is nontrivial. Not all processes are well documented, and they can often appear as informal, "unspoken" cultural norms. Determine each step in the product lifecycle and seek out your standard process—or create one if none exists. Don't wing it.

The process will broadly follow this pattern:

- **Identify and prioritize ideas**—Determine how potential initiatives are identified, captured, and prioritized. Initiatives might be decided in a top-down nature, or your organization may broadly canvas for candidates. Different levels of data, analysis, and approvals might be required at each step. They might take shortcuts with high-priority issues, disrupting other work in flight. Understanding how work is identified and prioritized allows you to add your own ideas or to influence others to advance the ideas you feel have the most potential.

- **Discover customer needs and validate solutions**—Understand how to schedule and complete your own customer research and to participate in the research activities of other departments. As your product takes shape, continue validation throughout discovery and delivery,

Create Value for Customers, First and Foremost

My client, a company that had recently had an IPO, had to deal with pressures typical of an organization now answerable to the stock market. Its core business was under competitive pressure, and its new digital businesses were still going through growing pains. All eyes were on the company's key quarterly metrics: top-line revenue and new customer growth (converting site visitors into paying customers). Not much else mattered. The roadmap focused on every conceivable way to optimize landing pages and convince users to register for the product. New pricing tiers, discounts, and payment options (such as international banking and credit cards) were introduced. Personalized email marketing campaigns were devised and delivered.

But the product manager felt something was missing—and he was right. In the effort to deliver on short-term business metrics, the team had lost sight of keeping loyal customers happy. Satisfaction was low, retention was falling, and competitors were catching up. With all the effort to gain new customers, the business had forgotten that its real purpose was to deliver sustained value to its customers.

I argue that focusing on long-term value for your customers should *supersede* focusing on short-term value for your business. Solve your customers' problems first, rather than optimizing for a business goal that has little to do with end-customer value. It is rarely that simple; however, balance pursuit of short-term goals with regularly delighting your customers with unexpected and high-impact solutions and, usually, sustainable business value will follow.

and after your product is launched and in-market. Never shortchange discovery and validation in the interest of "going faster."

- **Document specifications and manage requirements**—Figure out the tools used to document product needs. Use templates for consistency and to avoid overlooking essential details. Invite collaboration, be responsive to answering questions, and allow for flexibility as you learn from testing and other feedback.

- **Develop products**—Learn how work flows through the design and development queue. At what stages should you provide input and test out the emerging product? Which decisions are you simply informed about and on which do you have a direct say?

- **Launch and support products**—Ascertain the steps required to approve and launch your product, including risk management, bug management and resolution, and go-to-market steps.

3. The People *P* Stands for Collaborating with a Variety of Stakeholders to Be Successful

This book focuses on the human element of product management. This overlooked aspect of product management can also be the hardest to master and a major reason that product managers fail or their career growth stalls. Put into place the practices outlined throughout this book and you will increase the chance that you garner broad organizational support. You'll also earn a healthy reputation as someone who can be relied upon to drive outcomes for both your customers and your business.

Your most critical relationship is with your engineering and design counterparts. You must also be in regular communication and in sync with your direct manager. But while these are vital relationships to cultivate, others are also crucial.

Identify, recruit, and involve a broad set of stakeholders. Who provides input on product direction? Who will you rely on to make the product successful? You need trusted relationships so you can access customers, gather valuable market feedback, and drive adoption of your product. Trust is also essential when you inevitably make mistakes or when a product release fails.

And always keep the number-one priority in mind—as the product manager, you're the "voice of the customer." You are expected to know more about the customer than is any other person on the team. You build empathy for customers; you spend time out of the office talking with them and observing them. Yes, it's easy to slip into laziness, rarely venturing out of your office. You're their advocate and must consider any decision from their point of view. You might occasionally make trade-offs to maximize short-term business metrics or to please demanding internal stakeholders. Or you might take shortcuts in the experience so as to hit a deadline. But to be effective, you'll need to make sure customers' long-term interests are represented and considered when making decisions that affect them.

Product Manager Superpowers

As you develop your career as a product manager, in addition to "hard skills" such as your technical and business capabilities, you'll need to develop effective "people skills" to build rapport and support. After years of building teams and interviewing managers of product teams across the industry, I can say that anyone exhibiting some or all of the following "superpowers" is more likely to excel as a product manager.

These attributes appear to be innate, embedded in the attitude and behaviors they bring to work every single day. (That's not to say there won't be bad days.)

Superpower 1—Insatiable Intellectual Curiosity

You may be surprised to see intellectual curiosity listed as a people skill. In isolation, it is not. However, product managers can use their natural curiosity to discover insights about their customer and surface new problems to solve. Be tenacious when it comes to tackling demanding, ambiguous problems, breaking them down into smaller, manageable components. You must be analytical, seek out data, and make decisions based on the best information available. You must be highly detail-oriented and not afraid to go deep when needed.

Equally so, you must be comfortable in ambiguity, willing to go with intuition when data is not forthcoming. You should enjoy the challenge and relish finding solutions, perhaps taking an unexpected and innovative approach, and sharing new discoveries to excite the team around you.

Superpower 2—A Sense of Ownership

Outstanding product managers have a deep sense of ownership across all aspects of their product. They work to collaborate with any part of an organization necessary to define, build, launch, and drive the market success of their product initiatives. They collaborate widely, reaching well beyond their immediate design and engineering team members.

Step up to lead as needed—roll up your sleeves to help your team deliver. Don't limit yourself to doing only the work detailed in your job description—if something needs to get done, you must find a way to get it done. Product managers never say, "That's not my responsibility."

Have passion for your work and set attainable but tough goals for yourself, then strive to deliver or beat them. Ship product regularly, even if it's imperfect. Circle back to customers to be sure the solution successfully addressed the problem you set out to solve and take ownership for fixing critical issues. Great product managers live to address their customers' problems and are rarely satisfied until customers express delight in the solution—then they tenaciously get to work on the next problem.

Superpower 3—Overcommunication

Good written and verbal communication skills are essential in most professional, team-oriented roles, but a product manager needs to take it a step further. You have to be able to communicate effectively across all levels of seniority in a cross-functional organization. You must learn how to be an effective communicator one on one, in team meetings, and in presentations to large groups. You should be able to deliver highly structured, succinct business updates. You must be approachable and remain at ease when chatting informally, as you build personal relationships.

You have no direct authority over the team, yet you must find a way to build support. You must lead with trust—assume everyone is working with good intent. Be open to pushback and feedback, and embrace "healthy" conflict—the type of conflict where you discuss differences respectfully and constructively to reach a compromise.

Being able to inspire and motivate others is a definite plus. You don't need to be an extroverted evangelist, but you should have an infectious enthusiasm for the problem you are solving, remain optimistic when dealing with challenges, and be able to provide context for how the team's efforts positively impact the customer and deliver business results.

Superpower 4—Think and Act Strategically

When you are heads-down addressing issues or dealing with day-to-day demands, it's all too easy to neglect strategy.

Becoming a strategic thinker need not be daunting—it just requires you to invest time in deliberately exploring and planning for the future. All too often, the urgent, tactical issues get in the way. Switch your time between execution and strategy; which requires discipline because there will almost always be something else "urgent" demanding of your time. Acting strategically includes visiting and understanding customers, thinking about your overall vision and the progress you are making toward your goals, digging into interesting data or industry trends, updating your roadmap, and evangelizing the product within your company.

Superpower 5—An Egoless Existence

Don't let your ego get in the way. When something goes wrong, accept that there are things that you could have done better (and don't blame the team). When something goes right, step back from the limelight and liberally praise the team.

Great product managers are resilient to change. Your senior managers make many decisions and trade-offs. Customers can be unreasonably demanding even when you deliver them something they desperately need. Competitors do unexpected things. All of these things may impact you negatively. For instance, your company likely has a rich product portfolio, each product requiring its share of resources, and this may mean you can't get the resources you think you need. Perhaps a key initiative in another part of the organization is in trouble and getting it back on track comes at the expense of your project. Your company's business objectives might be reprioritized if revenue is slower than expected. Rather than resist, get with the program, quickly and with few, if any, complaints. You should seek to understand the context behind the decision and help get everyone else behind the change (for example, by talking about it in a positive light with your team members). You must be adaptable and able to support management if you are to be successful.

These skills will come to you in time, especially if you explicitly pay attention and invest effort into acquiring them. Don't let yourself become overwhelmed. Instead, learn to do the following:

- **Identify and play to your strengths**—Be aware of, and confident in, what you are good at. You will find that you will employ your strengths effortlessly. And you can build rapport with others by being willing to help them practice and develop those skills you are naturally good at.

- **Admit your weaknesses and learn**—Become aware of and improve a few areas in which you are weak. Achieving some proficiency might be all that is needed. Do not focus exclusively on your development opportunities but become very conscious of blind spots, as you never want them to be your Achilles' heel.

- **Leverage the strengths of others**—You don't have to do it all. Partner and learn from peers who have complementary strengths. By building trusted relationships with them, you can use them as sounding boards and trust them to take the lead when they can.

Advice for Non–Technical Product Managers

Some companies—those with enterprise products or complex platforms, or those with hardware, data-intensive, or engineering-driven cultures—may be unwilling to hire product managers lacking deep technical expertise and an engineering degree.

But at many companies, product managers do not need formal technical qualifications. This is especially true when the role emphasizes more interaction with customers, which is common for many consumer products and enterprise roles where the product manager often meets with clients. In a survey of job descriptions for entry-level associate product manager positions in mid-2017, only 30 percent *required* a technical degree or equivalent engineering experience. (Although many more *desired* a technical degree, they were presumably open to making the trade-off.)

A scarcity of engineering talent is not the only reason behind the reduced need for highly technical product managers. Development tools, processes, and team self-accountability have all matured, diminishing the need for product managers to manage day-to-day delivery. We're (thankfully) trusting developers more to be true partners in *what* the product will be and to let them own the question of *how* to get there. This is because of the following:

- Engineers can make perfectly good product decisions in collaboration with you when you provide context. They understand what the technology can do.

- Mature development processes entrust and drive accountability for developers, enabling them to commit to what they will deliver in a given timeframe rather than to a deadline they have no control over.

- Given the fast pace of modern technology companies, timelines or requirements can quickly become obsolete. What's needed is flexibility and collaboration in responding to new learnings and revised needs.

Strategies to Earn Technical Credibility

A product manager without technical training must still have technical curiosity and creditability. For instance, you must enjoy keeping current with the latest trends, earn the respect of your engineering counter parts, and communicate effectively in technical conversations (to keep up!).

Here are some specific activities you can do to build your technical expertise and earn creditability:

- Make a list of websites, podcasts, and blogs to read or regularly listen to (see http://www.influentialpm.com for a recommended reading list).

- Enroll in some credible online coding courses—consider "101" introductory courses and complete a few to develop a range of relevant skills.

- Join a coding boot camp or hackathon—work in a team.

- Complete a few coding projects of your own—build a website, application, or game and add these to your portfolio to show others.

- Ask your engineering counterpart to whiteboard the overall technology architecture for the product (and ask lots of questions).

- Learn the technical terminology frequently used in your company, so you can engage in and keep up with workplace conversations.

- Sit in as an observer on engineering "brown bags," architecture reviews, and other appropriate forums.

- Don't fake it—ask someone to explain when you don't understand.

Few product managers today would say their primary responsibility is to manage the development process, ensuring an engineering team turns detailed specifications into product deliverables. The real value of product management has become more outward-looking and strategic, connecting vision to execution, business goals to technology, and unmet customer needs to solutions.

Good product managers now spend more time with external customers and stakeholders. They are excellent communicators and empathizers and can articulate a vision in terms relevant to each audience. When product managers come from varied, non-technical backgrounds (such as business and economics, cognitive science, and communications), their diverse thinking, complementary skills, and interpersonal capabilities can more than compensate for the lack of a technical degree. Most companies will embrace smart, collaborative, results-driven product managers who can work with a team to solve a customer need.

No, you don't need to be able to code. But a modern technology company will still require that you embrace technology, love to learn new skills, respect engineers, and keep up with the latest technology trends. You also need to be confident in admitting when you don't understand something and be able to ask for help. You won't be successful without earning the respect of your development team.

Similarly, aspiring product managers looking for a company or industry change often ask me what domain expertise they need to have. Do you have to come into your role with an extensive understanding of the industry you will work in? Not necessarily. True, in highly specialized fields, some knowledge of the overall ecosystem, including key trends, regulatory environment, and incumbent industry players, remains essential. And given a choice between two otherwise equally skilled candidates, a company might opt for the one with greater inside knowledge.

However, I have now worked—and built teams—across many consumer and enterprise internet domains. Rarely was lack of domain expertise a problem—and on two occasions, I was hired specifically by industries ripe for innovation because I *didn't* come with the baggage of legacy thinking and practices. You, too, can come up to speed quickly in a new domain.

Looking Forward: Your Career Trajectory Isn't Linear

Most product managers are ambitious and highly committed to learning and developing. Because of this, though, some become frustrated when they are slow to earn promotions or lack opportunities to manage a team, yet are nonetheless given increased responsibility, receive less management oversight, and are expected to pick up more product ownership and accountability.

Product managers need to demonstrate a track record of repeated success in shipping quality products first. So much of a company's business success depends on the product manager carefully guiding a significant investment of time and resources to deliver customer and business value.

Consider a product manager guiding a typical team of six engineers and a full-time designer. A 2018 "State of Salaries" study by Hired reported the

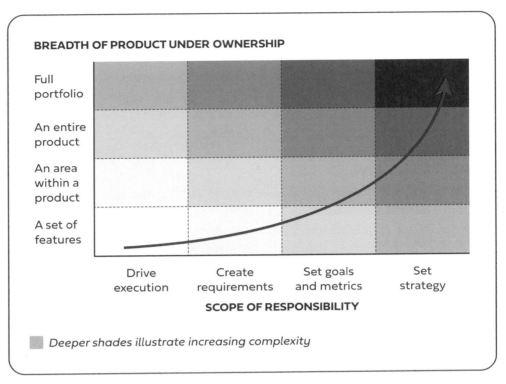

FIGURE 12.3 *A typical product manager's career trajectory*

salary of technology workers across 11 cities in the United States as averaging approximately $135,000 per year.[11] This equates to a million-dollar investment each year in your team. This shows that your company is putting a lot of faith in you.

You can map your development as a product manager against two dimensions—*breadth of product under ownership* and *scope of responsibility*—as illustrated in **Figure 12.3**.

As a junior product manager, you will generally be given a small part of a product to own, such as a few product features. As you grow, you will assume more ownership, with responsibility for an area within a product, and then a whole product. At your most senior level, as a product leader—perhaps with a team of product managers reporting to you—you might own a portfolio of several products, each competing for resources and serving different customer needs.

Now consider the scope of responsibility. As a junior product manager, you will usually primarily work with a team engineers and other stakeholders to deliver an already established plan. Your manager will provide guidance on requirements and desired outcomes, given the overall product and business strategy set at more senior levels. As you grow and demonstrate your ability to execute and consistently ship quality outcomes to customers, you will be trusted with more strategic tasks—starting with creating your own requirements and eventually leading to setting goals and metrics for the product area you own. As you understand customers and business needs at increasingly deeper levels, you may set and communicate a product strategy (and a roadmap).

Each step is orders of magnitude more complex to manage. Growth along these dimensions is not linear. Companies want product managers to demonstrate that they can deliver long-term value for a limited product component, developing more and more strategic skills in the process before they can earn greater ownership of a product or portfolio. Too much of the company's business success depends on the decisions a product manager makes.

Therefore, product managers tend to grow along the "scope of responsibility" axis first—successfully managing a set of features or product area over an extended period (perhaps several years). They show they can be trusted with more strategic tasks and build their reputation within their company as someone who can be delegated to address a complex and ambiguous problem and see it through. It may take many years—five to seven is not uncommon—for a product manager to be given ownership of an entire product.

Don't be frustrated by this—instead, embrace learning, become the expert on the product component you own, and ship! Generate quality outcomes for customers and your business, and the rest will follow.

All the very best on your exciting journey.

Notes

1. "Entrepreneurship and SMEs," European Commission website, https://ec.europa.eu/growth/smes/business-friendly-environment/sme-definition_en; EUR-Lex: Access to European Law website, https://eur-lex.europa.eu/legal-content/EN/TXT/?uri=CELEX:32003H0361; "2 percent of all companies are classified as medium-sized," The Business Journals website, https://www.bizjournals.com/bizjournals/on-numbers/scott-thomas/2012/07/2-percent-of-all-companies-are.html; The Small Business Administration's Office of Advocacy.

2. "Introduction to NAICS," United States Census Bureau website, https://www.census.gov/eos/www/naics/.

3. "Pareto principle," Wikipedia.com, https://en.wikipedia.org/wiki/Pareto_principle; Tatu Lund, "Product Manager's Pareto Principle," LinkedIn.com, https://www.linkedin.com/pulse/product-managers-pareto-principle-tatu-lund/; "Understanding the Pareto Principle (The 80/20 Rule)," BetterExplained.com, https://betterexplained.com/articles/understanding-the-pareto-principle-the-8020-rule/.

4. Ian McAllister, "What are the best ways to prioritize a list of product features?," Quora.com, https://www.quora.com/What-are-the-best-ways-to-prioritize-a-list-of-product-features/answer/Ian-McAllister.

5. Adam Nash, "What are the best ways to prioritize a list of product features?," Quora.com, https://www.quora.com/What-are-the-best-ways-to-prioritize-a-list-of-product-features/answer/Adam-Nash.

6. Innovation Games website, http://www.innovationgames.com/; *Innovation Games Creating Breakthrough Products Through Collaborative Play*, https://www.amazon.com/Innovation-Games-Creating-Breakthrough-Collaborative/dp/0321437292.

7. Noriaki Kano, "Life Cycle and Creation of Attractive Quality," Hebrew Union College Jewish Institute of Religion website, http://www.huc.edu/ckimages/files/KanoLifeCycleandAQCandfigures.pdf; "Kano Model," Wikipedia.com, https://en.wikipedia.org/wiki/Kano_model.

8. "Career Leaders for Batting Average," Baseball Almanac website, https://www.baseball-almanac.com/hitting/hibavg1.shtml.

9. Mike Cohn, *User Stories Applied: For Agile Software Development* (Boston, MA: Pearson Education, Inc., 2004).

10. Frederick P. Brooks, Jr., *The Mythical Man-Month* (Boston, MA: Addison-Wesley Longman, Inc., 1995 [1975]).

11. "State of Salaries Report: Data reveals where techies get paid most and the skills that get them there," Hired.com, https://hired.com/state-of-salaries-2018.

Acknowledgments

To Jeremy Templer, my ever-reliable and thoughtful editor—this book is so much better because of you. Keep challenging me to write succinctly, with clarity and directness. To Rich Mironov, Jen Marshall, Mark Cook, and Arthur Nichols for reviewing early drafts and providing me with pointed feedback, yet with much kindness and empathy. To James Huang, David Sherwin, and Meritt Thomas for loaning their keen design and photography skills, and to Kim Scott of Bumpy Design for bringing this book to life through her modern and elegant designs. To Jodie Sclafani and the Westchester Publishing team for seeing *The Influential Product Manager* through the production process. To my many peers—those I have worked with in the past and those I work with now—I appreciate your thoughtful input and contributions, which have made me a better product manager and colleague. To the staff of the Sutardja Center of Entrepreneurship and Technology at the University of California, Berkeley—particularly Ken Singer and Ikhlaq Sidhu— thank you for the opportunity to create and offer the popular 186 Product Management class. And for all the past, present, and future students of 186, I appreciate your feedback and tolerance as I try out new ideas and content to make product management more accessible to young professionals. A special thanks to student teams who agreed to share their examples in the book or as an online resource. To BK publishing, I would never have thought when starting this project that I would find so compatible a publishing partner, one that shares my values and is similarly passionate about helping professionals everywhere be their very best; I am humbled and thrilled to be part of the BK family. And finally, thank you to my parents for your endless support and for teaching me, through words and actions, the importance of education, lifelong learning, and writing. Because of all of you, this book is a reality.

Index

About the Author

Ken Sandy has led technology product management teams for over 20 years in the San Francisco Bay Area. He is an industry fellow and lecturer at the Sutardja Center for Entrepreneurship and Technology at the University of California, Berkeley, where he pioneered and now teaches the first product management course offered in the engineering school. His work draws on leading teams at fast-growth, early-stage companies as well as at larger companies attempting digital transformation amid industry disruption. At all these companies, he consistently defined, launched, and managed award-winning web and mobile products that were loved by customers and used by millions across 60-plus countries. He was vice president of product at the premier online learning companies MasterClass and Lynda.com. Prior to that, he was an executive at companies developing content and advertising platforms for independent publishers and startups creating mobile messaging and social networking solutions. He also led business units based in the United States, India, and China. He is an executive consultant and active mentor and advisor for startup and scale-up companies in the United States, Canada, and Europe, and a regular speaker at leading product management conferences. In his early career, Ken was a consultant at management consulting firm McKinsey & Co. He is an alum of Melbourne University, where he received bachelor's degrees in engineering and computer science. He is an avid traveler and photographer—backpacking, teaching, and working across the United States, Asia, his native Australia, Europe, and South America.

For more information, visit the following websites:

http://www.influentialpm.com/

https://www.linkedin.com/in/kensandy/

Berrett–Koehler
Publishers

Berrett-Koehler is an independent publisher dedicated to an ambitious mission: *Connecting people and ideas to create a world that works for all.*

Our publications span many formats, including print, digital, audio, and video. We also offer online resources, training, and gatherings. And we will continue expanding our products and services to advance our mission.

We believe that the solutions to the world's problems will come from all of us, working at all levels: in our society, in our organizations, and in our own lives. Our publications and resources offer pathways to creating a more just, equitable, and sustainable society. They help people make their organizations more humane, democratic, diverse, and effective (and we don't think there's any contradiction there). And they guide people in creating positive change in their own lives and aligning their personal practices with their aspirations for a better world.

And we strive to practice what we preach through what we call "The BK Way." At the core of this approach is *stewardship,* a deep sense of responsibility to administer the company for the benefit of all of our stakeholder groups, including authors, customers, employees, investors, service providers, sales partners, and the communities and environment around us. Everything we do is built around stewardship and our other core values of *quality, partnership, inclusion,* and *sustainability.*

This is why Berrett-Koehler is the first book publishing company to be both a B Corporation (a rigorous certification) and a benefit corporation (a for-profit legal status), which together require us to adhere to the highest standards for corporate, social, and environmental performance. And it is why we have instituted many pioneering practices (which you can learn about at www.bkconnection.com), including the Berrett-Koehler Constitution, the Bill of Rights and Responsibilities for BK Authors, and our unique Author Days.

We are grateful to our readers, authors, and other friends who are supporting our mission. We ask you to share with us examples of how BK publications and resources are making a difference in your lives, organizations, and communities at www.bkconnection.com/impact.

Dear reader,

Thank you for picking up this book and welcome to the worldwide BK community! You're joining a special group of people who have come together to create positive change in their lives, organizations, and communities.

What's BK all about?

Our mission is to connect people and ideas to create a world that works for all.

Why? Our communities, organizations, and lives get bogged down by old paradigms of self-interest, exclusion, hierarchy, and privilege. But we believe that can change. That's why we seek the leading experts on these challenges—and share their actionable ideas with you.

A welcome gift

To help you get started, we'd like to offer you a **free copy** of one of our bestselling ebooks:

www.bkconnection.com/welcome

When you claim your **free ebook**, you'll also be subscribed to our blog.

Our freshest insights

Access the best new tools and ideas for leaders at all levels on our blog at ideas.bkconnection.com.

Sincerely,
Your friends at Berrett-Koehler